The Man
Who Robbed
The Robber
Barons

The Man Who Robbed The Robber Barons

ANDY LOGAN

NEW YORK– W. W. Norton & Company, Inc.

The caricature of the "Town Topics"
proprietor, facing the title page, was
drawn especially for "The American" by
F. T. Richards, Foreman of the Jury,
and noted cartoonist of the time.

A part of this book appeared in
"The New Yorker" in different form.

Index prepared by Thomas Lyon

Copyright © 1965 by
W. W. Norton & Company, Inc.

FIRST EDITION

Library of Congress Catalog Card No. 65-13031
All rights reserved. Published simultaneously
in Canada by George J. McLeod Limited,
Toronto. Printed in the United States
of America for the publishers by the
Vail-Ballou Press, Inc.

1 2 3 4 5 6 7 8 9 0

FOR CHARLES

Contents

The Man Who Robbed
The Robber Barons

The Proprietor

ALTHOUGH COLONEL WILLIAM D'ALTON MANN, for nearly
thirty years the publisher of a New York magazine called
Town Topics, has been described as the ranking blackmailer
of American society, he was nothing like the stereotype of
his undercover trade, the sly, skulking figure with the mirth-
less smile who exacts his tribute in some shadowy rendezvous.
In the years just before and after the turn of the century, a
period when some of the most ruthless infighters of the Gilded
Age would respond to Mann's request for an interview by
arriving at his office within the hour, cash in hand, the Colonel
bore a striking resemblance to Saint—rather than Old—Nick.
"A rousing, bouncing, noisy, vigorous, open-hearted, choleric
old man," was the way one of his editorial employees of the
time described him, adding, "What wonder that everybody
loved him?"

Mann was born in 1839 and thus by 1905, when he suddenly became a prominent figure on many of the front pages
of the nation, was sixty-six years old. He had a mop of white
hair that sprang back from a lustrous bald spot, sparkling
blue-gray eyes, a large, fierce, red nose, and dense, untamed
whiskers that cascaded over his enormous diaphragm. The
Colonel was not only endowed with the physical attributes of
jolly old St. Nicholas, but he dressed almost as conspicuously,
regularly appearing in a glistening black plug hat and frock
coat, a pleated white shirt, a flaming red bow tie, often with
a vest to match, and striped trousers whose pockets bulged
with the sugar lumps he distributed every noon hour to all

horses along the way as he bowled up Fifth Avenue from the Fortieth Street office of *Town Topics* to lunch at the main branch of Delmonico's at Forty-Fourth Street and Fifth. Contemporary accounts of his progress abound with metaphor. He was described as "panting like an ocean-bound steamer," "cruising up the avenue under full sail," "breathing like a platoon of steam engines," and "exuding buoyant animalism from every pore." If he met anyone he considered worth impressing, he would stop, inflate his chest, wave his arms like a windmill, expel air from his lungs like a surfacing whale, and split the atmosphere with a loud report that sounded to one observer like "Waugh! Waugh! Waugh!" and to another like "the pumping of a battery of howitzers."

The Colonel's usual salutation as he burst through the door of Delmonico's was "Waugh, boys, I'm thirsty as a goat!" Subsiding into a chair by the window where he could keep a reportorial eye on the passing scene, he would then remedy the matter several times over, slanting his eyes upward as he drank and patting his waistband appreciatively with his palm. He approached the meal that followed, his daughter once said, "as devoutly as a Mohammedan at his prayers." The menu routinely consisted of six mutton chops, a mountain of boiled yams, two heads of lettuce drowned in dressing, a hamperful of hot biscuits—for which he had an initial serving of twelve pats of butter—and a quarter of a chocolate cake, all washed down with two bottles of champagne. The ritual over, he would treat himself to a dollar cigar and a brief snooze in his chair and then, after lavishly overtipping the waiters, give off a few resonant "waughwaughs" and take off down the avenue to stir up the decibels in the editorial rooms of *Town Topics*.

The full name of the publication that, according to F. L. Mott's *History of American Magazines,* was "the best-known urban weekly in America" during most of the period between 1891 and 1920 when it had the Colonel as its commanding officer, was *Town Topics, the Journal of Society.* Beneath this title on its glossy black-and-white cover, twined about specimens of dubious foliage, cigarette-smoking cupids, ads for millinery and tobacco shops, foot doctors, fashionable department stores, mind readers, fruit salts and other restoratives, and a centerpiece that showed two haughty-looking debutantes reading a minuscule copy of *Town Topics,* were curls of ribbon labeled "Drama," "Books," "Music," "Art," "Fashion," "Sports," "Finance," and "Politics"—all fields that *Town Topics* also covered in some depth. The magazine was actually turned out by Mann (who held the title of editor as well as publisher), three or four subeditors, and perhaps a dozen outside contributors, many of whom appeared there only once a week to deliver their copy. Nevertheless, during working hours in the middle of the week there were rarely fewer than fourteen or fifteen people in its narrow fourth-floor offices at 452 Fifth Avenue. The yachting columnist, for example, whose assigned chores occupied him for perhaps four hours a week during the summer months, arrived in all seasons at half-past nine each morning and settled down for a nap in his accustomed easy chair by the window, overlooking what had been the gray ruin of the old city reservoir that by 1905 had given way to the foundations for the new Public Library. A number of other occasional contributors also treated the magazine's outer editorial room, with its red carpet and dozen shabby desks, as an informal clubhouse. At eleven o'clock and again at four, except on the two days before the magazine went to press, all present and accounted for would engage in a flank movement to the outside world—most often Delmonico's—for liquid refreshment. The Colonel, who would usually make his morning appearance in the office at about the time they departed for their elevenses, gave no sign of resenting these extended recesses. Indeed, he appeared to share with Joseph Pulitzer over at the *New York World* the theory that if most of the members of his staff weren't practicing alcoholics, his paper was in trouble.

One visitor who was regularly on hand for the Delmonico pilgrimages was an artist who had no connection with the magazine at all, other than that of having years before painted the portrait of the Colonel that hung on the wall above the editors' desks. The artist continued in faithful attendance at the clubhouse even though his work was the butt of irreverent remarks any time the Colonel was out of earshot. On one occasion when an assistant editor declared that the whiskers in the portrait looked as if they'd been shot at, the painter, who had a bad stutter, answered back with "W-well, that's more than they w-w-were in the w-w-war," and joined in the general laughter symbolizing the staff's disbelief that the rolypoly buffoon who was *Town Topics* publisher could really be, as he claimed, one of the heroic survivors of the Union cavalry charge at Gettysburg. Most of them doubtless regarded with similar skepticism their employer's equally valid claims to having been, in previous professional incarnations, a civil engineer, a hotelkeeper, the inventor and purveyor of cavalry accoutrements, the entrepreneur of one of the first American oil companies, an Assessor of Internal Revenue, the publisher of one of the most prominent newspapers in the South, the proprietor of a large cottonseed oil refinery, a candidate for the United States Congress, the promoter of railroads in Alabama, the author of a book on military tactics, the millionaire inventor and manufacturer of railway sleeping cars, a founder of the company that continued—and continues today—to operate the Orient Express in Europe, the designer of one of the earliest railroad refrigerator cars, and the proprietor of slaughterhouses in Budapest.

Each afternoon when the Colonel stomped into the *Town Topics* office after his midday banquet, he would send a swift look around the editorial quarters that would cause all within its range, including the free loaders, to sit up straight and begin shuffling any papers that were in front of them. After this brief pantomime of power, he would give the tacit as-you-were by awarding each man within reach an indulgent cuff on the shoulder as he lumbered past their desks into his private office at the end of the room where, sitting in his over-sized leather swivel chair, he would be half-hidden from his underlings by an enormous rubber plant. Snug in his lair, he would park his heavy walking stick in the large wire waste-basket that, as it happened, was within easy reach of his right hand.

The Colonel, however, was never a man who enjoyed solitary confinement, and, fortunately, circumstances usually conspired to liberate him. The hour-to-hour house-count in the office fluctuated wildly, in large part due to what one re-porter called "the wealth of fluttering girlhood" with which Mann liked to surround himself. All day long clusters of young ladies in big flowered and fruited hats trooped in and out: friends of his daughter's, daughters of old army friends, and some of more dubious background. All of them would receive an uproarious welcome from the Colonel, who would bound out of his private quarters to give each girl a loud smack, an occasional tickle, and, if she was interested, a snort from the large store of Scotch and rye in his office safe, whose door always stood hospitably open. When a new re-cruit arrived and was introduced to him, he would bow as profoundly as the tension of his waistband would permit and, catching her right hand in his, would stroke it gently for some minutes with his left before ordering an extra round in her honor. When the visitors were colored ladies—and like many people who have spent impressionable years in the South, the Colonel had a large and affectionate acquaintance among Negroes in domestic service—they would be bussed just as soundly as his other female visitors and treated to a glass of spirits. As they left, he would customarily press on each of them a dollar bill from the drawerful he kept in his vast mahogany rolltop desk. Despite the whiskers, no one appeared to object to the kissing routine. He kissed typists. He kissed lady contributors. He kissed charladies. He kissed editors' wives. (One editor did remark that the Colonel's attentions to his wife were so extreme that "he wondered more than once how much farther he ought to permit them to proceed without at least demanding an increase in salary.") And he kissed the office cats. There were six of these outsized, fierce, prowling black animals: some of the staff pretended to believe they were the ghosts of rejected contributors. Anytime the noise in the outer office threatened to subside to a normal roar, the Colonel was likely to galumph past the rubber tree and address the cats in baby talk at the top of his lungs.

Mann also kept dogs—a pug, a black retriever, a setter, and a huge Newfoundland—who spent most of their time at Saunterer's Rest, his big red country house on his private island in Lake George opposite the town of Hague, a sedate resort with a large colony of retired Army officers who were always ready to hash over with him West Point gossip, old regimental feuds, or the latest strategy of the chief of staff. In March, 1904, a reporter for the "Men and Women of the Outdoor World" department of *Outing* magazine called on the Colonel at this retreat. Mann described to him the large parties he gave each August during the Lake George Regatta, the high point of which, as he told the reporter, was the pre-

sentation of the *Town Topics* trophy. "On other occasions
we invite in all the children we can get in the neighborhood,
and we have a bully time. I love my farm, my dogs, my
flowers, and every weed that grows. . . . I raise roses that
would put the professional florist to shame and asters and
chrysanthemums and splendid big grapes." "It did not require
much perspicacity," concluded the *Outing* reporter, "to read
the secret of the splendid vitality of the man who imbibed
the pollen of nature, who drew vitality from the animals he
loved, and who kept his lungs full of fresh air. . . . I began
to realize the secret of his material achievements and his in-
domitable energy as Nature and the animal kingdom returned
to him scriptural messages of affection."

They were messages the Colonel was generously willing to
share, and as a result the responsibilities of working for *Town
Topics* didn't end at the office threshold. Not only did he insist that every member of his staff dine at his West Seventy-
Second Street town house at least once a week, but from
April to November all editors and their presumptive wives,
along with a representative delegation of fluttering girlhood,
left Grand Central each Thursday evening and started back
Sunday evening, having spent the interval between imbibing
nature's pollen at Saunterer's Rest. For this weekly house
party the Colonel reserved the better part of a Pullman car,
using the pass of vast, amorphous powers left over from the
days when he had been a railway tycoon. The journey took
sixteen hours, including a stretch on a lake streamer and a
trip by naphtha launch at the other end. At the island the
Colonel's hospitality, like so much else about him, was demanding, ear-splitting, and prodigious. Fishing, hunting,
swimming, and canoeing were obligatory at appointed times
of the day (and, of course, the season) as were enormous
meals, Scotch-and-sodas for breakfast, and thereafter the al-

most continuous consumption of cocktails. Any shirking in this department, at play as well as at work, made Mann uneasy ("You don't want to turn into a prig, my boy," he would say sternly). The drinks were usually prepared by his daughter Emma in response to the Colonel's half-hourly signal of, "Say, ducks, aren't you dry?" Between rounds he would charge up and down the veranda with his man-sized dogs, who rarely let a day go by without taking a bite out of one of the visitors. It wasn't until late in the evening when he and his hounds had retired to their respective quarters that some of his captive house guests, rejecting the scriptural messages of affection, were free to speculate in whispers over how long they would remain on the *Town Topics* payroll if they turned down these strenuous weekends or, perhaps, to remind each other that their generous host owed them at least a week's salary.

Town Topics went to press on Tuesday nights. About nine o'clock each Monday morning the house party would arrive back at Grand Central where the grinning redcaps would crowd around their friend the Colonel to divide the spoils. ("Never guilty of paying money recklessly, he rarely let slip an opportunity of giving it away," an assistant editor once observed.) But from the time he stepped aboard the lake steamer for the trip back to the city, the Colonel's manner would begin to change. The noisy rampaging ceased. Pacing the forward deck, he turned silent and meditative. "He walked slowly along with his hands clasped behind him and his head lowered in an attitude of profound thought," was the way Harold Vynne, a *Town Topics* editor and frequent house guest of the Colonel's recalled these moments. "The expression on his face was that of a man battling with the gravest possible problems, and it lent to his fine eyes and forehead a dignity they never wore in his lighter moments. He might

have been a mighty statesman, considering the affairs of the
commonwealth . . . or a philanthropist, planning benefac-
tions to his race." His employees were reminded once again
that beneath the clownish mask was a powerful intelligence.
From Grand Central they would walk slowly behind him toward the *Town Topics* office where the Colonel's altered
mood would rule for the next forty hours until the new issue
of *Town Topics* was in the hands of the printers.

The magazine—or newspaper, as Mann always referred to
it—which reached most of its subscribers on Thursday mornings was quarto-sized, ten by thirteen inches, and printed on
heavy paper. The print was large and spaciously arranged in
double columns. The masthead listed the price (ten cents a
copy, four dollars a year), the names of half a dozen foreign
distributors, the information that the magazine was available
at consulates all over the world, and the notation: "Only Un-
exceptionable Advertisements Taken." Aside from the hodge-
podge on the cover, those ads that had passed muster were
usually dignified commercial messages from the nation's most
imposing financial and industrial institutions, such as the
Equitable Life Assurance Society, the Pennsylvania Railroad,
United States Steel, or Standard Oil. The last half of the
weekly twenty-four to twenty-eight pages was devoted to fiction and light verse and to reviews of events of interest in the
ancillary fields—finance, politics, music, books, and so on—
promised on the cover. The departments having to do with
the arts were signed with pseudonyms, but a number of them
were written during the Colonel's regime by men whom later
historians came to list among the more distinguished and in-
fluential critics of their time. It is doubtful, however, if a
single one of its weekly subscribers—the circulation total that
the Colonel informally laid claim to was a hundred and forty
thousand—bought *Town Topics* for its provocative and

learned essays on the arts. Their concern was with its advertised role as the *Journal of Society* and particularly with its first twelve or fourteen pages, which were given over to items of society gossip, often of a nature that the town's other society pages regarded as unprintable. Known as "Saunterings" and signed "The Saunterer," this department was also the primary interest and largely the work of the proprietor of Saunterer's Rest.

Colonel Mann had many reasons to be concerned with the content of "Saunterings"; in addition he laid down stringent house rules for its style, syntax, and grammar. "Avoidance of slipshod English is a matter in which I can insist on prominence," he wrote proudly in 1895, and he often urged his staff on with the reminder that, a couple of years later, a local magazine called *The Journalist* (eventually taken over by *Printer's Ink*) had described *Town Topics* as "the best-written paper in the English language." He felt a special responsibility to set a good example in this field since so many of his readers were socially prominent New Yorkers. "New York society cannot become more worthless, meaningless and theatrical than it is today," he wrote in December, 1895. "It is inhabited by jackasses, libertines and parvenus. But worst of all," he added, "nobody in it can write or speak good English." Besides insisting on the Saunterer's mission to divert his readers from the paths of slipshod literary usage, Mann liked to describe *Town Topics'* publication week after week of scandalous items, often of hideous import, as part of his crusade to convert the well-born from their undisciplined way of life. In testimonial support he sometimes cited Bishop Henry Potter, New York society's favorite man of the cloth at the turn of the century, who, Mann insisted, had once told him that he regarded *Town Topics* as "a great moral agency." "The world is more governed by fear than by love," the

Colonel quoted the Bishop as having said to him on a visit to the *Town Topics* offices. "The wickedly-disposed in society behave themselves through fear that your paper will expose them." "Viewed from every aspect," concluded Mann in an editorial in 1904, "there is no feature of my paper of which I am more proud than its informative and regenerative influence. To save the sinner by rebuking the sin is an achievement over which the angels rejoice."

Nor was this the sum of the Colonel's evangelical concept of the Saunterer's duty to his readers. He often fretted in *Town Topics* about the shallow frivolity of day-to-day interests among his socially prominent subscribers and made it his business in the last page or two of "Saunterings" to keep them informed about the problems of the world outside the Newport Casino or, at any rate, one thinking-man's view of them. This viewpoint was rarely of the sort the Newport set was likely to find persuasive, but Mann did not let this stop him, nor did he fritter away time examining both sides of any question. ("The Colonel's mind," an employee of his named Robert Rowe once complained, "was made up on every known social, moral, political or economic subject.") Over the years he took a stand in "Saunterings" for raising the "Maine," against Mary Baker Eddy, for the Democratic Party (but against Tammany and "the glittering mendacities of Populism"), for higher wages for workers, against labor unions, against the docking of horses' tails, for New York City as a separate state, for women's suffrage, against vivisection, for lynching ("perfectly understandable in the South"), against the meager pay of American diplomats abroad, against the raising of a statue to Jefferson Davis ("The South has been petted enough"), for lower tariffs, against the gas trust, for the appointment of Justice Holmes, against "soulless monopolies," for the reversal of the official reprimand of

General Fitz-Porter after Chancellorsville, against the acceptance of actors in society ("Stage people are social deformities. Their minds are like rugby footballs, filled with dried beans"), for a federal income tax, beginning in the 1890's ("I am satisfied that only by the imposition of such a tax can the ultra-rich of this country be induced to pay their due share toward the support of the national government"), and, as one might fairly expect, against any scientific kudos for Sir William Osler who had held, according to the Saunterer, "that all men over sixty were absolutely useless and should be chloroformed."

It was presumably this more general area of the Saunterer's weekly seminars that moved the *Des Moines Register and Leader* to note editorially in 1904 that "The comments of the Saunterer . . . are widely read and quoted because they are crisp, varied, sensible, humorous, and good-humored. . . . They maintain the tone of a thoroughly-informed man of the world, chatting after a good dinner about society, politics, journalism, music, theatres, charities, Europe, the city, the nation, the army, fair women, churches. . . ." "That is my ideal," responded the Saunterer himself, modestly, "and I endeavor to realize it."

In most circles outside those inhabited by thoroughly informed journalists, by frustrated agents of the law, and by the country's richer citizens, the Colonel's public image was that of an elderly, harmlessly flamboyant *bon vivant* and prosperous publisher of a somewhat rakish but highly readable magazine when, in the late spring of 1905, he left New York for a European holiday, accompanied by his third wife, Sophie. He traveled in style: according to a later story in the New York *Herald* his suite of rooms on the S.S. "Majestic" cost him a thousand dollars for the one-way passage. He almost certainly carried along with him cuttings of the *Des Moines Register and Leader* article to display to any of his old friends on the continent who might have been troubled by reports that "sensible" and "good-humored" were not the adjectives most often applied to the Saunterer's accounts of the goings-on in American society. No libel suit, he was probably also primed to remind them if they pressed the matter, had come to trial against the magazine since he had taken over its control fourteen years earlier. He presumably did not plan to offer as one possible explanation for this clean legal slate the fact that, as he himself later observed, "it has been my experience that ninety-nine men out of a hundred are moral cowards." Relying on these odds, the Colonel abandoned his weekly routine and, leaving *Town Topics* in the charge of an old friend, Judge Joseph M. Deuel, sailed aboard the "Majestic" on May 25th, mercifully unaware that before his return a tiny fraction of that discounted one per cent of the human race would set in motion a series of events that would turn his next years into an old man's nightmare.

"A Nest of Skunks"

BY THE SECOND WEEK IN JULY, 1905, according to a *Town
Topics* analysis of that year's summer edition of the *New York
Social Register,* 2,649 of the 7,616 personages listed in the
Register had left for the seashore, 3,925 had taken to the
mountains or other inland resorts, 195 were cruising on their
yachts, and 857 had departed for Europe where they were
doubtless congratulating themselves on their escape as each
succeeding edition of the Paris *Herald* reported more harrow-
ing details of New York's hottest July in a decade. Since the
Herald was reporting the vagaries of the weather, rather than
forecasting them, its stories were presumably more reliable
than the *Social Register's* roster of warm-weather addresses
which, as it turned out, was not wholly accurate. The *Register,* for instance, listed the dilatory domicile that summer of
Mr. Edwin Main Post, a popular member of the New York
Stock Exchange, as Tuxedo Park. His wife, Emily, was indeed established there, together with their two young sons.
Mr. Post, however, remained in town. Among the matters
that kept him in New York was a business appointment he
had at two o'clock on the afternoon of July 11 in the gentlemen's washroom of the Holland House at the corner of Fifth
Avenue and Thirtieth Street. At the prearranged hour he
kept the rendezvous with a slight, dapper young man named
Charles Ahle, to whom he handed over an envelope contain-
ing five one-hundred-dollar bills. Counting them, Ahle remarked that, as usual, the swag would be divided up among
various members of the staff of *Town Topics.* He indicated

that the broker was getting off easy. "We've had scandals worth twenty thousand dollars," he said, and then, patting the oversized black satchel he was carrying under his arm, added expansively, "In fact, *Town Topics* makes most of its money from the suppression of stories." At that moment, according to plan, Detective Sergeant Bernard Flood of the New York Police Department stepped out of one of the cubicles, confiscated the satchel and the envelope, and arrested Ahle on a charge of extortion. He then hauled his prisoner off to the Elizabeth Street Police Station; the following morning Ahle was arraigned at the Tombs and confined there in default of thirty-five-hundred dollar bail. Before leaving the Holland House with his quarry Flood stopped to telephone the good news to the District Attorney's office in the Criminal Courts Building on Centre Street.

The mimeographed handout, the public relations liaison man, and other modern journalistic conveniences were not part of the amenities at the Criminal Courts Building in 1905. Nevertheless, reporters then assigned there had certain advantages over those of today. The only telephone on the floor where the District Attorney and his staff had their offices was in a booth next to the long table at which the reporters assigned to the courthouse beat lounged, cut for deal, and, on this stifling July afternoon, brooded over the odds on something turning up to interrupt the monotonous menu of insurance company scandals the front pages had been featuring almost without variation since the previous winter, when an outrageously fancy dress ball given by James Hazen Hyde, vice-president and son of the founder of the Equitable Life Assurance Society, had sprung the lid on a Pandora's box of corporate chicanery. Even as they brooded, the District Attorney, William Travers Jerome, then at the height of a crusading career that had made him a nationwide sym-

bol of the incorrupt reformer, was in seclusion at his Lakeville, Connecticut, summer home, raking through a state
commission's report on the Equitable company for evidence
of indictable crime. In Jerome's absence Paul Krotel, one of
his assistants, took the call from Detective Flood. As soon as
the phone rang, the reporters' game of stud stopped dead in
the middle of a deal. When Krotel stepped back out of the
booth with a satisfied smile on his face, the eavesdropping
reporters fell upon him like starving men. In the newspapers
of the following day all word of actuarial peccadilloes had
been shunted to the inside pages to make room for the *Town
Topics* blackmail scandal.

When Edwin Post arrived on the floor of the Exchange
that morning, he got a rousing cheer from his fellow members, and trading was temporarily suspended while they
crowded forward to wring his hand and, in some instances,
to mumble that they "had been there themselves." Two days
later, while testifying at Ahle's hearing in the Centre Street
Police Court, Post told the story of where he had been. About
three weeks before, he recalled, he had had a phone call
from Charles Stokes Wayne, *Town Topics'* managing editor.
Wayne said Post "had better see" a man named Ahle whom
he was sending around the following day. Ahle had duly
arrived, armed with a letter of introduction from Wayne and
a galley proof of a paragraph that the managing editor proposed to run in "Saunterings." The paragraph Ahle brought
with him dealt at length with Post and "a little white studio"
in Stamford that it claimed he had shared with "a fair
charmer" who had a penchant for "white shoes with red
heels and patent leather tips." This idyllic report would be
withheld from *Town Topics'* readers, said Ahle, if Post cared
to fork over five hundred dollars to have a flattering write-up
of himself appear in a forthcoming society who's who to be

called *America's Smart Set*. Should Post prefer to pursue this second course, he would find himself in excellent company, Ahle went on, and fished out of his satchel subscription blanks endorsed by Colonel John Jacob Astor, William K. Vanderbilt, Jr., Hamilton McK. Twombly, and a dozen other prominent citizens, some of whom had apparently been so enthusiastic about the contemplated volume (not a word of which, it later developed, had been yet written) that they had paid fifteen hundred dollars apiece, or three times the going rate, for their copies. Actually, *America's Smart Set* would only cost about $50 a copy to publish, if indeed it was ever published, Ahle, a notably garrulous hold-up man had informed Post. But "the boys at the office are tired," Ahle had explained. "They need to go on a little cruise or something."

Post testified that he had told Ahle he would let him know his answer in a few days. He had then consulted his lawyer, who reminded him that the district attorney's office had been trying since the early nineties to establish proof of Colonel Mann's involvement in this kind of shady deal, but that to date none of the Colonel's victims had had the backbone to stand up in court and admit to having done anything of conceivable interest to a blackmailer. Post was having a bad year in the market and was aware of the habit-forming properties of successful extortion. He was also less spineless than some of his friends on the Street. He decided to nip the swindle then and there, but only if his wife—with whom he had been on rather distant terms for several years—would give her consent. An emissary was dispatched to Tuxedo Park to explain matters. The unflinching word that came back from Emily Post was to do the right, if humiliating, thing, *pro bono publico*. Post had thereupon notified the district attorney's office that he was willing to act as live bait for the trap, after which he had called Ahle and arranged their rendezvous. On the basis of his testimony and the corroborating statements of Detective Flood, Ahle was bound over for action by the grand jury and, still unable to raise bail money, was locked up again in the Tombs.

Meanwhile, local newspaper editors, liberated from their preoccupation with tontines, sequestered premiums, and other insurance company esoterica, were showing no intention of waiting around for the law to take its cumbrous course. The morning after the confrontation in the gentlemen's washroom half a dozen reporters invaded the offices of *Town Topics,* intent on staging a confrontation of their own with managing editor Wayne, who was also editor(up to then, at least, a journalistic sinecure if there ever was one) of *America's Smart Set.* Wayne, a bald, pudgy man in his forties, with large, melancholy eyes and a drooping moustache, put forward the notion that the whole trouble could be traced to some fearful misunderstanding on the part of Post who, he said, must be "half insane." For corroboration he referred his callers to Moses Ellis Wooster, a former employee of *Town Topics* who by this time was the director of *America's Smart Set* at 503 Fifth Avenue, two blocks north.

There, in a one-room office on the third floor, the reporters found Wooster, a blond, smiling, smooth-shaven young man, coolly waiting for them in the noonday heat. Raising his voice not a decibel, he expressed outrage over Post's behavior, and assured them that Ahle was well known as a most gentlemanly solicitor. As for the fact that some of the men involved in running the two publications were obviously wearing two hats (Wayne, for one, and, for another, W. L. Daniels, who was treasurer of *Town Topics* as well as secretary-treasurer of *America's Smart Set*) this, Wooster explained, was "sheer chance." There was no connection between the magazine and the book in spite of the interlocking mastheads or of the additionally confusing circumstance that Colonel Mann was publisher not only of *Town Topics* but of a magazine called the *Smart Set*. The Colonel himself would be glad to confirm this if he were on hand, Wooster added, but unfortunately he would not be back from Europe until the end of the summer. Pending his return, said Wooster, maneuvering his visitors toward the door, perhaps they would do well to consult Justice Deuel, presiding judge of the Children's Court, who, he understood, had been occupying the Colonel's office for the past few weeks—after court hours, naturally.

When the Children's Court adjourned late that afternoon in the basement of the Criminal Courthouse (four floors down from Jerome's office and next door to the Tombs where Ahle was now in residence) its presiding judge found a number of reporters waiting for him in his chambers. As soon as he saw them, Deuel, a stout little man of sixty with picturesquely curling white hair and a handlebar moustache, set aside his usual jovial manner. He also set aside any notion of Ahle as the innocent victim in the case. Ahle was "that wretch" who must be prosecuted to the full limits of the law, not only for his attempted hold-up of Post, but for his deception of managing editor Wayne, who had written Ahle the letter of introduction to Post "out of the kindness of his heart." The reporters, however, showing signs of having made an intermediate stop upstairs at the district attorney's office to consult its files on *Town Topics,* displayed less interest in Ahle than in an uncanny resemblance they detected between the plans for *America's Smart Set* and *Fads and Fancies of Representative Americans,* another projected vanity book that was an acknowledged *Town Topics* enterprise. Wasn't it true that the major selling point of these two publications was identical—pay up or get roasted in *Town Topics*—except that in the case of *Fads and Fancies* the boodle had been far more substantial than solicitors for *America's Smart Set* were trying to collect, ranging, in fact, from fifteen hundred to ten thousand dollars a write-up? And wasn't it also true that, although the subscription lists to *Fads and Fancies* had closed two years earlier and the book was still unpublished, its subscribers had remained curiously uncomplaining? How much had *Town Topics* cleaned up on *Fads and Fancies,* anyhow?

"Not a penny!" snorted Deuel, grabbing at the reverse end of the questionnaire. The idea for *Fads and Fancies* and the soliciting of subscriptions to it had been strictly Wooster's responsibility. *Town Topics* was to publish the book, that was all, and it would probably lose money on the deal, since it was the Colonel's intention to make it "the volume of the century." Each copy, Deuel went on, was to be printed on Japanese vellum and bound in the flawless hide of an entire calf; sometimes a hundred skins had to be discarded before one sufficiently worthy was found. Naturally this sort of thing took time. But *Fads and Fancies,* said the Judge, was "by no means a myth" and would be in the hands of its patient subscribers any month now. As for *America's Smart Set,* he knew nothing of that. And what, the reporters asked, was his official connection with *Town Topics.* None at all, Deuel replied, explaining, when pressed, that he was aware of a provision in the city charter prohibiting any member of the judiciary from engaging in the private practice of law. It was true, he said, that each Tuesday evening just before *Town Topics* went to press he was in the habit of spending some hours in the magazine's office reading over galley proofs of the forthcoming issue. But he assured them that this occupation had nothing to do with applying his knowledge of libel law. He undertook it, maintained the Justice, only for his own "pleasure, amusement, and delectation" and "as a personal advisor to my personal friend, Colonel Mann."

The July 13 issue of *Town Topics,* the first to appear after Ahle's arrest, bore witness that Justice Deuel's version of the misadventure had prevailed over Wayne's. Leading off the "Saunterings" department, a formal one-paragraph statement denounced Ahle "with all the emphasis of which I am capable" and, after promising to help bring him "to speedy justice," continued: *"Town Topics* is not in any way interested in the publication for which he canvassed. No one, for a pecuniary or like consideration, can buy his way into or out of the columns of this paper. Anyone making different representation is an imposter and, if arrested, *Town Topics* will assume the burden of prosecution." The paragraph was signed "William D. Mann," but it came as no surprise to those familiar with the Colonel's fanatical devotion to English syntax when, months later, court testimony revealed that the statement had been turned out in his absence by Justice Deuel.

On July 14 Wooster surrendered the books of *America's Smart Set* at the request of Assistant District Attorney Krotel. They showed that in the several months since the launching of the project eighteen subscribers to the volume had been relieved of $26,700, of which Wooster had got half. The rest, after deducting six hundred dollars for office space, stationery, and the like, had been divided among Wayne, Ahle, and Daniels. As for the roster of subscribers, John Jacob Astor had been the first to fall in line. Additional names revealed from the list included those of Clarence Mackay of Postal Telegraph, Judge Elbert Gary and Isaac Guggenheim of United States Steel, Harold McCormick of International Harvester, the architect Stanford White, and, among the Vanderbilts, not only William K., Jr., but his cousins Reginald and Alfred. With nothing further to gain from playing the town half-wit, Wooster agreed that he modeled his *America's Smart*

Set scheme on that of *Fads and Fancies,* which had proved to be a bonanza for him while he was still associated with *Town Topics,* as it had for Colonel Mann. He had tried to get Mann to come in on the new project, he said, but the Colonel had wanted too big a cut. He had therefore gone ahead without him, later (apparently without the Colonel's knowledge) taking in Daniels, Wayne, and Ahle from the *Town Topics* staff. During the time he had worked on the *Fads and Fancies* campaign, Wooster said, it had brought in some two hundred thousand dollars, of which he had got approximately a fourth, with the rest being divided among Justice Deuel, the Colonel, and the Town Topics Publishing Company.

A suggestion—never further documented—of the influence *Town Topics* could have had on the Judge's professional career was given in an anonymous letter received about this time by Edwin Post and turned over by him to the district attorney's office. It reported that two years earlier the Saunterer had been about to run a certain paragraph concerning Robert Fulton Cutting, founder of the Citizen's Union as well as president of the Association for Improving the Condition of the Poor. Cutting, according to the letter, had not only paid $25,000 to have the item suppressed, but had agreed to use his influence to have Deuel named to the Children's Court. Cutting issued a statement denying the story, although he agreed that the Citizen's Union had, in fact, endorsed Deuel. "This case appears to become more and more scandalous and serious," announced the district attorney's office.

For the moment the *Fads and Fancies* books remained under lock and key by order of Judge Deuel, who commanded the authorities to hold everything until the return of Colonel Mann, now revealed to have cut his trip short and to be on his way home from France. Krotel declined to be thus easily put off and set about trying to reach individuals believed to have subscribed to the mysterious volume. All at once it appeared that the summer edition of the *Social Register* had, if anything, understated the mass flight of the elect from their urban haunts. When Krotel tried communicating with their dilatory domiciles, however, he failed to flush them there, either. The piercing ring of the telephone up and down Newport's Bellevue Avenue went unanswered; gatehouse guards on the North Shore were reinforced. At Throgs Neck Mrs. Collis P. Huntington (now rumored to have paid the top price of ten thousand dollars in cash to make sure that the virtues of her late husband, the president of the Central Pacific Railroad, were fully covered in *Fads and Fancies*) decamped from her estate in the dead of the night on receiving word that a subpoena was heading her way in the care of Detective Flood, who had been attached to Jerome's office for an indefinite tour of duty. Returning to Manhattan, the frustrated Flood had to content himself with serving subpoenas on Daniels, Wayne, and Wooster.

Reporters poking around in the provenance of this trio for signs that they were old hands at the blackmail game were let down by Daniels. A bookkeeper for Colonel Mann since the late eighties, he had put a thousand dollars into the *America's Smart Set* scheme, got it back with a hundred and fifty per cent interest, and now blandly announced his resignation from that publication because of the pressure of his duties at *Town Topics*. Wayne, a pulp novelist on the side, had worked for the Colonel on and off for seventeen years, the unsteadiness of his employment being the result of a weakness for alcohol. Like Daniels, he had no discernible legal record, but in 1897, during one of his off intervals, he had turned up in Colorado Springs, where he had founded a magazine called *Facts,* a Rocky Mountain version of *Town Topics* devoted to more colorful (and possibly more factual) depictions of life among the local cotillion leaders than his readers were accustomed to find on the society pages. A few months later, threatened, literally, with tar and feathers, he had been obliged to leave town on twenty minutes notice and beat his way back east to a less headstrong clientele. Wooster, on the other hand, was no stranger to the district attorney's office. In 1900 he and an associate, Robert Irving, had organized the Blue Pencil Club in a loft on Spruce Street. Ostensibly an informal social clubhouse for newspapermen, it was soon attracting wealthy playboys eager to join in their revels, and from there it easily progressed to the business that was its primary purpose, the shakedown. It was eventually raided and closed, but its proprietors, after paying a fine for violating the excise laws on whisky, had walked off with a profit that some reports put as high as two hundred thousand dollars.

While local newspaper readers were being introduced to these and other members of the cast, Ahle, first in order of appearance, remained in the Tombs. Only a couple of years earlier he had arrived in New York as an obscure migrant from St. Louis and joined the circulation staff of *Town Topics,* where his wages were in the neighborhood of $20 a week. He had evidently found an additional means of prospering, however, for *The New York Times* reported that by late 1904 he had set himself up, together with a recently acquired wife, in a "luxuriously furnished home in Northport, Long Island, where they went out with the best people." None of the best people came to Ahle's assistance after the arrest, nor did any of his *Town Topics* colleagues. Meanwhile the heat wave continued unabated, and to add to the city's distress all local ice men were out on strike. On July 17 it was 95° in New York and the City's Health Department put the death toll from the heat at 137. The next day when the temperature hit 96°, the hottest July 18 then on record, seventy-five more New Yorkers died from the heat. Perspiring heavily, Krotel observed to the reporters outside his office that it was no kind

A "COLONEL OF INDUSTRY."

He Makes the "Captains of Industry" Surrender.

of weather for a man with friends to be in jail. That afternoon Mrs. Ahle persuaded Martin Engel, as Essex Street saloon keeper, to put up the $3,500 bail money to spring her husband from the cell in which he had sweltered through seven days and nights. It turned out to be a poor gamble on Engel's part. Within a week of his release the Ahles had sold everything they owned and had lit out for the cooler shores of the Continent where, if the fugitives encountered any former subscribers to *America's Smart Set* in the months or years that followed, the accident went unreported.

By the time Ahle was discovered to have cheated speedy justice, the plot was thickening so rapidly that his absence was hardly noticed. Judge Deuel, now also under subpoena, had finally agreed to allow Krotel to have a look at the *Town Topics* financial records in the presence of Daniels. Not ten minutes after Krotel started digging he came upon an entry of a $1,200 disbursement as an annual retainer to the Judge, at which point Daniels, plainly at the end of his tether, swooped down, snatched the books out of Krotel's hands, and locked them up again. Waiting for him back at the Criminal Courts Building, Krotel found William Travers, Jr., son of the Wall Street broker, wit, and Delmonico habitué for whom District Attorney Jerome had also been named, Jerome's father having been a crony of Travers, Sr. Young Travers, who had recently been divorced from his wife, one of the Harriman girls, had brought with him to the district attorney's office a copy of the current *Town Topics,* which dealt with him in its leading article. The gist of the piece was that he wasn't being invited out much these days. "It is an unwritten law in his set that sympathy must be extended to the divorced party occupying the place nearest the throne," the magazine's Newport correspondent had written. "Billy Travers is simply impossible. . . . He walks along the street without looking at anyone, and no one looks at Billy. He is a social outcast." Travers was astounded to learn that the district attorney's office did not regard being called a social outcast as grounds for criminal libel and was sent limping off to his bachelor apartment to consider the possibility of bringing suit in the civil courts.

On July 19 Krotel called in Robert Irving, the man who had been so profitably involved in the Blue Pencil scheme with Wooster. During 1902 and 1903, it developed, Irving had worked for Wooster and *Town Topics* as deputy solicitor for *Fads and Fancies*. In the past year he had been on the staff of *The New Yorker,* another society gossip magazine, which modeled its format and, it was widely suspected, many of its editorial practices on those of *Town Topics. The New Yorker,* never a healthy contender, had changed hands several times since its first issue of February, 1901. By mid-1905, its leading spirits were Robert Irving and Robert Criswell, the editor, who had just been arrested for criminal libel. A recent issue of *The New Yorker* had charged that Alice Roosevelt had been insulted during a trip to Ohio by being introduced to a Kentucky Congressman who had once been indicted "for snatching money from a farmer." The Congressman, who had never been indicted for snatching money from anybody, had brought a complaint. Released on $1,000 bail on July 15, Criswell was called back five days later for questioning by Jerome's office. Mention of Irving's name in the newspapers had refreshed the recollection of subscribers to still a third de luxe society album. This entry, according to Krotel's informants (who were, inevitably, unidentified) was to be called *America's Foremost Families.* Its presiding officers were substantially the same as those of *The New Yorker.* Like *Fads and Fancies of Representative Americans* and *America's Smart Set,* its patrons were to be written up in the book for a price—in this case a bargain $250 to $500 apiece. During the few weeks since this cut-rate operation had got under way $6,650 had been collected from the heads of foremost families, much of it, according to Krotel, from individuals who had already qualified both as Colonel Mann's representative Americans and members of Wooster's smart set.

As matters turned out, the full roll of these triply-distinguished citizens was never publicly called, nor was any of them asked in court whether the price of his third subscription had been handed over in order to avoid scandalous revelations in the regular columns of *The New Yorker*. There was also no evidence, however, that the editors had ever intended to publish the book at all, and preparations were made to arrest Criswell on a second charge, that of obtaining money under false pretenses.

With news of this third successful fleecing of the rich and mighty, the New York *Globe* sternly announced that the press must stop covering the affair as a three-ring circus and treat the revelations with the seriousness appropriate to a deep-seated problem of contemporary civilization. "We cannot allow our second and third generations, the class the old world looks to for the regeneration of its aristocracy, to be made the prey of the unscrupulous," declared the *Globe's* editors. But there continued to be no cry of *"Au secours!"* from the second and third—or even the first—generation victims. The District Attorney leaked the names of more $500 or $1,000 subscribers to *America's Smart Set:* Harrison Drummond of the Drummond Tobacco Company, Ogden Armour of the meat family, James W. Gérard, the corporation lawyer, Thomas Walsh, the Colorado silver king, and Mrs. Potter Palmer of the Chicago department store fortune. All remained discreetly incommunicado and out of reach of both the press and the process servers. When cornered at a public meeting, Theodore Shonts, the chairman of the Panama Canal Commission and a subscriber, as it turned out, to both *America's Smart Set* and *Fads and Fancies,* said only that he had paid over the money in order to help out his old friend, Colonel Mann, who he understood was in financial difficulties. Several newspapers printed a remark reported to have been made some months earlier by New York Senator Chauncey Depew to the effect that he had signed up for a $2,500 subscription to *Fads and Fancies* in 1902 because, at the age of sixty-six, he was about to take a young wife "and he wanted the boys to speak well of him." On July 20 Depew arrived from Europe in order to be, as he said, "in the storm center." The storm he had in mind was the Equitable Life investigation which later revealed that the company paid him a $20,000 annual retainer while he was holding public office. Reporters who met him at the dock, however, asked questions that elbowed him into at least the fringe of the tempest over *Town Topics.* "Colonel Mann? An excellent gentleman. I know him very well," was all the Senator cared to say on the subject.

The most forthright position in the matter was taken by Charles M. Schwab, a *Fads and Fancies* subscriber who went so far as to receive Krotel in the office he occupied as president of Bethlehem Steel. Schwab said he had paid $1,500 for a subscription to the book as the result of the widespread distortion in the press of an incident two years before involving his efforts to break the bank at Monte Carlo. This adventure had taken place while Schwab had still been president of United States Steel, and when he arrived home Pierpont Morgan, United States Steel's supreme commander, had reportedly called him on the carpet. "Anyhow, I didn't do anything to be ashamed of. I didn't do anything behind locked doors," Schwab had said, defensively. "That's what doors are *for,* Schwab," Morgan was supposed to have answered. *Town Topics,* Schwab now told Krotel, had been the only publication to carry an accurate account of the Monte Carlo matter, and "I felt such accuracy should be rewarded." Krotel asked him if there was any truth in the rumor that Schwab had recently rewarded the Colonel further with a $25,000 loan.

Schwab replied that the rumor was inaccurate. (It was indeed but, according to later court testimony, only to the extent that the loan was for a mere ten thousand dollars.) "But if I *had* been blackmailed," Schwab continued, "do you suppose I would talk about it?"

In a statement from Colonel Mann that appeared in the July 20 issue of *Town Topics*—authentic this time and cabled just before he had sailed for home aboard the Red Star liner "Zeeland"—the Colonel commended Edwin Post "most heartily" for his action in putting the kibosh on *America's Smart Set,* which he characterized as "that swindling undertaking." But, said Mann, *Fads and Fancies* was something else again. "We stand sponsor for that . . . beautiful book," he declared, adding that if admission to its pages had come rather high that was a matter for the subscribers to decide. "I have always supposed," he went on, "that men of wealth had the unquestioned right to buy such innocent luxuries as they desired and to pay for them what they chose." In this supposition the Colonel was joined by Krotel, who said he was aware that spending ten thousand dollars for a literary knick-knack meant no more to some people than parting with a dime did to others. "But we want to know with certainty," he added sternly, "that these large sums were paid out of vanity—and not out of fear." Krotel declined to speculate publicly on which motive had influenced the man who, according to the latest report sweeping through New York's city rooms, was among the subscribers to *Fads and Fancies:* Theodore Roosevelt, the President of the United States.

Every newspaper in town had a man on the dock to cover the Colonel's arrival at his own storm center when the "Zeeland" hove into port in the North River late in the evening of July 24th. When the sexagenarian publisher appeared on the "Zeeland" deck, his burly mane of white hair and vast snowy beard, his fierce blue eyes and beaklike nose in a face tanned from the Mediterranean sun combined to make the man from the *New York Daily Mail* think of a Biblical patriarch. His step was light and brisk, however, as he came down the gangplank, waving an outsized Panama hat and carrying the heavy, knobbed hickory walking stick that, several reporters noted in their front-page stories, he had been known to call "my very best friend" and that he always kept within hand's reach, especially at his office desk. Behind him walked his wife, Sophie, and behind her Albert A. Wray, a lawyer and former state senator from Brooklyn, who, apparently feeling that a conference was in order, had gone out on the government tug and met him at quarantine. Judge Deuel was first in line to shake the Colonel's hand. They talked earnestly for a few minutes before the publisher agreed to meet with the small army of newspapermen.

A certain preliminary briefing turned out to be necessary since the Colonel informed them with a straight face that he knew nothing of developments in the case, not having seen a newspaper since June 24. Brought roughly up to date, he expressed no surprise at the news that no further blackmail victims had followed Post's example in bolstering the District Attorney's case against Wooster's latest venture. Indeed, he formally backed Schwab's position that in such circumstances silence was golden. "The man who will give money in such a case is either a damn fool or a coward," he said, and added in a voice that may have been meant to carry, "In either case, he is going to keep his mouth shut about it." Asked about *Fads and Fancies,* the Colonel's reply was "I supposed that work was published by this time." In answer to another question, he said that when it did appear, Theodore Roosevelt would be represented in it at the President's own wish. The reporters then broke the news to him that Roosevelt had just issued a statement from Washington, denying that he had even heard of the proposed volume. The Colonel's eyes widened in shocked disbelief. "The President has forgotten," he then told them in a voice throbbing with forbearance. He would not go so far as others had, he said, and predict that *Town Topics* would lose money on *Fads and Fancies*. Probably there would be a small net profit. "But I pay little attention to these details. I am only interested in the artistic end of the magazine." When someone referred to Wayne as the editor of *Town Topics,* the Colonel cut him short. "*I* am the editor of *Town Topics,*" he said. (The magazine had never run a list of editorial personnel, but, beginning with its next issue and for the rest of the Colonel's life, there appeared directly under the masthead on page one, the pronouncement: "WILLIAM D'ALTON MANN, EDITOR.") Would he call *Town Topics* a scandal sheet, the reporters asked him. Certainly not, he told them. *Town Topics* was a clean newspaper although, heaven knows, with the prevalent state of public morals, it was a struggle to keep it that way. "I have often kept out a story I thought might work serious injury to some person or family," he told the press. "As a matter of fact," he went on, once again in a voice that may have been meant to carry, "at this very moment I have cartloads of stories locked up in my safe that would turn New York upside down if they were published."

A few hours before the "Zeeland" docked another practiced performer had returned to the city. District Attorney Jerome was back from his Connecticut hideaway, where he had concluded there was no indictable crime in the state commission's report on the Equitable company, a conclusion that was to cause him political embarrassment in years to come and give William Randolph Hearst an excuse to refer to him as "the brass-buttoned bellboy of the trusts." He was now ready to advance to stage center in the *Town Topics* affair. The next day's newspaper accounts of the Colonel's remarks at dockside supplied him with his cue. Jerome declared that, far from accepting Mann's appraisal of the situation, he had always considered *Town Topics* to be "a nest of skunks." This estimate was swiftly relayed to the Colonel.

"If there are any skunks in my office, I will soon find out," he snapped when, in midafternoon, he received the press for the second time in twenty-four hours, on this occasion more informally in the second floor bedroom of his town house on West Seventy-Second Street where he would be confined for some days, he told the reporters, having injured his back while lifting a truck on the "Zeeland." "However, that is a highly improper phrase for a district attorney to use. This man Jerome is a windmill." After a pause he added, "I used to know his father before he was born"—thereby putting the District Attorney in perspective. The spectacle offered by the Colonel *couchant* moved a reporter from the *Globe* to draw a fairly libelous analogy. "Propped up on the downy pillows of his handsome bedstead," he wrote, "the Colonel could have posed with advantage for a picture of the Old Man of the Sea." On the bedtable beside him, perhaps for contrast, was a photograph of Mann at twenty-three in the uniform of a Union colonel—"the youngest colonel then in the army," he told his visitors. On his dressing gown he wore the button of the Loyal Legion, the fraternity of Union officers of which, he noted, he was one of the earliest members. "That man Jerome must have twenty press agents," he told his visitors. "*I've* been to war," he added, hammering the bed for emphasis with a force that brought growls of protest from the pug dog at his feet. "*I'm* not a pop gun."

When asked about the $1,200 annual retainer *Town Topics* paid Judge Deuel, the Colonel explained that he had always regarded it as "a sort of a present." The Judge, he told them, "is as lovely a man as you ever saw. He and I play a game of pool every night." Reminding his audience that he had been the inventor of a railroad sleeping car, he said that Deuel, as private secretary to Roscoe Conkling, Mann's lawyer during the eighties had been very helpful with his patent work. After *Town Topics* had turned into "the best-paying weekly publication in America, bar none," it had seemed appropriate to reward the Judge in some fashion. Mann went on to disclose that Deuel had been further rewarded with his election as vice-president of the Town Topics Publishing Company in 1900 and, in addition, had been given thirty of the five hundred shares of stock in the company. The other four hundred and seventy, the Colonel said, were owned under a perpetual trust deed by his daughter, Mrs. Emma Mann-Vynne.

If *Town Topics* was so prosperous, the reporters inquired, how was it that his dear friend Theodore Shonts had given as his reason for subscribing to *America's Smart Set* and *Fads and Fancies* the fact that he understood the Colonel needed the money. This Shonts, Mann told them, was no dear friend of *his*. Shonts was a mere acquaintance he had run into the year before at Army maneuvers which, the Colonel pointed out, he himself had attended as a guest of General Corbin, chief of staff. Indeed, on thinking it over, he was of the opinion that Shonts wasn't an important enough man to appear in *Fads and Fancies*. The reporters then asked him what he thought of Depew's remark that he had subscribed in order to fend off ridicule in *Town Topics*. "Why, what did Depew have to be afraid of? He was my best friend," said the Colonel, smoothing his beard. He added with scrupulous accuracy that he did differ with the Senator politically from time to time. If there had been any funny business in connection with *Fads and Fancies,* he went on, he wanted it clearly understood that the responsible culprit was Wooster, who had turned out to be "an unsafe man, a scoundrel." At this point, the *New York Tribune* reported, the Colonel "kicked viciously at the bedclothes." As soon as his visitors left, he kicked them off entirely, rose—his back miraculously healed—dressed, and, announcing to a few straggler-reporters on the front stoop that "there are certain facts that I must get possession of at once," had himself driven down to the *Town Topics* office, where he went into a huddle with Judge Deuel and most of the regular staff. By the time their conference ended just before midnight Charles Stokes Wayne had been fired—either for his independent sortie into journalistic blackmail or for getting caught out at it.

When he returned to his office the next afternoon, Mann learned that Wooster had visited the District Attorney and had demanded that the Colonel be arrested on a charge of criminal libel for having called him a scoundrel. He would simultaneously file a $50,000 civil action for defamation of character, added Wooster. "I am not going to leave the country to escape any suits this youngster may bring," announced the Colonel, pulling seniority once more, and expressed doubt (well-founded as it turned out) that either action would ever be heard from again. Changing the subject, he announced the marriage in Burlington, Vermont, the day before, of his daughter Mrs. Mann-Vynne to former State Senator Wray, an event that was regarded in some quarters as support for the theory that the Colonel would go to any lengths to get free legal advice. The following evening, with the next issue of *Town Topics* on the presses, he departed for his usual long weekend at Saunterer's Rest. Also as usual, he and his wife were accompanied by half a dozen members of the *Town Topics* staff.

On the following Monday morning, which was the last day of July, District Attorney Jerome announced his intention to file for re-election as an independent, anti-Republican, anti-Tammany candidate, and in the afternoon dispatched Detective Flood to *The New Yorker* offices to bring in editor Criswell and his henchman Irving for further questioning. Flood was unable to find them. Neither man was seen again until two nights later when Criswell, "wearing a blue outing suit of fashionable cut," turned up on the subway platform at Broadway and Seventy-Second Street. In this summer of 1905 Criswell was fifty-five years old. Two decades earlier, according to an article that appeared later that week in the *Fourth Estate,* a local trade paper, he had "enjoyed a reputation as a humorist and satirist, and there are many newspapermen who remember his work." He had written successful children's books, had been owner and editor of a paper in Oil City, Pennsylvania, for several years, and, later, managing editor of the *Cincinnati Inquirer.* After coming to New York he had served as an editorial writer on the *World* for some years before becoming involved with *The New Yorker,* with the Colonel's former employee, Irving, and with derivative soak-the-rich schemes. Just before eleven that night, after half an hour of pacing up and down the platform, Criswell avoided arrest in one criminal action against him and forfeited bail in the other by jumping in front of a southbound express train. A few days after the funeral Irving was arrested on the same libel complaint, the one filed by the congressman acquaintance of Alice Roosevelt, and removed to the Tombs in default of $1,000 bail.

Ambush

By COINCIDENCE, it was also an article about the social activities of Alice Roosevelt that led, if not to tragedy, at any rate to a calamitous interval in the life of the editor whom Criswell had recently taken as his model. During the previous year Teddy Roosevelt's older daughter had turned twenty and had broken away from the rambunctious night-nursery atmosphere that surrounded the younger members of the family then in the White House. The preoccupations of another era are often ephemeral, and only members of a senior generation today recall with what avid attention her subsequent advance into society, her dance cards, her changes of coiffure, her Alice-blue wardrobe—indeed, everything that had to do with Princess Alice, as she was archly referred to—was reported in the nation's newspapers. Colonel Mann, however, harbored a practical grudge against her father. A few years before, he had invested a large sum of money in a plot of land on West Thirty-Eighth Street near Ninth Avenue. His idea was to sell it to the government for a considerably larger sum as the site for Manhattan's new main Post Office, then still in the planning stage. Notwithstanding *Town Topics'* weekly editorials urging the virtues of this location ("Let us waste no more time poring over a map of New York!") Washington had resolved to build a few blocks to the south— a decision that Mann, a devout Democrat, interpreted as a personal rebuff from the leader of the opposition party. About a month after this decision was announced in the fall of 1904 Alice Roosevelt made her first excursion to Newport.

In the next issue of *Town Topics* Mann led off the "Saunterings" department with a paragraph deploring her behavior there. The young woman's last name was never mentioned, but her anonymity was *Town Topics* style: she was identified as being the daughter of a figure on the highest level of national life and her host as a man "named after a distinguished American to whom the world of steam navigation is deeply indebted." (Among the men whose families Miss Roosevelt had been visiting was Robert Fulton Cutting.) During her Newport debut, reported the Saunterer, "from wearing costly lingerie to indulging in fancy dances for the edification of men was only a step. And then came a second step—indulging freely in stimulants. Flying all around Newport without a chaperone was another thing that greatly concerned Mrs. Grundy. . . . If the young woman knew some of the tales that were told at the clubs at Newport, she would be more careful in the future. . . . I was really surprised to hear her name mentioned openly there in connection with . . . certain doings that gentle people are not supposed to discuss." ("When I danced the hootchy-kootchy on Grace Vanderbilt's roof at Newport," Alice Roosevelt Longworth wryly commented to Cleveland Amory a few years ago, "you would have thought the world was coming to an end.")

The Saunterer's paragraph created a private furor, but, as was so often true of *Town Topics'* more outrageous capers, any public protest was muffled in compliance with the fiction that no respectable person ever read it. When *Town Topics* turned up on a hand-rubbed library table beside the latest edition of *The Well-Bred Girl in Society,* it had been "picked up by mistake in the club car" or was "that horrible paper the servants take in." Yet, one way or another, as Edwin and Emily Post's son, Edwin, Jr., recently recalled in his biography of his mother, *Town Topics* "found its way into almost every cottage in Tuxedo Park, as it did into the cottages, villas, and mansions at Newport. It was read upstairs, downstairs, and backstairs."

Among the Newport cottages into which a copy of *Town Topics* found its way the weekend after the Alice Roosevelt paragraph appeared was one occupied by a stocky, patent-leather-haired, ebullient young man named Robert Collier, who became so indignant after he read the ungallant account that he kicked over a nearby basket of firewood. It was but the first, and least effective, maneuver in a campaign he thereupon launched to show up the Colonel and his ways. Twenty-eight years old at the time, Collier was the son of the founder of *Collier's,* or *Collier's Weekly* as it was then known, and for the past six years had been its publisher while his father, Peter Fenelon ("Pat") Collier, tended to other aspects of the Collier empire. The elder Collier had come over from Ireland at the age of seventeen, started out as a door-to-door book peddler, and eventually worked his way into the more lucrative publishing branch of the literary game. By 1904 he had sold some forty million books—for the most part low-priced library sets of standard authors, offered on the installment plan—and the magazine, begun in 1888 as a sideline, was also a respectable success, having reached a circulation of three hundred thousand. P. F. Collier's wealth had been accumulated early enough in his life so that during his middle years he had been able to indulge his passion for fox hunting, which had opened the way to social circles, including those at Newport, that were not ordinarily hospitable to former peddlers from County Carlow. As *Town Topics* had described the feat a few years before, "Pat Collier is the first man to ride into the heart of swelldom behind a pack of hounds." In his role as self-appointed arbiter of society, Colonel Mann was a traditionalist and regularly took a stance hardly less disapproving of the society gate-crasher than that of Mrs. Astor herself. From time to time in the decade before the Post-Ahle rendezvous the Saunterer had sniped at the parvenu Collier for his alleged bandy legs, his eye for the ladies who had no eye for him, and his grammatical lapses. The sniping had become infrequent, however (perhaps in line with the unwritten law about the parties nearest the throne) after July, 1902, when young Rob Collier, a few years out of Harvard, married Sara Van Alen, Mrs. Astor's granddaughter. Some months before the Alice Roosevelt paragraph appeared, the Colonel had even seen fit to describe the young man as "attractive, with a clear head and charming manners."

Young Collier's savage reaction to the item may have been attributable to a long memory and pride of family, or, more probably, to genuine moral indignation and a sound sense of journalistic values. The editor of *Collier's Weekly* in that fall of 1904, Norman Hapgood, described him many years later as "at the time the most brilliant magazine mind in America" and a man whom "it was a stimulation, an education, and a joy to work with." Hapgood also commented on Collier's "dramatic nature" and was probably not too startled when, the Monday morning after his Newport weekend, the publisher stormed into the office and flung the *Town Topics* clipping at the editor, pronouncing it "the most vicious paragraph that ever appeared in a magazine." He declared his intention of using the pages of his publication to fight the Colonel, and, as a first step, asked for an editorial against Mann's methods in the next issue of *Collier's Weekly*. Hapgood obliged. "The most degraded paper of any prominence in the United States," he wrote in the issue of November 5, "is a weekly of which the function is to distribute news and scandal about society. The mind which guides such a publication tests credulity and forces one to take Swift's Yahoo as unexaggerated truth. The editor . . . in question leads a somewhat secluded life, and well he may. . . . A recent issue of his sewer-like sheet contains as its leading feature an attack on a young girl who happens to be the daughter of the President. It uses her first name only. That is a little way it has. It charges her with all the errors that hurt a woman most, and it makes these charges in the most coarse and leering way. That any steps could or should be taken to suppress such unclean sheets we do not believe. Paternalism, official regulation, once started goes too far. . . . We can only say that whoever refuses to read the journal we refer to or to advertise in its columns performs a public service. As to personal recognition, we can hardly imagine that many decent men would consent to meet the editor." Collier himself added the final sentence, which declared that "the editor's standing among the people is somewhat worse than that of an ordinary forger, horsethief or second-story man."

With the next issue of *Town Topics* the attacks on Pat Collier were resumed with a vengeance although, apparently out of ignorance of the true perpetrator, the Colonel generally left young Rob out of it. The elder Collier was described as lecherous, leprous and unable to write his name. He was also, *Town Topics* pointed out, currently debauching the youth of the country through the serialization in his magazine of *Raffles,* the adventures of a society jewel thief. These installments were intended to tempt young men of good family to a life of crime, the Colonel held, and he thereafter referred to Collier as Pat Fagin. In May, 1905, just before he sailed for Europe, he suggested that the publisher's connection with crime was more direct. Some jewels had been reported missing after a house party in Collier's neighborhood at Newport, and Mann advised the police that the case might be solved if they would take a close look at Pat Fagin's new scarf pin.

At the time of Ahle's arrest two months later the maligned elder Collier was away in England, following the hounds, but Rob Collier was on hand to rejoice at the development. He was also in a fever of curiosity over what would happen next. The day following Jerome's return from his Connecticut recess the District Attorney therefore had a visitor. Collier had sent down Norman Hapgood, by a fortunate coincidence Jerome's friend since his boyhood, to get the lowdown on how things were going. Jerome told the editor that the only solid evidence of extortion involved the *America's Smart Set* operation, with which the Colonel's connection, if any, could not be proved. The men who had been caught out were small fry. It was too bad that the real culprit—"the big spider" was the way Jerome put it according to Hapgood in his later autobiography—would apparently escape. Men like the Colonel, he reminded Hapgood, were too shrewd to let themselves in for any criminal charge, and at a civil suit they were, of course, worth nothing. At this juncture in the discussion it apparently occurred simultaneously to Jerome and to Hapgood (who had graduated from Harvard Law School before turning to journalism) that if Hapgood's magazine were to denounce the Colonel and the whole *Town Topics* operation, including Deuel's part in it, in blunt enough language the Colonel—and perhaps Justice Deuel also—would feel obliged to sue for criminal, rather than civil, libel. The District Attorney's office would thus be brought into the case, whereupon Jerome, as prosecutor, could call them as witnesses testifying in their own behalf and leave it to the defense to tear them apart during cross-examination. Hapgood went directly back to his office and wrote for the August 5 issue of *Collier's Weekly,* whose name had by this time been abbreviated to *Collier's,* an editorial urging the termination of

Deuel's judicial appointment, which had until 1913 to run. "He is paid $9,000 a year by the people," wrote Hapgood, "and is clothed with an honor that should be worth more to him. . . . What is his return? He is part owner and one of the editors of a paper of which the occupation is printing scandal about people who are not cowardly enough to pay for silence. What kind of public opinion would allow him to remain upon the bench until 1913? Every day he sits upon it is a disgrace to the State that endures him." As Hapgood pointed out afterward, he never actually accused *Town Topics* of blackmail but simply described exactly what the magazine did—an evasion that Jerome, a Columbia Law man, admiringly dubbed "libel, Harvard style." In the same issue Hapgood reprinted the editorial, now liberally intersticed with Mann's name, that measured the Colonel's reputation as rather less than that of an ordinary forger, horsethief, or second-story man.

The Colonel's response was to inform the American News Company, distributors of *Collier's,* that, since the article was "grossly libelous," he would hold them responsible for allowing the magazine to reach the public. Rob Collier countered with a letter indemnifying the distributors and pointed out that if libel was involved, no direct legal notice had been given of it. On August 21 the Colonel announced to the press with a flourish that he, Judge Deuel, and the Town Topics Publishing Company had each sued *Collier's* and Hapgood for $100,000 in civil damages. Deuel and Mann charged injury to their good names while *Town Topics* claimed loss of advertising and circulation revenues. In all of these cases, however, certain formalities were overlooked: no arrangements were made to serve papers on the defendants. "Colonel Mann, of course, is indulging in feeble bluff," declared *Collier's* in its next issue. "If we can goad him into daylight, the happier we. Fancy him in court putting figures to the injury to his fair name. . . . No, Colonel Mann, your course is to remain quiet and be thankful you are in your carefully guarded office instead of in the rear of prison bars." Mann lashed back with the accusation that Hapgood and Collier were dodging the process server (Hapgood had gone to York Harbor and Collier to Newport for the weekend) and to urge them "to come into the city of New York and place yourselves within the jurisdiction of the court." "We have no hope that the suit will ever come to trial," Collier told a *World* reporter gloomily. He then craftily added that if the Colonel were really convinced that a crime had been committed, he would file charges of criminal, not civil, libel. In its next issue *Collier's* reprinted all of its editorials against *Town Topics* "in compact form for the Colonel's convenience" and young Collier announced that he would be in his office every afternoon the following week hopefully awaiting arrest.

On September 11 the tireless Detective Flood appeared at Collier's office at last, but when the publisher stepped eagerly forward, Flood brushed past him to arrest Norman Hapgood instead. Moreover, the charge of criminal libel had been brought on the complaint, not of the Colonel, but of Judge Deuel. The following day, accompanied by three Collier lawyers and five Collier writers, Hapgood was arraigned in Jefferson Market Court and bound over for action by the grand jury. "Apparently the Colonel is pushing his partner into the foreground, hoping to escape behind him when trouble comes," Rob Collier told the *Tribune* indignantly. "The principal villain is Colonel Mann. It is not our fault if Justice Deuel chooses to lay his body athwart the track." He challenged the *Town Topics* publisher to give over his craven ways and swear out a warrant in his own name.

It had been a dull summer—the Nan Patterson murder case was over and the murder of Stanford White yet but a gleam in Harry Thaw's fevered eye—and these maneuvers and counter-maneuvers by the two magazine owners were reported in detail not only by the local press but by newspapers all over the country, exhilarated by glimpses of moral turpitude, celebrated names, large sums of money, and aging evil confronted by youthful righteousness. Dozens of papers were moved to come out editorially against such newsworthy sin, including the *Philadelphia Public-Ledger,* the *LeSeuer* (Minnesota) *Sentinel,* the *Norfolk Virginian-Pilot,* the *Rockford* (Illinois) *Republican,* the *Havana Post* and the *Richmond Times-Dispatch. Collier's,* whose contents until a year or so before had run largely to sentimental fiction, occasional war correspondence, college humor, and Gibson Girls, found itself hailed as an ornament to crusading journalism. "When a man has arrayed himself against clean living and good manners and has become a menace to the community, the journal which rebukes him earns the gratitude of the community's respectable elements," declared the *Charleston News and Courier.* The hostile attitude of the southern journals must have particularly dismayed the Colonel, who often remarked that he considered himself half a southerner because of his several years of post-Civil War residence in Alabama and who liked to remind people that he had been admitted to membership in the local Southern Society by special dispensation of its board of directors. Only the *Mobile Register,* which he had once owned, stood by him, and even its editor noted that the Colonel must welcome the opportunity to clear his name in the courts.

On October 26 the grand jury handed down an indictment against Norman Hapgood on the charges filed by Justice Deuel. Four days later the editor, Robert Collier, and

P. F. Collier—for once dismounted—were finally arrested for criminal libel on a warrant sworn out by Colonel Mann. In the minds of the conspirators, he was netted at last.

Even before the Colonel's capitulation the long prologue of the case had changed the lives of some of the minor figures involved in it. Distressed by Criswell's suicide, the Kentucky Congressman had withdrawn his charges against Irving, who had again become a free man. Charles Stokes Wayne and Moses Wooster had gone on the Colliers' payroll as "advisors" at salaries of one hundred a week, plus expenses. The rights, title, interest, and office furniture of *The New Yorker* had been sold by the sheriff for $1,100. (In the succeeding months four or five sets of publishers vainly tried to keep it going on a respectable basis. It went under for good with the issue of August 1, 1906, and when Harold Ross started a magazine of the same name in 1925 he had never heard of this earlier opprobrious namesake.) Martin Engel, the unlucky saloon keeper, had departed for Europe, announcing that he would pursue Charles Ahle to the ends of the Continent and if necessary wring the $3,500 bail money out of him by brute force. Emily Post had filed suit for divorce from Edwin Post under the laws of New York. (Mrs. Post had already written several novels, to the consternation of her well-bred family, but it would be seventeen years before *Etiquette: the Bluebook of Social Usage* would appear and immediately displace Papini's *Life of Christ* at the top of the best-seller list.) And on the last day of September Billy Travers had become the second minor member of the cast to take his own life, shooting himself through the head in his Madison Avenue apartment. Although he appears to have been a man with numerous problems that had nothing to do with the printed word, every obituary in town mentioned his deep distress over the recent attack on him in *Town Topics*. In one upstate paper news of this death had been given banner headlines. Confused by the names involved, the newspaper had reported the suicide as that of District Attorney Jerome. The latter had read his own obituary with interest and had expressed his satisfaction over being able to thank Governor Odell personally for his heartfelt condolences to the Jerome family.

A decent interval followed the handing down of the indictment against Hapgood on Deuel's complaint while all concerned marshaled their forces. Jerome then set about getting an indictment against the Colliers *et al.* on Colonel Mann's charges. Presenting evidence before a grand jury is only one means to an indictment, and Jerome now chose the alternate route, a public hearing before a magistrate, which opened on November 27 in Tombs Police Court. In the tedious manner of such real-life performances, it went on for two days, recessed for three, sat for a half day, adjourned for three weeks while Magistrate Charles Whitman took a vacation, sat for a day and a half, recessed for Christmas, and sat for a final day just before the end of the year, when it took what turned out to be a permanent recess. The chief lawyer for the defense in this proceeding was James W. Osborne, a tall, transplanted North Carolinian with a jutting chin, a booming voice, and a deceptively jovial manner, who was regarded as one of the great man-eaters of the contemporary bar. He and Jerome appeared to be on the best of terms although Osborne had just wound up several weeks of sustained public attack on Jerome's discretion and integrity in the course of unsuccessfully running against him for the post of District Attorney.

Colonel Mann went on the stand early in the hearing to deny that *Town Topics* was, as Hapgood in Harvard style had defined it, "a paper of which the occupation is printing scandal about people who are not cowardly enough to pay for silence." When, in cross examination, Osborne referred to certain countering evidence reflected in the Post-Ahle episode, the Colonel shrugged his massive shoulders and re-iterated that if there had been any hanky-pank on the part of his employees, he had known nothing of it. "In other words," said Osborne, stepping in delightedly with a punning paraphrase of a popular song lyric of the day, "everybody works but father. Everybody works but our old Mann." "Here," reported the *New York American,* "an interpolated song by the Colonel would not have been at all out of place." A poet on the *New York Daily Mail* went even further and offered, if not an interpolated song for the Colonel, one that would, at any rate, have served as a rousing first act curtain:

> "Everybody works but the Colonel,
> He sits around all day,
> Reading spicy gossip
> And *vers de societé.*
> Daniels and Justice Deuel
> Get the best they can.
> Everybody works the public
> But Colonel Mann."

As if this sort of thing weren't diversion enough, the hearing was further enlivened during its second week by the publication, two years after the closing of its subscription lists, of *Fads and Fancies,* whose full title—and full it was—turned out to be *Fads and Fancies of Representative Americans at the Beginning of the Twentieth Century, Being a Portrayal of Their Tastes, Diversions and Achievements.* There was still no evidence that any of its subscribers had brought pressure on the Colonel to give them something tangible for their money, but Jerome had continued to issue statements to the newspapers calling attention to their curious hesitancy in instituting fraud charges against Mann, and *Collier's* had described the volume in a November issue as "a book probably never intended to be published." It was therefore with a gleam of triumph in his blue eyes that the Colonel now watched as a copy of the glossy album, at Jerome's request brought down to the courtroom by Mann's Negro servant, was carried into court by the bailiff and introduced as a prosecution exhibit. After the day's session reporters, leafing through the 226 pages of the giant volume— it was a foot wide and nearly a foot-and-a-half tall—found write-ups, ranging from two to eight pages long, of the selected diversions of eighty-six highly unrepresentative Americans, including almost the entire roster of men whose names were then synonymous with the nation's financial and industrial power and whose high-handed and often felonious maneuvers against the interests of their fellow Americans historians have been exposing, at full tilt, ever since.

Colonel John Jacob Astor, New York's mightiest landlord, had consented to appear in the book, along with three Vanderbilts, William K., Reginald, and Alfred of the New York Central Railroad family. Other railroad tycoons accounted for were A. J. Cassatt, president of the Pennsylvania, Collis and Henry Huntington of the Central Pacific, James J. Hill, known as the "Colossus of Roads" for his monopoly of rail lines in the Northwest, and Chauncey Depew who had been president of the New York Central before his election as United States Senator from New York. Other Senators honored were Nelson Aldrich, the Rhode Island traction magnate, and New Jersey's John F. Dryden, founder of the Prudential Insurance Company. Henry Hyde, the founder of Equitable Life, was also in the book, as were such leaders in the tobacco industry as Pierre Lorillard, Benjamin Duke,

and Harrison Drummond (the same man who, like a number
of others on the Colonel's subscription list, had also paid
over money to be immortalized in *America's Smart Set*).
The textile man, A. D. Juilliard, Bromo-Seltzer's Isaac Em-
erson, T. R. Woodruff (typewriters), Charles H. Cramp
(shipbuilding), Levi Leiter (department stores), and Bethlehem Steel's Schwab were represented. Samuel Newhouse, who
had made his money in Colorado copper mines was there,
as were William Leeds, the tinplate tycoon; Thomas Walsh
(silver); Clarence Mackay, whose legacy from the Bonanza
silver mine was now reaping him further bonanzas in the
commercial cable field; Thomas W. Lawson, the spectacular
plunger in the copper market; Pembroke Jones (rice); E. J.
Berwind and Stephen Elkins, coal barons; and Standard Oil's
Henry Flagler and Daniel O'Day. Charles Yerkes, the Chicago street-railway mogul who would later sit for the portrait
of Frank Cowperwood in Dreiser's *The Financier, The Titan,*
and *The Stoic,* had sat for *Fads and Fancies;* so had William C. Whitney and Thomas Fortune Ryan of New York's
street railway combine and James R. Keene, the freebooting
stock market manipulator, who had also invested in a write-up
for his playboy son, Foxhall. Hetty Green's son, Edward H.
R. Green had subscribed for himself. Stanford White was on
the list. In the world of high finance the Colonel had started
at the top with J. Pierpont Morgan; among the other banking
names in his album were Oliver Harriman, Perry Belmont,
and Levi P. Morton, who was, in addition, a former governor
of New York and onetime vice-president of the United States.
All of these men—or their families in the case of several
who had died since signing up for the project—had provided
pictures of their summer and winter homes, their billiard
rooms, their favorite horses, their collections of mooseheads,
uncut gems, rubber plants, Alderney cows, or "very valuable

paintings," usually of the Barbizon school. The *Town Topics* staff had then put together a suitable prose accompaniment, whose sociological tone may be conveyed by its retrospective description of the financial brigand, Commodore Vanderbilt, as one who had "radiated pure sunshine in his life and character," and of the rapacious Yerkes as in reality "a sensitive, reserved, quiet gentleman of most refined tastes, absorbed in the beauty he has gathered around him."

The Colonel's minimum price for these fantasies, as Wooster had already repeated under oath at the hearing, was fifteen hundred dollars. Astor, Perry Belmont, Ryan, Lawson, Mackay, Leeds, Newhouse, and Hyde, along with Peter Marié, whose inherited money came from the West Indian trade, John H. Patterson, of the National Cash Register Company, and Henry C. Pierce, a southwestern oil man, had ponied up the money for a double spread of literary unctiousness. The longest write-up—eight pages—had been devoted to Collis P. Huntington in return for his widow's ten thousand dollar investment. Also in *Fads and Fancies* and wrought with the same reverent, loving care, were three testimonals that, as Wooster later testified, were on the house: one of Bishop Potter; one of the only living ex-President of the United States, Grover Cleveland; and a third devoted, as the Colonel had advertised, to the current occupant of the White House. The Roosevelt described in these pages bore no resemblance to the "human fiasco of politics" or the "professional cowboy" whom constant readers of "Saunterings" were familiar with. He had been transformed into a pre-eminent statesman, widely noted for his "high ideals," "modesty," "swift judgement" and "brilliant exploits." The President's appearance in *Fads and Fancies* despite Roosevelt's indignant denial of having cooperated with the enterprise, or, indeed, of having heard of it, came as no surprise to Jerome. To prove his point the

Colonel had, sometime before, sent the District Attorney proofs of the article that included private family photographs, provided by the President, showing him jumping a horse and enjoying a family tennis game at Sagamore Hill; the White House had even made some corrections on the proofs. The pictures, Mann explained, had been obtained for publication in the album several years earlier by Mrs. Wade Hampton, Jr., daughter-in-law of the noted Confederate General, who had then been a member of the *Town Topics* staff. It appeared from later testimony that, armed with a letter of introduction from her distinguished relative, the lady had made an appointment at the White House, where she had murmured something about a little book to be devoted to the hobbies of famous men. The President had amiably given her the photographs, and proofs of these, with a write-up to go with them, had undoubtedly been useful in conning other *Fads and Fancies* prospects into joining up.

When this unique record of its time, bound not in the advertised unblemished calf but in green Morocco leather, bordered in gold, was brought into the courtroom, it was encased in a Flemish oak box, the total load being so heavy that the bailiff entering with it staggered and dropped it with a resounding thud on the courtroom floor. The volume, which Mann had already described in *Town Topics* as "an exquisite example of the highest attainment in the art of book manufacture at the beginning of the twentieth century, a souvenir and an heirloom combined," received further rough treatment later in the day when Osborne asked Mann about an article in it, and the Colonel replied that he had never read the book.

"You charge $1,500 for a book and then don't consider it worth reading?" Osborne demanded. He then inquired whether the witness thought the success of the *Fads and Fancies* subscription drive could have been related to Mann's previous comment that "you had stuff in your safe which, if published, would turn New York society upside down."

"I did not say that," answered the Colonel, tartly. "I merely told the reporters that I had cartloads of scandal in my office which I had refused to publish."

Soon after the laughter over this distinction had subsided, a new face appeared at the defense table beside those of Wooster and Wayne. The new recruit was Robert Irving. Irving's testimony had become available as the result of an event highly gratifying to Jerome, who had announced every week or so since the previous summer that additional *Town Topics* victims were about to come forward to expose the scourge of American society. His fantasy had gone unrealized until young James Burden of the Troy ironworks family turned up at his office on December 15, thanks to the persuasive efforts of Robert Collier, a Newport crony of his. Burden declared that four years earlier Colonel Mann had made an appointment for him to see Irving, that when Irving arrived he had demanded $1,500 for a subscription to *Fads and Fancies,* and that when Burden refused Irving had urged him "to consider the matter very carefully," adding, "The Colonel wields a trenchant pen." Burden had nevertheless showed Irving the door, he said, and the following week articles had begun to appear in *Town Topics* charging him with public drunkenness, attendance at houses of ill repute, and other behavior difficult to explain at home. Burden added that two years later Irving had approached him again and demanded a cash contribution in return for suppressing an article in *The New Yorker*. This time Burden had denounced him before witnesses as a blackmailer. At Jerome's order Detective Flood now arrested Irving on a charge of attempted extortion and locked him up when he was unable to make bail. Help was at hand, however. Two days later, having, according to the newspapers, been offered immunity if he would testify for the defense, Irving turned up in the Tombs courtroom, cheek by jowl with the Colliers' other captive witnesses.

Shortly after Irving was called to the stand Colonel Mann rose from his chair on the prosecution side of the courtroom, declared that he wasn't sure he even knew this fellow, and asked to be excused for the day because of a jumping toothache. Among the disappointed spectators in the crowded courtroom when the Colonel continued on sick call the following day was Mark Twain, who sat at the defense table with Rob Collier. The Colonel sometimes boasted to the *Town Topics* staff that he had been one of Twain's earliest editors. Not surprisingly, the celebrated author gave no sign of associating the complainant in the case with W. D. Mann, owner of a newspaper in Mobile, Alabama, to which he might have contributed forty years before. After Burden, a handsome, sporty-looking young man, had given the details of his interview with the *Fads and Fancies* solicitor, Osborne produced half a dozen letters from the Colonel to Irving, whose files were clearly now at the Colliers' disposal. One introduced the younger man to Grover Cleveland and another dispatched him to Newport where, the Colonel had written, "there are a great many eligible people. I hope you gather them all in." The hearing then recessed to allow Hapgood to prepare for his impending trial on Judge Deuel's charges.

Later that afternoon a group of reporters called on the *Town Topics* publisher, once again granting an audience to the press from sick bay. He now diagnosed his trouble as neuralgia and blamed it on the drafty courtroom. The reporters asked him if, considering the evidence that was already in, he was about to withdraw his libel complaint against Hapgood and the Colliers. "The Colonel's militant spirit was manifest in a moment," reported the *Tribune* man. "It has been my experience that ninety-nine men out of a hundred are moral cowards," he told his visitors, but added that he himself was not of this predominant persuasion. "I am sixty-six years old," he said, "and with the career I have made, open as the day, if there has been any testimony given in this case that reflects upon my honor, I must fight to the end." As for his alleged correspondence with Irving, "I note that the letter purporting to carry my signature is without date," the Colonel told his callers, "something I would not be likely to omit. Furthermore," he added, "there is an utter absence of any form of courteous finish to the letter, and it lacks the conciseness of expression that would ordinarily characterize any letter I might write to anyone. It does not bear my earmarks of composition," he concluded, in the manner of one who has put an end to the matter, once and for all.

Others of the principals involved took a different view. Back downtown, in the room just beyond the press table, the reporters found Jerome deep in conference with attorney Osborne. "Everything so far," Osborne told them on his way out, "was just a curtain raiser for what's ahead."

From Gettysburg
to Oily Gammon

IF COLONEL MANN SUFFERED real distress over the impugn-
ing of his honor by *Collier's,* his self-esteem would hardly be
repaired by the names he would be called in other publications
during the months that followed. He would find himself
described as "the proprietor of a transparent bunco game"
(*New York Evening Post*), "a colossal grafter, without peer"
(*Scrantonian*), "a jackal, feeding on dead scandal" (*New
York Sun*), and the publisher of "worse than a vermiform
appendix of legitimate journalism" (*Knoxville Tribune*). "A
more crapulous journalistic Mafia man never leered his goat-
like way through life," were the words the *New York Evening World* used about him. These motions would be sec-
onded in variant terminology in such newspapers as the
Brooklyn Eagle, the *Minneapolis Times,* the *Norfolk Land-
mark,* the *Auburn* (New York) *Advertiser,* the *Roanoke Times,*
the *Boston Record,* the *Providence Journal,* the *Kansas City
Journal,* and the *Seattle Times.* Only a few scattered words
would be offered in his defense, including an editorial in the
Birmingham Ledger in March, 1906. Taken all in all, wrote
the *Ledger,* the Colonel had been "a remarkable man."
"While Colonel Mann is undergoing a terrific punishment
in the press of the United States," it was only fair to remember, added the Alabama paper, that in another place and
time, Colonel Mann had been "a real soldier in a real war."
When the *Ledger's* reminder was reprinted in *Town*

Topics, this authentication of Mann's rank and claim to a combat record probably astonished most readers who had watched the Colonel's name being jolted from one incriminating newspaper headline to another during the preceding months. By the turn of the century the rank of Colonel was bestowed as a jocular courtesy on a large share of the surviving officers of the Civil War, old men, by this time, whose tales of ancient exploits were received in the same sceptical spirit. The scepticism was naturally compounded in the case of a man who was by now widely identified as "that *Town Topics* Colonel," an association that implied all kinds of misrepresentation when convenient. For that matter, if there had been no other evidence against him, the Colonel's frequent overacting of the role of the retired military personage of high rank would have cast doubt on the possibility that his eagle had been honestly come by. As for his occasional references to important achievements, or at least temporary success, in half a dozen other fields during his lifetime, his own employees at *Town Topics* weren't the only ones to treat them with an elaborate wink as soon as his back was turned. Most of his 1906 contemporaries, including newspaper writers of the day, regarded these tales as further bluster from the proprietor of a transparent bunco game. Serviceable headlines require simple premises, and it is not considered cricket for the principal figure they deal with to have had as various and protean a history as that of Colonel Mann in the half-century or so before he settled in as publisher of *Town Topics.*

The *Ledger's* "remarkable man" was born in Sandusky, Ohio, on September 27, 1839, of what he described as "Puritan stock," perhaps descending from the Kentish Manns who began to arrive in Massachusetts in 1627. His French middle name remains unexplained; since he made no point of it, more often than not signing himself with the bare middle initial, it was apparently no high-flown afterthought. (When "d'Alton" was spelled out, he insisted upon the small "d", but when he used the initial it was capitalized and the apostrophe dropped.) Of his parents all that is known is that his mother's name was Ford and that his father, William R. Mann, was a Jeffersonian Democrat, to which political philosophy the Colonel remained faithful all his life. In his later years he sometimes told people that his father had fought in the War of 1812, but what William R. Mann did for a living thereafter he never thought interesting enough to mention. The elder Mann lived long enough, at any rate, to father a son as late as 1855. Besides this son, Eugene, and the future Colonel, there were several other children, one of whom was named Horace, but Mann never claimed any kinship with the distinguished educator. As a young boy in the 1840's, he reported two decades later, he had stood in the Ohio fields and watched "long trains of great Dutch wagons or 'prairie schooners,' each carrying a hundred and fifty or two hundred bushels of grain, drawn by four or six horses, slowly wheeling along to the city of Cleveland." Soon afterward the railroads had come through and their revolutionary effect on the area, making some towns and breaking others, had made a deep impression on him. Early in the 1850's he rode on one of the new railroads as far as Chicago and noted for future reference the discomforts of the overnight part of the trip.

By 1855 the Mann family had moved thirty miles across the state border to Adrian, Michigan. William d'Alton Mann left the fold about this time to be "educated as a civil engineer," as he later described it in the first edition of *Who's Who in America*, without specifying his alma mater, if any. By late 1858, according to certain internal references in the Saunterer's later commentaries, he was living in New York

City. Whatever his source of income, it was sufficient to keep him in good standing at the Astor House on lower Broadway, still one of the town's fashionable hostelries, and to allow him frequent visits to the theater which, six decades later, he enjoyed comparing, to its vast advantage, with the Broadway fare available after the First World War. His acquaintance in those early days, either in New York or on a visit to South Carolina, included Wade Hampton, one of the country's largest cotton planters and a grand seigneur of the South. Sometime during 1858 he took out one of the earliest policies issued by the Connecticut Mutual Life Insurance Company. Presumably the beneficiaries included a wife he had acquired along the way. At any rate, a daughter, Emma, had been born sometime during 1857 or 1858, in the fall of which year Mann celebrated his nineteenth birthday. During the summer of 1865 when he was on trial as an oil swindler this precociousness baffled one of the men from the district attorney's office.

"He swears he is only twenty-five years old!" shouted the prosecutor. "He has a child eight years old, is married to a second wife, and he swears he is only twenty-five years of age."

"I arrived at puberty at an early age . . . , and all I can say is I can lick *you*," Mann answered him smartly.

In 1859 a relative of Mann's died and left him a hundred acres of farmland near Grafton, Ohio. On the property was a run-down building that had once been a country inn. Apparently the outlook in New York had turned unpropitious. Mann, now all of twenty, moved his family to Grafton and re-opened the hotel. It was not the Astor House, however, nor was Grafton New York. When he abandoned the project, and the town, in the spring of 1861, he left a trail of debts. He wasted little time brooding over the disaster. Fort Sumter had fallen, and crossing over to his parents' adopted state he arranged, in accordance with his policy of always traveling first class, for a captain's commission in the First Michigan Cavalry. The First Michigan arrived in Washington in the early summer, moved on into Virginia and, according to Mann, was the first volunteer cavalry regiment to take the field. Late that same summer the First Michigan, fighting under General Pope, took part in the Second Battle of Bull Run.

The northern cavalry troops amounted to only a few thousand in the early days of the war and were, for the most part, used as vedettes—mounted sentinels in advance of the picket forces. "Whoever heard of a dead cavalryman?" General Hooker snorted about this time. During the following winter and spring the fifty thousand Union troops deployed in northern Virginia for the protection of Washington spent much of their time fending off the raids of Confederate General J. E. B. Stuart's cavalry division, hardly a tenth as large. Armed with sporting rifles and fowling pieces, Stuart's men, fed and quartered by the friendly Virginians, would swoop down on troop and supply trains, burning and looting them, and be off in the hospitable hills before the northern forces could lumber up to engage them. According to a pamphlet, "The Raiders," which he published in 1876, Mann was prominent among those who proposed that the North should fight mounted rifleman with mounted rifleman and that the ideal mustering place was the West—by which he meant the Middle West—where the citizenry were still more at home on the horse than the horse car. "This view prevailed," he wrote, and in the spring of 1862 "under orders from the Secretary of War," as he recalled it, he was sent back to Detroit, where he organized the First Mounted Rifles. Along with two horse artillery companies which he also raised, this became the

Fifth Michigan Cavalry, "the first of a large number of regiments of volunteers speedily raised from among the farmers of western states." At his suggestion, he later claimed, they were armed with the new rapid-fire magazine gun. In the late summer of 1862 he organized a second regiment, the Seventh Michigan and was given its command, receiving his colonel's commission shortly after his twenty-third birthday. Command of the Fifth Michigan went to another youthful volunteer, Russell Alger. With a third local cavalry regiment, the Sixth Michigan, Alger, Mann, and their mounted troops cantered East to join the First Michigan at the Virginia front, the four regiments—actually the second brigade of the Third Cavalry Division—being unofficially known as the Michigan Brigade.

By the end of 1862 Lee's army, including Stuart and his cavalry, had moved North and West. Colonel John Singleton Mosby, Stuart's favorite scout, remained behind, deep within enemy territory, to continue the hit-and-run harassment with a force that rarely numbered as many as a hundred men— stragglers, deserters from other branches of the Confederate Army, and other venturesome free souls, whom Mosby described as constituting "almost as motley a crowd as Falstaff's regiment." During the next eighteen months the raiding operations of this bold and impudent little band kept the occupying forces so demoralized that the four Virginia counties nearest Washington were known, in grudging tribute, as "Mosby's Confederacy," and an entire cavalry division of six thousand men, under General Julius Stahel, was deployed there just to keep his depredations at a minimum. When, decades later, the army finally got around to issuing a manual on guerrilla warfare, it leaned heavily on Mosby's memoirs, and in the 1950's he reappeared as a television hero in a series called "The Gray Ghost." To the Union Army in the spring of 1863, however, he was no hero but a maddening symbol of their ineffectuality, "a lurking and mocking spirit," as Edmund Wilson has described him, who added dire insult to injury when, in late April, he captured a northern general and a hundred of his troops without firing a shot.

An exploit that is dwelt upon at as great length as any other in Mosby's memoirs was his firing of the Orange-Alexandria train at the end of May, 1863. Most of his previous damage had amounted to the stealing of horses, the taking down of chain bridges, the occasional shooting of sentries, and to general loss of face as well as sleep. ("I have often thought that their fierce hostility to me was more on account of the sleep I made them lose than the numbers we killed and captured," he later wrote.) Stuart now sent a courier to suggest that Mosby emulate one of his own more ambitious feats and put out of commission the supply train that brought food and ammunition from Washington to the occupying troops stationed deep in Virginia. Mosby sent back word that for this assignment he would need a small cannon, and a mountain howitzer capable of delivering curved fire was dispatched to him.

Colonel Mann, whose regiment was part of General Stahel's division, had his headquarters at Kettle Run in Mosby territory, between the Rappahannock and Bull Run Rivers. On the evening of May 28 he reported the return of five different searching parties who had spent several days vainly looking for Mosby. At that moment, with forty-eight recruits and his new gun, Mosby was bivouacked a few miles away on a hill above the railroad track near Catlett's Station, the men sleeping on pine needles in a protective circle around the howitzer. When reveille from the nearby Union camp woke them the next morning, they slipped down, cut the telegraph wires, removed a rail from the track, watched as the twelve-car train was derailed and then exploded its boiler with a shell from the howitzer. When the guard fled, Mosby's men, who were always short of rations, began to loot the train of its contents, with special attention to a load of fresh shad. While Mosby and a few stalwart helpers burned the train, most of the others stopped to fry the shad on the spot and then went after a salvaged load of candy. Knowing the cannon fire had alerted the enemy, Mosby wrote in his memoirs, "I wished I was somewhere else." A few minutes later Mann came galloping up with some of his own men as well as detachments from the Fifth New York and the First Vermont Cavalry regiments. They charged Mosby's forces on the shad-reeking hillside. A shot from the cannon scattered them, but Mosby's motley company didn't make its getaway at once. "I was fighting on a point of honor. I wanted to save the howitzer," Mosby later recalled. Both sides regrouped, with Mosby's men deploying themselves at the top of a nearby hill where Mann's troops charged them. "They came up quite gallantly, not in dispersed order, but in columns of fours, crowded in a narrow lane," Mosby wrote to Stuart the next day in a report that cast some doubt on the sophistication of Mann's military tactics. If the Union men had separated and attacked him from several directions, guerrilla style, it would have been all over with him, Mosby noted. Mann and his troops were twice driven back by the cannon fire, but rallied each time, and when Mosby ran out of ammunition, moved in and took the howitzer. Mosby and most of his men escaped. The Union side had lost four men, with fifteen wounded, and reported Mosby's casualties as seven men. Mosby insisted he had lost only one, with four wounded. As for the gun, he pointed out grumpily that it had been the Union's anyhow, having been captured from them eighteen months before at the battle of Ball's Bluff. Nevertheless, the Federal forces were exultant about even this measure of victory over the infernal Mosby. "We whipped him like the devil and took his artillery," Stahel wired Washington, and gave Mann credit for the feat. "It was the main Mosby engagement in Virginia, the only time he stood and made a determined fight against a Union force," the Colonel boasted in a note on Mosby's death fifty-three years later.

The high point of the war for Mann, however—as for so many Civil War buffs today—was Gettysburg. His regiment there was under the command of General George Custer. In the West Point class of 1861 Custer had ranked thirty-fourth in a class of thirty-four. During the fall of 1863 he had vainly applied to the Michigan Governor for command of the Seventh Michigan. The Governor had replied that such commands customarily went to the officers who were responsible for raising the regiments. It was this commission that had then gone to Mann. At the beginning of June, 1863, Custer was still a first lieutenant with the Fifth Michigan. On June 18, however, in a minor engagement at Aldie, Virginia, he led a wild and effective charge against one of Stuart's forward detachments, a report of which caught the eye of the commanding cavalry general, Pleasanton. Twenty-four hours later, in a move that causes some blinking on the part of Custer's most idolatrous biographers, Pleasanton named Custer general of the Michigan Brigade. Two months younger than Mann, he was twenty-three years old, the youngest general in the army.

The move north to Gettysburg began four days after this startling promotion. Even among cavalry officers, whose sartorial independence was notorious, Custer cut quite a figure in his black velveteen and gold-braided jacket and trousers, his gray cloak with a red rose in its lapel, his star-studded cavalier's hat, his scarlet necktie, and his shining golden ringlets that hung to his shoulders. The Michigan Brigade with its four colonels, whose stunned and disgruntled frame of mind Custer happily described in letters home, fell in behind this gaudy knight, crossed the Potomac in a heavy fog, and, after a forced march, reached the battle scene. Their major engagement came on July 3, the third and culminating day of the battle, and was fought on Rummel's farm, three miles east of Cemetery Ridge. Pickett's famous charge on the Union forces was from the west. Jeb Stuart, according to a plan devised by Mosby, was to engage the rear. But as Stuart moved toward the main arena across Rummel's cow pasture, he was attacked by the Union cavalry, including Custer's brigade. Though heavily outnumbered, the northerners held the field from midmorning till seven in the evening. By that hour Pickett had been driven back, and the battle was over. "A few miles to the east," writes Bruce Catton in *This Hallowed Ground,* "all but unnoticed by the armies themselves, Union and Confederate cavalry were fighting a desperate mounted battle, charging lines crashing into each other at full gallop as if these troopers by themselves would win the day and the war; and if Stuart's worn brigades had managed to break through, they would have gone all across the defenseless rear of the Army of the Potomac, where they could have made vast trouble. But they did not break through. They drew off at last with heavy losses—and afterward all anyone could say was 'Oh, yes, the cavalry fought at Gettysburg, too, didn't it?' " In the opinion of other historians, who have called it "the great cavalry fight of the war"—and of all cavalrymen— the fierce tournament in the cow pasture provided the margin of victory at Gettysburg, itself traditionally the turning point of the rebellion.

The charge of Mann's Seventh Michigan came in the early afternoon. Screaming, "Come on, you Wolverines!" Custer led them off, but then turned aside, and Mann and his regiment, 407 strong, "sabres gleaming and colors flying in the breeze," in the words of an eyewitness, "dashed into the open field and rode straight at the Confederate line where they discharged their revolvers in the very faces of the foe." Horses reared and rebounded, and Mann charged again; then "for minutes, which seemed like hours, amid the clashing of sabres, the rattle of small arms, the agonized imprecations, the demands to surrender, the undaunted replies, and the appeals for mercy, the Confederate column stood its ground." Eventually the Seventh Michigan fell back, but "Colonel Mann is entitled to much credit," Custer declared in his official report to Pleasanton. "From his ornate report of that day's fighting," noted one of Custer's biographers, Frederic Van De Water, "it would appear that (Custer) and the Seventh Michigan alone broke the Confederate assault." By the end of the day General Hooker had heard of a dead cavalryman. Custer's brigade had suffered 219 casualties, almost a tenth of its strength. Of these, an even hundred were from Mann's regiment.

After Gettysburg Stuart headed South and crossed the Potomac with Custer's brigade among those in hot pursuit. In a few days the Union cavalry was back where it had started, in the dense forest growths bordering the banks of the Rappahannock. At Brandy Station in September Stuart came within a stirrup's width of trapping Custer's entire brigade. At Buckland a few weeks later they were described as "running for their lives." Thoroughly out of sorts, Custer dug in for the winter in the southern reaches of Mosby's Confederacy. "Throughout '63 I not infrequently had to do with Mosby and once again came mighty near to making him prisoner, but that is another story," the Colonel declared in his obituary note on the elusive scout. Mosby remained at large, however, and, as his raids continued, Custer's disposition did not improve. Many months later, after some of his men captured six of Mosby's scouts in a freak encounter, he not only ordered all of the prisoners summarily executed in accordance with an order from General Grant but had one of them, a seventeen-year-old boy, dragged through the streets in back of a horse and then shot in the presence of his mother.

In the tedium of garrison life the incubating ill-feeling between the arrogant, be-curled twenty-three-year-old general and his inferior officers—many of them twice his age—inevitably flourished. Custer took to ordering morning and evening inspection and frequent drills, once calling seven in twenty-four hours. His was not a large nature, and it seems unlikely that he was partial to Mann, who had got the commission he'd gone after a year before. Certainly, another of the original Michigan Brigade colonels later felt the force of his antagonism. In August, 1864, apparently in a fit of bad temper, Custer ordered Russell Alger dismissed from the army for being AWOL. By the time the order went through channels Alger had been moved to another post, and it was never carried out. A senatorial investigation many years later concluded that the AWOL charge was probably baseless. Alger afterward was brevetted a major-general, became commander of the Grand Army of the Republic, Governor of Michigan and Secretary of War under McKinley, and died a United State Senator, but the furor over the old dismissal order, dug up in 1892, was enough to disqualify him in the race for the Republic nomination for President in that year.

A *Tribune* story in 1880 would call Colonel Mann "an adventurer who left the army under a cloud." There is apparently no record to support this version of his departure from military life, but it seems possible that the atmosphere of Custer's garrison had given him a premonition of a sudden end to his army career much like the one Custer eventually tried to arrange for Alger. Fortunately for him, Mann now had other plans for his future. Sometime in the fall of 1863 it appears that he had gone on furlough to Washington and, after meeting with a lawyer, had visited certain government offices. Back in camp he kept a sharp ear out for mail call as the third winter of the war closed in. Early in February, 1864, having got the letter he was waiting for, he resigned from the Army.

On December 8, 1863, Mann had been granted a patent on an improved method of "so arranging the slinging attachments, accoutrements and equipments of infantry and cavalry soldiers that when in use the weight of the cartridge box will be counter-balanced by the other accoutrements usually worn upon the body, and the weights of the whole held upon the shoulders." Mann's Patent Accoutrement Company was incorporated early in June with an office at 240 Broadway, a few doors north of A. T. Stewart's department store, the Marble Palace. In May, 1863, even before going through this formality, he had an order from the Secretary of War for thirty thousand of his yokelike contrivances; twenty thousand more were ordered in August and another thirty thousand in November. One way or another Mann had solved the problem of initial capital, possibly by way of his second marriage, which may have taken place about this time; it was in July, 1865, that he was described in court as having a second wife, and in the same proceedings he was quoted as having spoken the previous winter of a wealthy mother-in-law. (The first Mrs. Mann had apparently disappeared from the scene sometime before, perhaps as a result of one of the obstetrical accidents that made domestic histories as various a hundred years ago as divorces do today). Orders for Mann accoutrements were arranged for by tried and true methods: the

Colonel's farewell to the cavalry was a case of *au revoir* but not goodbye. He spent most of the spring and summer of 1864 touring the army camps around Washington, renewing old friendships, and, incidentally, accumulating endorsements. Apparently Custer never obliged him, but he did considerably better. Enlisting a Colonel William Hillyer, who had been on Grant's staff at Vicksburg, Mann dispatched him to Grant's headquarters at City Point, just north of Richmond. The commanding general obligingly signed a letter calling the invention indispensable to the war effort. Mann also added to his staff the clerk of the Military Committee of the House of Representatives, George Kellogg, who carried the appropriate message to his superiors. By the end of 1864 Mann's personal profit on his invention had reached $50,000. Unfortunately for his plans, however, one of his earlier promotion schemes had now developed into an historic success. According to his account of matters in *The Raiders,* the 1876 book on cavalry tactics, his proposals for using the Union cavalry as a mobile force of outriders, rather than as sentinels, had been dutifully carried out by Sheridan and Wilson and had "turned the tide of the war in favor of the national forces, and contributed vastly to, if they did not actually secure, the concluding triumphs of Grant and Sherman." As these triumphs came thick and fast and the war drew to a close, new orders for military accoutrements inevitably slumped to nothing.

Just over five years earlier the first oil well in the world had been sunk in Titusville, Pennsylvania, thirty-five miles east of the Ohio border. As the *Tribune* later described matters, Mann in early January, 1865, "had a 'golden inspiration' about some neglected and worthless property he owned in Grafton, Ohio, near the Pennsylvania line." Within a few weeks' time the resourceful ex-accoutrements tycoon was in the oil business. His corporate assets included the hundred acres of Ohio land left from his hotelkeeping days, the magic properties of the word "oil," the avalanche of mustering-out pay about to be loosed on the victorious Union forces, and the stubborn ignorance of geographic points west of Philadelphia on the part of the average easterner. (The *Tribune* writer was no exception: Grafton lies not "near the Pennsylvania line" but a third of the way across Ohio, a hundred miles west of the Pennsylvania border.) Colonel Mann made a western swing, laid down a $45 deposit on two hundred acres not far from his almost-forgotten holdings, hired a caretaker, and on his way home stopped off to lay down another small deposit on a single acre in Verango County, Pennsylvania, near the fabled Titusville. Back in New York, he set up the United Service Petroleum and Mining Company and, ordering some stationery, shortened the name on the letterhead to "U.S. Petroleum and Mining Company," implying some measure of government cachet. The officers included Kellogg and Hillyer (whom he persuaded to plow back into the new venture the commissions he owed them from the accoutrement venture), the editor of the *Army-Navy Journal,* and a former governor of the Dakota Territory. The president of the Company was Major-General Winfield Scott Hancock, one of the celebrated northern commanders at Antietam and Gettsyburg, whom Mann had somehow talked into contributing to the enterprise not only an impressive façade but a thousand dollars of his own money. The company's vice-president and general superintendent was Colonel Mann. He immediately arranged to have U.S. Petroleum's executive committee designate him as their trustee with full powers to buy all land necessary for development and meanwhile to have custody of all company funds.

Even before the company had been formally organized, Mann had got up a prospectus "written in magniloquent style," reported the *Tribune* later, and "fairly daubed with oil," that listed the site of its holdings as "mainly Verango County, Pennsylvania, near the famous Joy Farm," the site of a big oil strike in the summer of 1864. Taking a remarkable chance, he emphasized that none of the properties "is in mythological or unknown regions." "Successful drilling will be completed in sixty days," the prospectus went on. There was "no possibility of loss: the reputation of all concerned makes this certain." Eager investors need not wait for a salesman to call, the circular went on to point out. "Persons at a distance or in the army can send Treasury notes, drafts, government bonds, post office or paymaster's orders to our office at New York." Advertisements crammed with similar helpful hints were prepared for the *Army-Navy Journal* and for *Harper's Weekly*. Armed with a suitcase of these come-ons as well as a small bottle of lubricating oil which he described as the product of some preliminary prospecting on the Grafton acres, Mann in early March transferred his point of operations to Washington, where he took rooms in Owen's Hotel and held open house for officers returning from the front. To his guests he explained that U.S. Petroleum was issuing a hundred thousand shares of stock with a par value of three dollars, but that before the general public got a chance to gobble them up, a hand-picked group of investors would be given a crack at them for a mere dollar a share. During the next few weeks Mann succeeded in handpicking— and collecting a total of $57,500 from—forty-five investors who made the mistake of showing up at his suite. They included five brigadier-generals (the commander of all army prisons was one of these) and a dozen lieutenant-colonels and colonels, one of the latter being his crony from the Michigan Brigade, Russell Alger. (Probably he hoped also to include Custer, by this time a major-general, in his privileged circle.

On March 8, 1865, Mrs. Custer, who was living in Washington, wrote her husband: "Colonel Mann is so polite. He sent me a lovely basket of violets and camellias. . . ." But Custer, fortunately for his bank account, was otherwise occupied north of Richmond, fending off the last-ditch assaults of Jubal Early.) As fast as a ranking officer forked over his money, the brassy weight of his name was added to the U.S. Petroleum prospectus.

The war ended on Palm Sunday, April 9. Two days later Mann marched down Pennsylvania Avenue with the rest of the Army of the Potomac to the tune of "Ain't We Glad to Get Out of the Wilderness," and then, in hot pursuit of the three-dollar customers, scurried off to City Point, where he unloaded thousands of his handouts just inside each company paymaster's tent. The men were warier than some of their general officers, however, and no more than seventeen hundred dollars came in from troops in the field during the next two months. By the end of this period distribution of the circular had been called off by U.S. Petroleum's executive committee, and all hell was breaking loose at company headquarters in New York.

At a meeting in March the Colonel had informed the committee that the price of the company land came to $45,000. This disbursement had been authorized although none of the stockholders then—or at any time in the future— saw any deeds or other evidence of money paid out. (The papers had been held up by the recorder's office, Mann explained to them.) Late in the next month Mann had arranged for his caretaker in Ohio to send a telegram announcing the bringing in of a gusher on property adjoining the Grafton acres. By early June, however, with no oil of their own in sight except for the sample that the Colonel carried around in his pocket and with the sixty-day deadline long past, his overprivi-

leged investors, none of whom had laid eyes on Grafton, began to regard the name of the town as ominous. After a council
of war, the ex-Governor of the Dakotas was delegated to go
out and see what was going on. Mann, getting wind of what he
called their "contemptible subterfuge," wired his caretaker to
start digging, to pretend the pumping machines were temporarily somewhere else, and to "CRACK EVERYTHING
UP HIGH RUSH THINGS FOR GOD'S SAKE." But the
jig was up. On the twenty-sixth of June, after the scout had
reported back, four of the stockholders swore out a warrant
for Colonel Mann's arrest on a charge of obtaining money
under false pretenses. Apprehended in his quarters at the
Astor House, he was arraigned the next day at Jefferson
Market Courthouse and released on fifteen thousand dollars
bail.

The trial lasted all summer and into the fall. It was well
attended. Oil was moving into the national limelight, along
with some intimation of the great fortunes it would bring.
Mann's was one of the first—perhaps *the* first—important trial
involving peculation in the new commodity. Morever, he had
hired an attorney who was bound to draw a crowd: David
Dudley Field, the most famous trial lawyer of his day, a stalwart and impressive figure and one noted for his colorful
skirmishes with opposing counsel. The trial so often occupied
space on the front pages of local newspapers that the *Times*
could begin one account of the proceedings with the words,
"Assuming that everyone knows the history of the U.S.
Petroleum Company to the present time. . . ." Half a dozen
papers had representatives there daily to cover "The Celebrated Oil Bubble," "The Great Petroleum Swindle," or what
the *World* aptly called "The Oily Gammon," a gammon, in
backgammon, being a double game won by the player who
bears off all his men before his adversary removes any.

Part of Field's strategy was to take advantage of the post-war reaction against the military. The former cavalry colonel was transformed into just an ordinary civilian youngster who was being ill-used by uniformed arrogants. "Gentlemen in the army can wear fine coats and ride long-tail horses, but they cannot override us," he boomed at one point. It was the steady emphasis on Mann's youth that, late in July, precipitated the prosecutor's challenge of his claim to being only twenty-five years old ("He looks to be over thirty," the *New York Daily News* noted) and Mann's response to the effect that he had been sexually precocious. An exchange followed involving comparative virility that had the judge calling for "decency." The newspapers ruled it unprintable, but their references to "the racy nature of the proceedings" brought out the SRO sign in the gallery. A few days later, waiting for the judge to arrive, one of the spectators remarked that "he just had to see the play out." "Do you think it will turn out to be a farce or a tragedy?" the prosecutor asked him. "Either way, the defendant is no Hamlet," said Attorney Field.

As the summer wore on, the audience at Jefferson Market Courthouse heard testimony that all but one acre of U.S. Petroleum's holdings were some hundred and twenty-five miles west of "the unctuous region around Titusville," that a large share of the holdings consisted of vacant and abandoned acreage that had been owned by the defendant since 1859, that on inspection they had been found to be "not an oleaginous location" but totally worthless except for the former hotel—"a mere shanty, anyhow," that "Mann run away from in 1861," as the prosecutor put it, with less grammar than accuracy—and one recently dug well, quite empty and going down only ten feet. Not only had the defendant paid himself $45,000 for this and other unpromising acreage, but the balance of the company treasury, amounting to nearly $14,000, had also disappeared, appropriated for the rental of an office (Mann's old accoutrement headquarters at 240 Broadway), stationery, and "miscellaneous." Nevertheless, early in October, after two thousand pages of prosecution testimony, Field moved for dismissal of the charges. Three months later, on the twenty-seventh of January, the Judge agreed to the dismissal on the ground of lack of jurisdiction. Most of the money, he pointed out, had changed hands in the city of Washington. In any case, he added benignly, if there had been "a bit of overstatement" in Mann's claims, all concerned were "highly respectable parties." Interviewed by the press, the Colonel described himself as "highly gratified" by the outcome. The *Tribune's* subhead over their report of this verdict was "How Mann Escaped His Just Due."

The judge had noted that the complainants, if they cared to, could pursue the matter in the civil courts. None of them was so minded, and the hapless trickle of U.S. Petroleum share orders that continued to come in during the next few months was soon being routed to the dead-letter office. The events of the trial were recapitulated on the front pages of the Republican press on July 9, 1880, the day after General Hancock (who had taken no part in the trial) was nominated by the Democrats to run for President of the United States against Garfield. It was in an accompanying editorial that the *Tribune* referred to Mann as "an adventurer who left the army under a cloud." In spite of this detailed reprise, when Mann, a quarter of a century later, was suffering nationwide notoriety in the series of trials involving libel, perjury, and extortion, not a single reporter dug around in the morgue and connected the hoary journalist with the youthful perpetrator of the Oily Gammon. Nor, apparently, did any of the principals who were still extant, including Senator Alger, care to bring the matter up. When the *Birmingham Ledger,* in its staunch apologia for the Colonel, declared that "before he took charge of *Town Topics,* no word had ever been uttered against his good name," no word having to do with oil swindles was uttered to the contrary.

Artist Frederick's study of the overflowing whiskers of Colonel Mann, with "society row" as a relief.
MRS. NORMAN HAPGOOD.   MRS. ROBERT COLLIER.   MRS. NAST.

Carpet Bag
and Boudoir Car

"As a youngster, prior to the war, I had visited different portions of the South, had many acquaintances among Southern people and, while doing my utmost as an officer of cavalry in the Union Army to defeat the Confederate forces, I had always close to my heart a deep sympathy with the Southern people in the sufferings and deprivations which their attempts to disrupt the Union had brought upon them. The war over, my thoughts turned to the South, and I was so strongly moved by the conditions existing there that I determined to take the somewhat considerable means of which I was possessed— largely from royalties arising from my invention in army accoutrements—and go to the old city of Mobile, cast my lot with its people, and do what in me lay toward its material . . . upbuilding." Thus, half a century later, the editor of *Town Topics* explained his oblique change of course shortly after he had retrieved his $15,000 bail money from the clerk at the Jefferson Market Courthouse in the winter of 1866—and almost managed to conceal in the welter of lofty verbiage the fact that the reticule he carried with him was a carpet bag.

The Birmingham *Ledger,* in its 1906 statement in his defense, had also noted that as a resident of Mobile after the war the Colonel had "helped to expose the terrible infamy of the reconstruction period. He made a gallant fight for the South in those dreadful days." If he was now in trouble, wrote the *Ledger,* "Alabama has thrown no stone at him." Remarkably, the Birmingham editor found it as easy as the Colonel to gloss over the circumstance that Mann had invaded the postwar South as what southerners of the time also called a "carrion crow." After the long wait for the verdict in the oil case, he must have been on the lookout for a likely berth, an assignment that would get him way out of town as well as improve his cash position, no doubt somewhat depleted after he had paid off David Dudley Field. The New York papers in these months were full of correspondence from the ruined Confederacy. Mobile was, according to the *Tribune,* "the most desolate of cities." With its "low and mean buildings," its narrow streets, "overrun with mules and mosquitoes," its "thirty thousand languid citizens, maundering of yellow fever," it had altogether "the most melancholy atmosphere that our healthful land knows." On the other hand, it was Alabama's largest city, the commercial center of the state, and had been the country's busiest cotton port after New Orleans. In the spring of 1866, probably through the influence of his many friends in high places to whom Field had continually referred during the U.S. Petroleum trial, the twenty-six-year-old Colonel turned up in Mobile as the Federal Assessor of Internal Revenue.

In the first years after the war Mobile women would "go far out of their way to avoid meeting a Federal officer and, when forced to pass one, would sweep their skirts aside as if to avoid contagion," reports Walter Fleming in *Civil War and Reconstruction in Alabama.* Representatives of the Federal government, he adds, were "mercilessly ostracized." Mann was not only such a representative but a member of an agency authorized to capture and sell the abandoned property of all men who had fought for the Confederacy and, if a local citizen balked at paying his taxes, to have him arrested and tried

by a military commission. The annual Federal revenue from
Mobile during his first two-and-a-half years in office was more
than four million dollars. The position of Assessor was obviously one offering abundant opportunity for personal enrich-
ment. "Under the military constitution," wrote an historian
living in Mobile at the time, "the art of taxation reached its
most tortuous trickery." He added that at least one Federal
revenue man in an upstate Alabama city had been murdered
in his bed. Nevertheless, the front page of *The New York
Times* for August 4, 1869, carried the announcement that,
according to early returns from Mobile, W. D. Mann, Federal revenue officer, had been elected to Congress from the
First Alabama District, having run as the candidate of the
Redeemers, or Democrats, the bitterly anti-Reconstruction
party of most of the white people in the South.

This unlikely development probably came about because
the Colonel was a devoutly convivial man. One of his first
moves after he arrived in Washington as a cavalry captain in
the fall of 1861 had been to enlist in the Knights Templars.
In his later years he was rarely a member of fewer than a
dozen clubs at a time. In or out of the fraternal orders, presumably in his youth as well as in his old age, he was forever
convening a crowd around him. The social life of a Union
partisan was clearly impossible during the Reconstruction
years in Mobile. In early 1866 there were five thousand
northerners in Alabama, come down to enjoy the spoils of
victory. Within a few years all but a handful of newcomers
had departed, done in by the side-swinging skirts and the
long, solitary evenings. The Colonel, however, had solved the
problem by going four-square over to the other side. Such a
conversion must have appeared highly suspect, but his plau-
sibility under fire had recently been proved in a court of law.
Moreover, a tax assessor is in a position to make friends as

well as enemies. When, three years after his arrival, the Colonel was accused of diverting to his own use enormous sums of money due the United States Treasury, he arranged to have a spokesman reply that if any such money had failed to reach Washington, it was because it had stayed in the pockets of his Mobile friends. "There are many merchants in this city," said his informal defense counsel, "who know that Colonel Mann saved them thousands of dollars that they would have lost had he rigidly and vindictively strained the regulations of the revenue department for the purpose of catching the unwary in the meshes of the law." From whatever source, the Colonel also had cash in hand and was soon applying it where it would do his social—and political—cause the most good.

When the war ended, there were four daily newspapers in Mobile, the *Evening News,* the *Register and Advertiser,* the *Times* and the *Tribune,* all in advanced stages of financial disrepair. In the view of *The New York Times* a few months before Mann arrived there, their proprietors, without exception, were "a disloyal gang," constantly stirring up trouble for the Reconstruction forces. Mann threw in his lot with three of this recalcitrant crew, the men who controlled the *Evening News,* the *Register and Advertiser,* and the *Times.* As he described the process twenty-two years later in the *New York Tribune:* "The editors of the three papers were friends of mine. I accommodated them with loans until I had quite an amount invested." He had then taken over the *Mobile Times* outright sometime during 1866 when, in his own version of things, the owner became embarrassed about owing him so much money. By the following year he had paid enough over the amount owed him by the publishers of the other two papers to purchase them also. He then combined the plants and began to put out a single paper with a morning, evening, and weekly edition, which he called the *Mobile Register*. In case the usurper's proclamation that he had been "born and bred in the principles of Jeffersonian Democracy" and had cast his first and only vote for John Breckinridge didn't put the local Redeemer mind at rest, he announced that he was entirely in agreement with the political philosophy of the *Register's* predecessors. A number of the members of the "disloyal gang" continued to work for the hybrid journal and their friendly loan shark from the North. The *Register,* which now had by all odds the largest circulation in town, inveighed day after day against "the mousing and treacherous reconstruction grimalkins" and continued to assert for the benefit of the local colored people "the natural and indefeasible superiority of the white man on all occasions . . . a supremacy that God has created." During Mann's regime it became such a symbol of southern intractability that when the *Louisville Courier-Journal* announced in 1870 that it was giving up its fight to repeal the Fifteenth Amendment, the editors defended themselves by pointing out that in all other respects they had hewed as faithfully to the Confederate line as even the *Mobile Register.*

The first of the *Register's* four-to-six pages, during the years when Mann was its proprietor, was given over to commercial notices, with the exception of the two columns on the right which offered the irreducible minimum of foreign and national news. Inside were dispatches from "Our New York Correspondent," who, even in those days, was praising the virtues of the Lotos Club, and "Our New York Fashion Reporter," who on one occasion advocated the wearing of extra-long skirts by ladies indulging in that new craze, the riding of velocipedes, since there would then be "no need to wear false calves to make a fine show, for the calves need not be exposed at all." Otherwise the *Register,* after its daily rebel rallying cry, gave its attention to municipal reports, directions from Lee's former generals on how the French could win their war against the Prussians, and essays on such topics as whether or not Byron had committed incest. (Absolutely not. Harriet Beecher Stowe said he had, and "the author of *Uncle Tom's Cabin* can't tell the truth about anything.") The *Register* ran no society news. On one occasion in 1870 it denounced a short-lived northern magazine called *Our Society,* which printed items about its subscribers at fifty cents a line. The *Register*'s editorial writer pointed out that no genuine society person would dream of allowing his private affairs to be aired in the public press. The following year an editorial about a fake count who had married into a prominent New York family struck what would become a familiar posture, calling the incident "a ridiculous revelation . . . which lays bare the utter rottenness and corruption of what is called fashionable life in the metropolis."

Mann's total previous literary production, so far as is known, had consisted of the magniloquent oil prospectus. Nonetheless, the proprietor of the *Register* was publicly accused from time to time of also writing some of its editorials —although such charges by the opposition press usually referred to puffs for business ventures in which he was interested. In later years he was not backward about claiming credit for all aspects of the *Register* during his association with it. Although a naturally modest man, he wrote half a century afterward, he had no choice but to call most impressive his early success in a profession he had entered almost inadvertently, "for I succeeded in making a paper which at that time had a wider circulation and was deemed more important than any other published south of Louisville." Nor was he the only person impressed, he added. In 1886 when he had called on Henry Grady, the noted publisher of the

Atlanta Journal, Grady had told him that it was reading the *Register* in the Mann era that had given him the idea of going into the newspaper business. Grady had greeted him, according to the Colonel's self-serving recollection, as "my journalistic father" and "the man whose work determined my life."

Looking back from another century, Mann liked to cite with special pride two examples of his enterprise in the Mobile days. In 1867, he said, the annual message of a President of the United States had never been sent by wire further south than Richmond. When Andrew Johnson delivered his message to Congress in that year, the Colonel wrote, he had had it telegraphed to the *Register.* It had cost him a little over nine hundred dollars, but he had published it at the same time the New York papers did and had showed them, in his view, that the South was not so backward after all. Sometime before this he had decided to introduce some comic relief into the weekly edition of the *Register,* and, Mobile then being short of humorists, had cast about for some outside talent to give it a light touch. "Mark Twain had begun to attract attention by his witty sketches. I wrote and asked him to contribute to my paper. . . . I said he could choose his own subject," was the way the Colonel later remembered the episode. "He very promptly replied, accepting my proposal, which was that he should have the munificent honorarium of $15 an article. He wrote, 'I see by the copy you have sent that you have an Agricultural Department. As I know nothing about agriculture, I will write on that subject.' That was very characteristic, and I am happy to say that Mr. Clemens continued as a contributor until long after he had acquired such fame that he could command his own prices for his work, but he never raised the ante on me." The experience, if Mann's recollection was accurate, was presumably the basis for

Twain's article called "How I Edited an Agricultural Paper," published in *Galaxy* magazine in 1870. He had taken on the job, wrote the humorist, on the theory that "the less a man knows about a subject, the bigger noise he makes." During his tenure, which was "of short duration," he claimed he had repeatedly confused a furrow with a harrow and on one occasion had referred to the moulting season for cows. Later this piece became the basis for one of Twain's most successful turns on the lecture platform.*

The Colonel's standing with the white electorate of Mobile was undoubtedly enhanced when, not long after he took over the *Register,* he was visited at his office by his antebellum acquaintance, Confederate General Wade Hampton who, ironically, had been one of the southerners wounded in Mann's cavalry charge at Gettysburg. But what probably had made the Colonel eligible for the final password into former enemy circles was his role in an affair that the New York *Tribune* in 1888 would describe as "one of the most memorable incidents of the Reconstruction period" and John DuBose in *Alabama's Tragic Decade* called "the opening salvo of organized southern opposition to federal rule." Early in May, 1867, a delegation of northerners was scheduled to arrive in Mobile under the leadership of Congressman William Kelley of Pennsylvania, also known as "Pig Iron Kelley" because of his advocacy of a high tariff on that commodity. The invaders' announced mission was to lecture the townspeople on the rights of their Negro fellow citizens who by this time, encouraged by the Reconstruction forces, were threatening to take over the local government. The *Mobile Times,* by then the Colonel's property, ran an editorial expressing the pious hope that the white people of Mobile would not become so inflamed by Kelley's message

* Possibly it was the lecture that gave Mann the idea of claiming Twain as a contributor. Twain was not named as the agricultural editor in any copies of the *Mobile Weekly Register* that survive.

that they would imitate the people of Boston who had once torn another Irish Catholic limb from limb on the Boston common. Baffled, perhaps, by the information that the owner of the offending newspaper was a northern office holder who had arrived in town little more than a year before, Kelley confronted Mann in his rooms at the Battle House, Mobile's leading hotel. The Colonel not only endorsed the editorial, but declared that he had written it himself. During the street-corner speech that evening, as Kelley later described the event, he was "attacked by a very bad lot" who were led by Mann, whom he called a "cutthroat." "He meant to kill me. The platform was swept by bullets of the assassins, and several men were slain by my side. It was a fearful scene, and that villain was solely responsible for it. . . . I would not like to harbor in my breast that wretch's conscience." Three men had, in fact, been killed and ten wounded. The next morning, fearing further violence, Mann's old commanding general, Pope, then in charge of the Third Military Occupation District of which Alabama was a part, sent in a special boat, and Kelley and his party, including a highly nervous representative of the *New York Herald,* were ignominiously removed from the city. Public assemblies were banned after nightfall, all firearms were confiscated, and, as one Alabama patriot described it, "despotism of the sword followed."

The events of the bloody evening were hashed over twenty-one years later when Kelley gave an interview to a Washington paper that was widely reprinted elsewhere and made the front page of the New York *Tribune.* Kelley expressed his astonishment over having recently run into his would-be assassin at West Point and discovered him to be a highly-respected summer resident there as well as a friend of many of the Academy's officers. "He drove around in a stylish rig," reported Kelley, "and I scattered him every time by simply moving toward him when he stopped. He was evidently very uncomfortable, fearing perhaps that I would expose him to the crowd." Mann responded to this newspaper attack in true Alabama style, challenging Kelley's son to a duel since Kelley himself, he said, was "too aged." Calming down, he described the statements of the Republican Congressman as "an unwarranted attack on someone who is now out of politics," and expressed the hope that it would not have a disastrous effect on Cleveland's campaign for the Presidency against Harrison. As for having led the unfortunate riot in Mobile, he insisted that he had not even been present at the disturbance, having that night, as he recalled with his characteristic attention to detail, "attended the second and last concert of the Patti company at the Odd Fellows' Hall." At the time, however, a Congressional committee that investigated the incident upheld General Pope's contention that local newspapers had been largely responsible for the riot. In retaliation Pope cancelled the government's printing contracts with the plants of the Colonel's papers, an important source of their revenue, and also withheld all Federal, state and municipal legal advertising. When the Reconstruction government was turned over to civilians, they continued the ban. For the next three years Mann thus publicly suffered under the tyranny of the conquerors along with other residents of Mobile. In the minds of the leading citizens of his adopted city the former enemy colonel had proved himself to be true blue—or rather true Gray—when it counted. Besides, as one prominent Alabama citizen testified in 1871 before another Congressional committee investigating the Ku Klux Klan, the term "carpetbagger" was not generally used to describe "northern men of character and responsibility, who came to live in the South and identified themselves with the best interests of the community." Moreover, he added, it "is never applied to a Democrat under any circumstances."

"In those reconstruction days," the Colonel wrote many years afterward, "there was little for a southerner to do but make things hot for the northerners, hunt, fish, and run for Congress." John Forsyth, the editor of the *Register,* was a former mayor of the city and a power in local Democratic circles. The *Register*'s agricultural editor, C. C. Langdon, was a onetime Congressman from the First Alabama District, which included not only Mobile but such now-celebrated cultural centers as Camden and Selma. These two new friends probably pointed out to the Colonel the possibilities for him in the unusual political circumstances that then prevailed in Alabama. By the summer of 1869 Alabama had formally reentered the Union, and a special Congressional election was to be held on August 3. The House of Representatives has the privilege of passing on the qualifications of its members, however, and feeling against the South was still running very high. The House insisted that no member could be seated who had ever sworn to uphold the Constitution of the United States and had then supported the rebel cause in the war. Almost every likely Democrat in the state was thus disqualified from running for the Congressional seat. The candidate of the Radicals, as the Republican party was then known in the South, was a more orthodox carpetbagger from the state of Maine named Alfred Buck, who held not one but five separate state, county, and municipal offices. The Democrats in the First District were convinced that they had no chance of keeping Buck out of Congress unless they put up against him another northerner, but in this case, as the *Register* outlined the plot, a northerner "whose every action and deed while amongst us has proven his devotion and fidelity to the Constitutional Liberty of the South." And who amongst us, asked the *Register,* fitted this description better than Colonel Mann? He would serve as "our perfect Trojan horse to introduce into the enemy's walls." There were two other contenders for this subversive role, but on June 22 Mann was nominated on the first ballot at a meeting in Mobile's Mammouth Hall. He described himself as astonished and overcome. ("May I not be pardoned for a diffidence that amounts to almost a distrust of myself?") He stood, he said in his acceptance speech, as "a living refutation of the malignant representations that bitterness and hate toward all northern men, and especially Federal ex-soldiers, rule among the people of the South." The county Democratic leader described him as having come to the city "overshadowed by a dark, a sable cloud" that had then been "pierced by the golden rays of intelligence, of truth. It is the heart which makes the man."

A few days later, accompanied by Langdon, Forsyth and a small band ready to play "Dixie" at every opportunity, the Colonel set out on the campaign trail through the upper reaches of the district, traveling by horse, stage coach and river steamer. This was indeed Alabama's tragic decade, but it had its comic opera episodes. Extraordinarily, the slogan of Mann's campaign was "Down with the Carpetbaggers!" ("We must not relax our efforts till every absquatulator is sent back howling to his hole in the north.") Even more remarkably, the ex-Assessor of Internal Revenue—he had resigned this office the day after the nomination—never failed to denounce in particular "the carpetbaggers who exhaust our substance by cruel taxation—under which we are groaning—for no other purpose than to fill their purses." His speeches, according to not only the *Register* but other Democratic-Redeemer papers in the State, were well received. "So telling were his blows," reported the Camden *Vindicator,* "that one could almost imagine he heard the dying groans of the venal crew who pollute with their presence the sacred precincts of our halls of justice." "He came amongst us unknown and without a reputation as an orator," noted the *Selma Argus,* and then described one of his addresses there as "the best political speech made in the county since the war. It was plain, earnest, practical, logical, truthful. His presence here has acted like magic." "We wish there were a Mann of the same stripe in every district in the state," declared the Tuscaloosa *Observer.*

The Colonel's manner on the hustings continued to be a study in diffidence. "I come to you as a simple, almost-stranger," he would often begin. "You have received me with more welcome and more consideration than I had a right to expect." Supporting players in his retinue described him to the assembled crowds as "honest and upright," "high-toned and chivalrous," "quiet and unobtrusive." They also remarked upon more enduring elements in his character. ("He is imbued with great energy, and a more industrious man does not live.") There were certain gaps in the Colonel's official biography that he recited to the crowds. He made no mention, for example, of petroleum ventures or of having supplied military accoutrements to the Federal forces. He had served in the Union army, he told them, until February, 1864, when he had "found the policy of the Federals was that of making war upon defenseless non-combatants and on private property." He had then resigned his commission and "thanked God that this was before Sheridan's scenes in the Shenandoah Valley and Sherman's march to the sea." "With no puritanical or partisan prejudice, I then came here among you to make my home, bringing my little portion with me. I know no other home. My ambition is simply to be such a citizen among you that I may be permitted to spend all the rest of my days in Alabama."

All former office holders in Alabama were at this time disenfranchised. Even so, the city of Mobile had a considerable white majority among registered voters; voters in the First District as a whole were about equally divided between Negroes and whites. Although speeches by Mann's supporters were full of reference to "our saddle-colored servants" and to the opposing candidate as "not quite a nigger but a Buck," the Democrats were convinced that they had won over a considerable body of Negro voters "who understand where their real interests lie." Apparently the local Reconstruction government also began to be concerned over the possibility that the Colonel might win. Four days before the election an agent of the United States Treasury Department arrived in the city and announced that Mann was about to be arrested—some Radical newspapers reported that he had *already* been arrested—on the "overwhelming evidence" that he had misappropriated $1,500,000 worth of Federal revenue. At any rate, observed the *Huntsville Advocate,* a Radical journal, "it is certain that he made an immense fortune since the war on a salary of $3,500 a year." This was the cue for the *Register*'s explanation that "if by Colonel Mann's administration of the office $1,500,000 were diverted from the Treasury (which is an absurd falsehood) then that amount was kept by the same token in the pockets of Southern planters and merchants. There is no earthly doubt that he did save thousands of dollars to the latter that would have been filched from them had a Radical malignant held his place." The Colonel, added the *Register,* was, in fact, a *poorer* man because he had come to Mobile. (According to a rumor printed in newspapers as far away as Buffalo, he was at any rate poorer by $25,000, the amount the election had reportedly cost him.) Colonel Mann, the *Register* concluded, "has shown himself to be a true friend of the people, and they will stand by him as such. *Cease viper, for you bite against a file!"*

By election day riots had broken out in some sections of Mobile, and President Grant moved in Federal troops to supervise the voting. The first tally showed that Mann had won about sixty per cent of the Mobile vote, and telegraphed reports from the northern counties in the district were equally triumphant. The Democrats proclaimed him the winner and held a huge victory celebration in Mammouth Hall. "The air rang with loud and vociferous shouts, . . . and all seemed mad with joy," reported the *Register.* Mann's acceptance speech was received "with deafening plaudits." Cheering throngs of Democrats, including marching bands, paraded through the Mobile streets, stopping at intervals to give three cheers for Mann, and cannons were fired. "It was a general glorification," declared the *Register.*

The glorification was premature. Mann had carried Mobile county by fifteen hundred votes out of about seven thousand, but the Reconstruction authorities reported a gross informality in the first count of Negro ballots in outlying rural districts. Nor had he carried Camden or Selma (which was then known throughout Alabama as the "Gibraltar of Radicalism"). There was also strong evidence that many white Democratic voters had decided to pass up the privilege of choosing between a pair of carpetbaggers. Two days after the election the Radical candidate was declared the winner by about two thousand votes.

The Colonel was not a gallant loser. Under the heading "The Lessons of the Election," the *Register* ran an editorial that began: "The black people have drawn the line broad and deep. . . . It means that they will govern this state and all the states of the South. It is for us to take up the gage they have so rashly thrown down. We are eight millions against their three millions, and we must at once give them to understand that we intend to exert that power and at all hazards to rule this country." A few days later they declared that "carpetbaggers, scalawags, and hostile negroes will be finally disposed of. . . . We mean to meet force with force. We mean to kill. . . ." On the night of August 5 the Radical partisans met at the corner of Government and Royal Streets, the site of the Kelley riot, and lit tar barrels for their own victory celebration. The ceremony, they had proclaimed ahead of time, would include the burning of Colonel Mann in effigy. As the dummy figure appeared, a loud voice called out "Hurrah for Mann!" and the shooting began. The police and government troops moved in, but by the time the city was quiet again three Negroes had been killed and a dozen other citizens, black and white, had been wounded. In a reflex that would come as effortlessly to many southerners nearly a century later—though with a different reference—the *Register* blamed the bloody affair on "foreign Radicals in our midst."

Colonel Mann never acknowledged the accuracy of the election verdict, and in his final years often described himself as "the last surviving member of the Forty-first Congress." The *Register* had accurately defined the election-eve embezzlement charge as "a dirty electioneering trick." Although even in the all's-fair of politics, a million-and-a-half dollars seems quite a sum to accuse a man of making off with if there is no evidence in hand—at the very least it implies considerable respect for his talent for larceny—it appears that the Colonel was never, in fact, arrested. Perhaps it was a case of cooler heads prevailing. Some weight may have been given to the interesting circumstance that one of the five offices formerly held by the winning candidate, Alfred Buck, had been that of *Deputy* Assessor of Internal Revenue. In any event, turning a shrewd and eloquent recreant loose on the stand to testify to the operations of an internal revenue office in the postwar South probably, on reappraisal, looked like too much of a risk.

The Colonel's well-publicized brush with the law did not impair his standing in Mobile in the slightest. To most white citizens of Alabama legal authority then meant only the tyranny of the enemy and lawlessness came very near to godliness, conceptions that would not die easily. For his first Mobile Christmas in 1866 Mann had given a dinner at the Battle House for his friends in the newspaper business, apparently the first of the thousands of such maneuvers in his long lifetime that were designed to insure him congenial companionship among unfriendly natives. The dinner had become an annual ritual, and that in 1869 was the best-attended of them all. Its invited-guest list included the staff of the *Register,* editors of Democratic papers all over the deep South, and civic leaders of Mobile. A hundred and twenty people turned up at the Battle House for a thirteen-course dinner that featured haunch of venison and pressed buffalo tongue. Afterward the Colonel was given a standing ovation by the assembled company, and the head of the Mobile Board of Trade made a speech which hailed him as "one of Alabama's greatest capitalists" and concluded with the rousing endorsement: "May the pride of the South in its adopted son be excelled only by his own distinguished merit."

Although Mann was no longer an office holder, he was hardly in retirement. In the spring of 1869 he had invested about $100,000 in a cotton seed oil refinery near the Mobile wharves, one of the first in the South and—or so he liked to describe it in later years—the largest then in existence anywhere. Its name, as it happened, was the Mobile Oil Company. In the next years the new tycoon made frequent trips to see his commission agents in New York and Boston, on one occasion taking along a specimen of iron ore from the mines in northern Alabama. When a New York mining expert pronounced it, according to his report, "positively unequalled by any iron on this continent," he began to invest in the mines in the part of the state where Birmingham stands today. But his most compelling new interest was in railroads.

In the middle years of the century the Alabama citizenry held it as an article of faith that all that was needed to make the state rich and mighty was to connect its northern and southernmost counties by rail. Its legislators, Radical and Redeemer alike, generously voted large sums to any group that promised to make these arrangements. Mann entered the railroad picture as a promoter. Presumably his major assignment in this field, at least at the start, was to provide favorable publicity through the columns of the *Register,* but an Alabaman who held a similar job at about the same time later wrote in his memoirs that the primary responsibility of a railroad promoter in the years just after the war was to shuttle sacksful of cash from the offices of the railroad companies to those of the legislators, who naturally expected a percentage of each appropriation to find its way back to them. If in this process the Colonel ruefully observed the rewards of politics, he also must have noted those of the railroad business: most of the companies, once their owners' pockets were full, would default without laying a track. Of the dozens of railroad ventures that Mann touted editorially in the *Register* only one became a reality during his sojourn in Mobile. This was not a north-south affair but what he described as "a latitudinal necessity," a hundred-and-thirty-eight-mile line between Mobile and New Orleans. It appears that in this case the Colonel sold not only the public but himself on the project. His involvement was well outside the grab-and-run tradition. Besides being a company officer, he also held the contract for actually building the road.

The Colonel was delegated to drive the spike for the first rail in November, 1869. He made the ceremony the occasion for an hour-long plea to all Mobilians to "disenthrall our minds, our business energies, from the shackles of Old King Cotton." The city's industry should be diversified, he told the crowd. Instead of shipping cotton north, Mobile should manufacture cotton goods of its own. With all the iron resources near by, railroad cars should be built in Mobile instead of being imported from the Troy iron works. (Had this notion been carried to the point of giving real competition to the source of the Burden wealth, the Colonel might have met the members of that family on other terms than those that he resorted to many years later.) Mann also urged Mobile's civic leaders to give most serious attention to the tourist business since, unlike most southern cities, it was out of the track of tropical hurricanes and had a climate "known to be absolutely healthful," a commercial message to which he felt obliged to add a rather large reservation—"save between the months of July and December when there are possibilities of that over-dreaded scourge, yellow fever." Mobile was a lucky city, he said, adding that "being more superstitious than most men, I early learned to avoid unlucky people, places and things." The weather on the day of the rail-laying ceremony had been gray and cheerless, but as he drove the first spike in place "to deafening cheers," the sun burst through the clouds and he quickly hailed this as "the dawn of a brighter day to Mobile's prosperity."

The name of the new railroad was the New Orleans, Mobile, and Chattanooga; a few months later, reversing its direction, it became the New Orleans, Mobile, and Texas. Either terminus turned out to be an overstatement since the line never went beyond the two rival gulf cities. Much of the territory between Mobile and New Orleans was an engineers' nightmare of spongy marshes and bayous, at some points so junglelike that in order to be sure of their direction the workers laid the tracks toward the sound of a bugle blown by a Negro stationed on muleback a quarter of a mile ahead. The understructure of the line was in danger of being swept out to sea at high tide and had to be anchored like a boat. As soon as this was done, its untreated wood supports were attacked by a species of salt-water termite. Cars finally began rolling over the road in December, 1870, and it survives today as part of the Louisville and Nashville complex. But the construction contract was hardly the financial bonanza that the Colonel presumably had had in mind. Early in 1871 he paid off one subcontractor, Isaac Donavan, by turning over to him his interest in the *Register*.

Meanwhile the Colonel had become deeply engaged in an even grander railroad scheme to bolster Mobile's prosperity and gave every evidence of intending to see that this one also became a reality. He proposed to make the port city the terminus of a line that would deliver to it the products of the rich grain fields of Kansas and Nebraska, crossing the Mississippi at a point opposite Helena, Arkansas. To this end he got up another persuasive prospectus and by early 1870 had organized the Mobile and Northwestern Railroad, chartered not only in Alabama but neighboring states. The city of Mobile voted a hundred thousand dollars toward the enterprise, but the Alabama legislature was beginning to recover from the railroad delirium of the immediate postwar years and now favored a policy of paying over appropriations on the basis of how many miles of track had actually been laid. Two years later Mann was still beating a path to the state capital at Montgomery, pleading the case for what the *Register* called his "bold dream." "Colonel Mann is here doing some good lobby-

ing, but he is none too well satisfied tonight with the conduct
of affairs," reported the *Register's* Montgomery correspondent
in February, 1872. Construction was begun on a speculative
basis soon afterward, but in mid-1873, when twenty-four miles
of track had been built going out of Mobile and a few more
miles at the Mississippi River end, money ran out. The line
was then abandoned. By this time, however, the Colonel was
not around to take part in the obsequies.

Early in the summer of 1872 Mobile's loudest drum-beater
had departed the city. Within a few weeks after his 1869
speech describing its immunity from tropical windstorms a
hurricane had struck just north of the town. In the late summer
of 1870 Mobilians were hit by a severe yellow-fever epidemic.
One northern paper reported there had been four thousand
cases there, two-thirds of them fatal. Whatever the toll, Mobile
became for many months not a tourist mecca or a thriving
manufacturing center but a ghost town. Soon after the quarantine was lifted a northern visitor to the Battle House, where
the Colonel lived throughout his Alabama years, wrote to the
Register to complain that his sleep was constantly being dis-
turbed by the barking of alligators in the open ditches that then
bordered either side of the unpaved streets. *Pro bono publico*
—or in the interest of his own nights' rest—Colonel Mann dug
into his pocket and arranged to have the stretch of Royal Street
that ran past the hotel surfaced over with patented wooden
pavement. Within a week the new civic improvement had sunk
to the bottom of the mire. It was not long after this discouraging development that the Alabama legislature posted its unco-
operative notice about railroad appropriations. Finally, in the
spring of 1872, the Mobile Oil Company burned to the ground
and, through the error of a bookkeeper, turned out to be un-
insured. According to an historian writing in the *Register* about
this time, the name of Alabama is derived from an Indian word

meaning "Here We Rest." Apparently Mann—now in his thirty-third year—concluded that he had rested there long enough. Invoking his superstition about unlucky people, places, and things, he sold everything he owned in the state and left Mobile to enter another branch of the railroad field as a manufacturer of sleeping cars.

In January, 1872, retrieving his inventor's franchise, he had been granted U.S. Patent Number 122622 for what he called a "boudoir car," equipped with a double bed that was hoisted up on pulleys during the day. Sleeping cars were no novelty by 1872. Only five years after the first American passenger train had gone into service in 1831 between Albany and Schenectady, a sleeping car fitted out with a primitive system of folding boards had been introduced on the Cumberland Valley Railroad between Harrisburg and Chambersburg. But such early cars offered little more than a horizontal option. In their candle-lit interiors the men passengers stretched out fully-clothed while the ladies sat bolt upright, protecting their virtue through the lurching nights. As railway journeys lengthened, the problem became more acute. In 1859 an Illinois cabinetmaker named George Pullman started tinkering with abandoned railroad cars, trying to work out more genteel bedding-down arrangements. The first Pullman car, the Pioneer, was completed in 1864 and went into service on the Chicago, Alton, and St. Louis line in time to treat some of the more important mourners on Lincoln's funeral train to a good night's sleep. For this boon to humanity a midwestern professor of literature was declaring to his classes a few years later that George Pullman was "superior in creative genius to Shakespeare, Homer, and Dante." By 1872 the name of Pullman, now a millionaire, had become not only the common synonym for the term "sleeping car" but a common noun, replacing it. As a late starter in the field, Mann prudently decided to move his boudoir car operations to Europe, where shorter distances between points had retarded commercial interest in locomotive sleeping provisions.

For affluent southerners, especially those who had served in the war, there was only one London hotel in 1872. This was the new Langham, whose manager was a former Confederate colonel. Bull Run and Chancellorsville were fought and won again in its gaslit dining room hardly less often than they were back in Mobile's Battle House. Mann kept rooms at the Langham off and on for the next eleven years, although he spent some time in Oldham, two hundred miles north, where his boudoir cars were first built, and later across the channel where, in 1873, one of them was put into service on the Munich-Vienna line, the first sleeping car ever provided for public use on the continent. The Colonel had arrived in England with considerable capital, and whatever arrangements he made for additional backing left him in full charge of the new enterprise. An advertising brochure printed in Paris in 1873 noted that "the general direction and special supervision" of the Mann Railway Sleeping Carriage Company, Ltd., was entirely the responsibility of Colonel Mann. England, with its low-mileage runs, continued to be a resistant market, but by 1876 the company had fifty-eight *chemins de fer-wagons-boudoirs pour éviter la grande fatigue*—as the brochure proclaimed them—in operation in half a dozen European countries, including Russia, and was maintaining offices in Paris, Vienna, Berlin, and Brussels.

Mann followed Pullman's practice of leasing his cars to the railway lines on a contractual basis, and during the next years had the European market virtually to himself. The interior design of his sleepers, however, departed sharply from Pullman's long double row of curtained berths, separated by a central aisle. Modeled on the old stage-coach architecture, his *wagons-lits* were divided into eight compartments, each nearly the width of the car. In his earliest version passengers stepped directly from them across a narrow footboard to the station platform. Each stateroomlike compartment accommodated anywhere from a single person to a family of four, giving his cars a capacity of thirty-two where Pullman's— which were also somewhat longer—could sleep fifty-two. During his decade in Europe and the first years after his return to the States, Mann took out ten patents to improve the bedding-down, heating, plumbing, and ventilating arrangements in his cars. The pulley beds gave way to intricate folding berths, and the later boudoir cars were even equipped with primitive air-conditioning consisting of filtered ducts through which air was forced over blocks of ice. Reserved, unlike the more democratic Pullmans with their higher population density and their flimsy green baize curtains, for travelers who could afford to value their comfort and privacy, Mann's cars were fitted out accordingly with gold-fringed upholstery, teak gaming tables, Italian Renaissance paintings, Oriental carpets, gilded flower holders, crystal chandeliers, embossed spittoons, and similar amenities previously available only to nomadic princes of the realm. This impression of accommodations suitable for royalty was fortified when, early in 1874, the future Edward VII of England borrowed Mann's own private boudoir car for the trip across Europe to St. Petersburg to attend the marriage of his younger brother, the Duke of Edinburgh, to the Russian Princess Marie. The crowning endorsement came in 1876 when Mann was commissioned to build a private car for Leopold II of Belgium. The result was so opulent that Brussels socialists got up circulars denouncing its appointments as the stuff revolutions were made on. It may have been in the course of fulfilling this assignment that the Colonel met George Nagel-mackers, an engineer from a Belgian banking family. In December, 1876, he and Nagelmackers founded the Compagnie Internationale de Wagons-Lits. In return for all European patent rights and tangible assets of the Mann Railway Sleeping Carriage Company, Ltd., Mann received about sixty percent of the shares in the new enterprise, with a par value of just under three-quarters of a million dollars.

Back in his Mobile days Mann's inventive mind had busied itself briefly with the dilemma of how to transport fresh meat by rail, and he had made at least one excursion to Texas to discuss with cattlemen there the matter of suitable refrigeration. He had also conducted some experiments with chemical preservatives. Soon after he joined forces with Nagelmackers he doubled back on the problem. In 1879 he took out a patent for a refrigerator car with an inner storage wall of ice and had several of them built in Brussels. Three years later (after stopping off in Vienna to unload on the Austrian Army the remaining supply of his old cavalry accoutrements that had been gathering dust in a New York warehouse) he built two *abattoirs* in Budapest, handy to the Puszta, the vast Hungarian cattle-grazing lands, and began shipping meat to the cities of western Europe. For whatever reason, this venture—or, at any rate, his connection with it—was short-lived. In September, 1883, the Compagnie Internationale de Wagons-Lits launched its most ambitious and now legendary project, the Orient Express, whose sleeping cars, built according to Mann's original patents and specifications, were soon bearing travelers in nocturnal comfort all the way from Paris to Constantinople. But Mann was not on hand for the premier *"Attention, au départ"* ceremony. Whether because of personal differences with Nagelmackers or a craving for more negotiable assets, he had allowed his

Belgian associates eleven months before to buy out his interest in the company for just under two million dollars.

The decade Mann spent in Europe left curiously little mark on him. He apparently had no gift for languages, and even in England only a few friendships survived his departure. Always an opera and theater buff, he did, according to his own account, get to know Adelina Patti and Henry Irving, the latter through Joe Jefferson, the American actor whom he had first seen in New York in 1858 at the opening of *Our American Cousin* and had later met during one of the actor's stands in Mobile. But he seems to have put down no roots during his years overseas, living always in hotels or on a siding in one of his boudoir cars. In documents he continued to list his address as Mobile. After his return to America his only nostalgia appeared to be for the Langham, to which he had gone back again and again to re-form old battle lines with visitors from the South. From time to time, posing as an important military figure, he wangled invitations to European army maneuvers. In 1876, perhaps stimulated by one of these excursions, he brought out in London his small book called *The Raiders*. Old style cavalry, laden down with its sabres, pistols, and carbines, was now useless, he wrote ("Could anything but a Balaklava result from fighting cavalry against modern artillery and small arms?"). He proposed instead an independent branch of the army to be known as "The Raiders." Its troops would ride on amphibious, iron-clad wagons, each drawn by four horses and equipped with Gatling guns. The wagons would not only give the men speed and mobility but would serve as bastions during an attack. This primitive outline of an armored tank corps—and a pointed essay on where the necessary "bold, energetic leadership" for it might be found—apparently sank to the bottom of the book stalls without a trace. When the Colonel arrived back in New York early in 1883, he had acquired a taste for certain offshore luxuries such as French wines, Spanish cigars, and British tailoring and in London had also got in the habit of carrying a walking stick, preferably one with a heavy handle. Otherwise all that his travels had apparently broadened was his financial base. With his foreign spoils he immediately set to work on the scheme he had probably been mentally nurturing since his departure eleven years before: to challenge on home ground Pullman's rule over the sleeping car business.

The Mann Boudoir Car Company was incorporated with a capital of $1,000,000, much of which was immediately disbursed for the building of forty-one of his uncommon carriers at a minimum of $18,000 apiece. By the end of 1883 several of these, their wooden bodies painted a stylish seal brown and their roofs a gaudy yellow, were in operation on the Boston and Albany line, and soon afterward others were on the move in the west between Chicago and St. Joseph and Chicago and St. Paul on the line that became the Chicago Great Western. Mann's sales talks were especially effective among his old friends in the South, and by the mid-eighties his traveling boudoirs were also avoiding *la grande fatigue* on the Louisville Southern, the Queen and Crescent, the Mobile and Ohio, the Wabash, St. Louis and New Orleans, the Georgia Pacific, the Alabama Great Southern, and the Vicksburg and Memphis routes. Reflecting his operatic interests, many of them bore such names as "Rigoletto," "Il Trovatore," and "Carmen," and among the several private cars he built was an especially rococo one for Adelina Patti that got almost as much attention as the florid soprano did during her repeated farewell tours. Another such car was commissioned for actress Lily Langtry by a New York admirer. According to one story, the gentleman happened one afternoon to be standing beside the Colonel in the bar at Delmonico's, pondering out loud over what heart-warming trinket he could give the lady for her birthday. As it happened, the Colonel knew just the thing, and it wouldn't cost a penny more than fifty thousand dollars. Apparently the gift was favorably received. (As Mrs. August Belmont noted in her autobiography, *The Fabric of Memory:* "A private railway car is not an acquired taste. One takes to it at once.") Miss Langtry's car was called the "Lalee," which she claimed was East Indian for "flirt." It was painted a royal blue on the outside with green silk brocade covering its interior walls and was equipped with a grand piano and the Colonel's primitive version of an air-conditioning system. Suggesting, according to Miss Langtry's biographer, "nothing so much as Cleopatra's barge under full sail," it has been called probably the most highly publicized rolling love nest in history. Mann also built for hire several cars with more appropriate names such as "Davy Crockett" and "Izaak Walton" to accommodate hunting and fishing safaris to the Far West. Though the marquetry and frescoed ceilings of his rolling stock sometimes turned out to be painted canvas, their basic construction was notably durable: four of his cars, built in the mid-eighties, were discovered in 1960 plying regular overnight runs in the sheepherding provinces of Australia.

For the iron-horse tournament with Pullman, however, Mann had come on the field too late—or possibly too early—in the game. In 1887, when he had forty-one cars on the rails, Pullman had nearly a thousand and through his membership in American industry's fraternity of interlocking directorates was a Goliath in the railroad world. Moreover, the private stateroom arrangement of Mann's cars, while fit for a king or for commoners interested in a luxuriously appointed setting for adultery—a possibility that caused them to be featured over and over in lurid contemporary cartoons in the *Police Gazette*—was unsuited to economic competition with Pull-

man's fifty-two passenger design. History would prove the
Colonel right. "Despite the gaudy overtones of Colonel
Mann's bravura performance on the New York scene," de-
clares Lucius Beebe in *Mr. Pullman's Elegant Palace Car*, a
panegyric to the palace car era, "his instincts as a carbuilder
were strangely prescient. Almost alone in his time he . . . .
built cars composed of private sleeping apartments. The concept was half a century in advance of its general practice. . . .
The compartmented corridor was not to emerge on a large
scale for years to come. Beyond all doubt," Beebe concluded,
"the boudoir cars of the versatile Colonel Mann paved the
way for all-room cars" that in another generation would put
the open section sleeper out of business. Mann also showed
prescience in his patent, secured in this country in 1878, for
a vestibule at either end of his sleeping cars and a longitudinal
corridor along one side, an improvement that Mann boasted in
1906 "has done more . . . for the comfort and safety of the
travelling public than any single improvement ever made in
railroad cars." Before this innovation the only method of
traveling from one sleeping car to another was by perilous
means of a running-board along the outside of the train. By
the mid-eighties, with the growing popularity of dining cars,
the vestibule arrangement that allowed passengers to move
easily from car to car became more and more essential. In a
legal dispute involving an 1887 vestibule patent of the Pullman company, Mann was aligned with Pullman's adversaries,
the Vanderbilts, under far different circumstances from those
that would link their names in New York's Criminal Courts
Building two decades later. In May, 1889, however, the
United States Supreme Court ruled against them, severing
the Colonel's last connection with the railroad business—although not with the fortunes it had made.

Except for 1887, when its net earnings were $6,000, the

Mann Boudoir Car Company had steadily lost money, and by 1888 its only assets were its rolling stock and its patents. In December of that year, in a desperate penultimate maneuver, it was merged with another fading vestige of Pullman's competition, the Woodruff Parlor Sleeping Coach Company. Six weeks later the corporate hybrid, known as the Union Palace Car Company, was taken over by Pullman in what the *New York Herald* called "one of the quickest transactions on record. . . . absolutely without dickering." For the three million dollars' worth of Union Palace stock Pullman paid a reported fifty cents on the dollar. Mann's share of the proceeds was not enough to cover the large sums he had laid out to keep his company going. According to his own testimony, he had been transformed in five years from a man who was "several times a millionaire" to one who was a hundred thousand dollars in debt. Fortunately, a means of recouping his fortunes lay at hand, one for which it soon appeared that he had been predestined by nature.

Not for Babes,
Prudes,
Idiots or Dudes

A FEW DAYS AFTER he stomped down the gangplank of the "Zeeland" and into the eye of *"l'affaire Town Topics"* in July, 1905, Mann outlined for a reporter from *The New York Times* his elevated concept of his mission as proprietor of the controversial magazine. "My ambition," he declared, "is to reform the Four Hundred by making them too deeply disgusted with themselves to continue their silly, empty way of life. I am also teaching the great American public not to pay any attention to these silly fools. If I didn't publish *Town Topics,"* he said—the *Times* noted that at this point he laid a fatherly hand on the reporter's shoulder—"some one else without moral responsibility would do so. I am really doing it for the sake of the country."

When Mann first began to feel the stirrings of this patriotic vocation is uncertain, but he placed his earliest glancing association with a magazine of society news during the years when he was in and out of London, building and promoting his boudoir car. By his own account of things, he was consulted in 1874 by Edmund Yates, then European correspondent for the *New York Herald,* who was about to start a British weekly magazine called the *World* that would cause him to be hailed in his obituaries twenty years later as "the inventor of society journalism." According to an edict of the

London *Times,* at any rate, published in 1912 after the death of Yates' major collaborator, Henry Labouchere, the founders of the *World* were the originators of this form of newspaper enterprise—the gossipy reports of life among the upper classes, laced with intimate trivia and revelation of indiscretion that were also, the *Times* noted, known as "personal journalism." In the early part of the nineteenth century, the *Times* went on, "the old Books of Beauty and Annuals"—glossy biographical volumes that, in fact, bore a close resemblance to Mann's *Fads and Fancies*—"occupied themselves in a remote and rather amateurish fashion with the personalities and pursuits of the 'fashionables' and the nobility. But this kind of literature never penetrated to the multitude and . . . gradually died out." Yet, in the 1870's, the *Times* recalled, "there were great numbers of highly respectable persons who looked with an avid, but for the most part futile, curiosity on the gilded and brilliant existence of those who formed the world of pleasure and leisure, of high politics and high birth." Yates and Labouchere, the *Times* declared, had seized the opportunity to satisfy this curiosity in publications of some stature and substance and thus had founded a new branch of journalism.

Yates, who at the time he started the *World* in 1874 was a minor novelist as well as a newspaper correspondent, had first attained a certain fame on the British literary scene sixteen years earlier. A penny-paper attack he had then made on Thackeray, accusing him of undue obsequiousness toward the nobility, had so incensed the author of *Vanity Fair* that he caused Yates' expulsion from a cherished hangout of his, the Garrick Club. Yates' unsuccessful campaign for reinstatement, directed by his friend Dickens, had split the London literary world and caused a breach between the two best-selling titans of the day that had only been partially healed a few months before Thackeray's death in 1863. In his anger at Yates Thackeray had inserted into later editions of *The Virginians* literary caricatures of him, bearing such names as "Young Grub Street" and "Tom Garbage." The famous novelist's embittered attention to the bumptious young man (whose primary means of livelihood at the time was in the dead letter department of the London post office) had given Yates' literary career a boost that eventually enabled him to quit Her Majesty's civil service. It was while he was in America as a junketeering lecturer in 1872 that he had persuaded James Gordon Bennett to hire him as European correspondent for the *Herald.*

Writing in *Town Topics* for October 19, 1916, the issue celebrating the silver anniversary of his taking the magazine in charge, Colonel Mann recalled that in January, 1874, when Yates had been on his way back from St. Petersburg where he had covered the story of the marriage of the Duke of Edinburgh to the Russian princess, he "fell in with me at Berlin." Mann, who had gone to that city to retrieve his private boudoir car that the Prince of Wales had borrowed for the wedding, was in the habit of giving free rides to itinerant journalists in return for their company and, presumably, the opportunity to explain that he used to be a newspaperman himself. Yates, the Colonel went on, had traveled with him across Europe to Calais. "En route he disclosed to me a project that he said had been in his mind for some time. It was to start a weekly paper in London to be devoted mainly to social news and gossip with, incidentally, a short fiction story, a city financial article, and some political and general comment. He ended by asking me to join him with some capital in the venture. Finally I said, 'Mr. Yates, go ahead and carry out your scheme. . . . If not successful, I will advance you from week to week any amount you may need up to a thousand pounds as a loan, and we will leave the return of it to your convenience.' He was greatly gratified." Thus Mann pointed out, somewhat imaginatively, "it is perhaps worth noting that in a measure I was responsible for the founding of the first publication devoted to social news ever issued." Sensing, perhaps, that this account, offered so many years after the death of the possible corroborator, had a somewhat *ex post facto* ring, Mann offered further *ex post facto* details. "A few years later, before my sailing for America, Mr. Yates gave a dinner to me, present at which were a dozen men in the literary and publishing world." Among these, he recalled, were Chevalier Wykoff, a *Herald* correspondent then resident in London; Hiram Fuller, brother of Margaret Fuller; the publisher of *Pall Mall* magazine; and Lawson-Levy, owner of the *Daily Telegraph* "afterwards raised to the peerage." At this dinner, "Mr. Yates related the little story of our trip from Berlin and how the encouragement I gave fixed his determination to risk his all in founding the *World.*" He had never been called upon to live up to the agreement, the Colonel added, since the *World* had been a financial success from the start.

Laying claim to a further place for himself in the history of society publications (and locating *Town Topics* in the direct line of descent) Mann wrote in his later years of having also known Yates' colleague, Henry Labouchere, a notably vigorous, talented, and unconventional figure who during his long life—he was eighty-one when he died in 1912—alternately exasperated and dazzled not only Fleet Street but the British diplomatic service in which he served, the London financial and industrial worlds in which he was a powerful figure, and Parliament, of which he was a Radical member for almost thirty years. Labouchere, who was widely known as "Labby," had left Yates' *World* after two years and in 1877 started a magazine of his own called *Truth.* ("What is *Truth?*"

one of his friends asked him. "Why, another and better *World,*" said Labby.) At the last moment he had a different notion about its name, and it was only with difficulty that he was persuaded not to call it the *Lyre.* Having inherited a large fortune, Labouchere wasn't on the lookout for a financial sponsor. In the same anniversary issue of *Town Topics,* Mann recalled, however, that one day in 1877 he had happened to run into Labouchere "in Threadneedle Street, City. He asked me to dine with him that night at the Reform Club. After dinner he took me to the 'Strangers' Room'," a special lounge set aside in the better English clubs, Mann explained, "where non-members might enjoy burning the weed with their host" without discommoding other members by their presence. "We seated ourselves on a luxurious sofa," he went on, "and Mr. Labouchere drew from his pocket a rolled sheet, opened it, held it before me, and said, 'What do you think of it?' It was the original sketch with the figure holding up the title 'Truth' which became the well-known front cover of that forceful periodical." Labouchere told him, according to Mann, " 'You are the only person other than myself who has seen this, which the artist completed this afternoon.' " Labouchere had then described his plans for the new publishing venture, which would not fear to tread on any toes, however well-shod. "I said, 'Bully, for you!' ", reported Mann. "So here I was in at the birth of the *second* society journal."

Whether or not Mann's alleged conferees Yates and Labouchere had accomplished anything else, declared the *London Times* after Labouchere's death, the two pioneers of British society journalism had been completely successful in invading the heretofore sacrosanct privacy of the nation's most privileged classes, having for the first time brought what the *Times* called "the *arcana imperii* into the back kitchen" and "set us all to listening at the keyhole." Yates, the *Times* ruled, had done this "with no particular aim other than making money." But Labouchere had run his magazine "with a keen perception and with a certain didactic, or at least a satirical purpose that lent piquancy to the adventure." Labouchere, like Mann, even professed to view his role as less that of a scandalmonger than of a man with a mission. "I believe," recalled the *London Times* correspondent, "that Labouchere himself maintained that he was engaged upon a thoroughly democratic task. I remember hearing him reproached with the fact that he, a . . . convinced Radical, should make money by gossiping about the personal affairs of titled people, but he retorted that all this was a step toward the eventual undermining of classes and that leveling of artificial distinctions which a Radical might be disposed to admire."

Though Colonel Mann, for his part, often appeared to admire the artificial distinctions, it seems possible that the wide-ranging style of Labouchere's career, which was reaching its height during his years in England, stirred the imagination of the also flamboyant and versatile American. Labouchere, with his financial and political as well as literary resources, lectured kings, caused Parliamentary heads to roll, exposed as shams some of the most sanctimonious figures of his day, and rampaged the length and breadth of the late-Victorian scene in his irreverent paragraphs in *Truth*. As a consequence, according to Hesketh Pearson in his 1936 biography of Labouchere, not only society but members of "every institution, from the Crown to the Treasury, from the Church to the Army," shook in their boots on the morning of *Truth's* weekly appearance. Labouchere's bravura performance may have been especially vivid in Mann's conscious or subconscious mind when he later sat down to write the biting paragraphs of commentary on the political and social issues of the day that concluded the Saunterer's weekly stint. Unfortunately for the Colonel's dreams of glory, this was probably the one area of "Saunterings" that went largely unread.

A less intrepid man than the Colonel, observing Yates' and Labouchere's careers from whatever distance, might well have been discouraged by the risks to life, limb, and liberty encountered by editors of *chroniques scandaleuses*. In 1883, for example, the *World* printed a blind paragraph reporting the "elopement" of a married master of the hounds with a young and titled lady. Immediately the Earl of Lonsdale and the daughter of the Duke of Westmoreland identified themselves as the principals involved, denied the allegation, and, in spite of Yates' abject apologies, brought a complaint against him for criminal libel. Yates was eventually sentenced to four months in prison, an experience from which, according to his friends, he never recovered. ("It was his misfortune," wrote Labouchere in his 1894 obituary of Yates, "to exemplify in his own person the monstrous absurdities of our libel laws; and although he bore his imprisonment with great pluck, it left a permanent mark on him.") Over the years Labouchere himself was beaten, caned, and from time to time horsewhipped on the street by irate victims of *Truth's* revelations. On one occasion he got off easy, however. A man he had attacked in *Truth* came upon him unexpectedly in the street and shouted that public revenge would now be taken. A crowd gathered. But, reports Pearson, "like most persons of that period, when he wished to chastise another person, he could only think in terms of one instrument." The announced assailant was reduced to asking members of the crowd one after the other, "Do you happen to have a horsewhip about you?"—while Labouchere escaped around the corner. As for attempts at legal retribution, Labouchere was so often sued for libel (usually unsuccessfully) that some doubt has been expressed that any other individual not directly connected with the legal profession ever appeared in court so frequently. According to Pearson, Labouchere even developed a ceremonial *mot* for such occasions. "I wish they had not put that libel case down for Tuesday," he would say plaintively, "since that's the day when I *write* my libels."

But no matter how well primed he was on the hazards of the trade, it was probably Mann's nature to reflect only on the financial success of the two London publications (Yates had told him he was clearing $40,000 annually from the *World,* an enormous sum in the eighties, and Labouchere eventually left an estate estimated by the *London Times* to be ten times what he had inherited) when word reached the Colonel that a journal of society news had come on the market in New York in the spring of 1885. At this period he himself was preoccupied with the high-level corporate maneuvers of sleeping car manufacture, but he may well have encouraged his younger brother Eugene to take on the bankrupt publication, which already bore the name of *Town Topics.*

This periodical that would become the abiding interest in the Colonel's life had been founded in 1879 as *Andrews' American Queen* by W. H. Andrews, a businessman, recently arrived in New York from Cincinnati, who had put it out as an adjunct to his pattern company, Andrews' Pinned Paper Fashions. In taking this step he may have been deliberately following in the trail of James McCall who six years earlier had brought out a magazine called *The Queen* (later *McCall's*) as a promotion gimmick for *his* patterns. But whereas the McCall publication's full title in the seventies was *The Queen: Illustrating McCall's Bazar Glove-fitting Patterns,* and it dealt entirely in fashion news, the formal name of Andrews' twice-a-month periodical was *Andrews' American Queen: A National Society Journal.* In order to live up to this billing, it carried society reports from some fifty Ameri-

can cities, dispatches that ran largely to massive lists of invited guests with the bulk of further editorial attention devoted to what the ladies had worn. When this limited fare
failed to draw off circulation from *Godey's Lady's Book*—or
presumably to sell patterns—a sprinkling of fiction, humor,
and, eventually, criticism was introduced, the fifty-city territory being cut down to the four or five major social capi-
tals on the eastern seaboard. The admixture proved ineffective.
The magazine then became a weekly, and its fifteen-cent price
was reduced to ten. Despite these measures Andrews found
at the end of 1882 that he had lost a fortune the New York
Home Journal put at several hundred thousand dollars, and
one night in January, 1883, he simply left town, abandoning
the magazine to its creditors' mercies. In the next two years
it was taken over by successive platoons of young society
gentlemen, some of whom had done a little book reviewing
for the *New York Sun* or otherwise dabbled in journalism. Beginning in January, 1885, the editorial incumbents were Louis
Keller who, two years later, made a more durable contribution to the fashionable scene by founding the *Social Register,*
and James B. Townsend, whose claim to fame is that he is
sometimes credited with having invented the word "dude."
It was during their brief tenure on the weekly that its name
was changed to *The American Queen and Town Topics,* abbreviated with the issue of March 7, 1885, to *Town Topics.*
A few weeks before this conversion the editors had inaugu-
rated a department called "Table Talk," consisting of short,
informal paragraphs about society doings. The new department occupied two pages at the beginning of the fourteen-
page magazine. "It is the aim and hope of its editors," they
announced, "to make this department intelligent and reliable
and to avoid in every way possible offensive personalities
and attacks and slurs upon character." A few weeks later

they were bravely insisting upon the magazine's prosperity which, they declared, "proves that journalism can be clean and decent and yet thrive." Even as they wrote, they had reason to mistrust the rewards of virtue. They were in deep trouble with their creditors, and by early May the magazine was again bankrupt. Its printers, having acquired it by default, sold it to Eugene Mann. After "the amateur journalists who started *Town Topics* . . . lost all the money their confiding backers could be induced to put up . . . a real journalist stepped in," was the way the magazine called the *Journalist,* described the event some years later.

Eugene Mann's qualifications as a real journalist are not obvious from the surviving record. Born in 1855 in Adrian, Michigan, he was educated—perhaps by the Colonel, who was then in funds—at Kentucky Military Institute and Cornell. In the mid-seventies he followed his older brother to Europe, where he studied political economics in Munich and Paris and for a time acted as Munich agent for Mann's sleeping car interests. Later his name appeared as the patentee of record for an improved railway car window. In 1881 Eugene Mann returned to Adrian, studied law in a local attorney's office, was admitted to the Michigan bar, and for a time was part of the corporate entourage of Henry Villard, the president of the Northern Pacific Railroad. This timetable gave him only a year or two to work up a reputation as a bona fide newspaperman before he took over *Town Topics* in his thirtieth year, but his credentials were apparently authentic. In his custody the magazine rapidly became for the first time a viable enterprise and took on much of the appearance and form it was to maintain for a generation. By late 1885 its coverage had vastly expanded. It now described itself as *Town Topics, A Journal of Society, Fashions, Drama, Music, Art, Books, the Club, Racing, Yachting, Military, Flowers,*

Household, Etc. A few months later this clutter had been pruned to *Town Topics, A Journal of Society,* but most of the departments dealing with the kaleidoscope of human interests continued to appear. Paul Potter, a former London correspondent and dramatic critic for the *Herald,* was an early editor under Eugene Mann and for a time owned a third interest in the magazine. Potter apparently attracted a staff of talented young refugees from more decorous local publications. By the beginning of 1886 *Town Topics* was running each week under its editorial flag the boast that it was "the newsiest, brightest, wittiest, wisest, cleverest, most original, and most entertaining paper ever published."

This self-proclaimed printers' bundle of superlatives was naturally happy to quote the more detached verdict of the *Sun,* ("We highly recommend *Town Topics*") and that of the *New York World* critic, who found it "entertaining and trustworthy" from cover to cover. The reviewer for the *World* made no exception of the department of society gossip at the beginning of the magazine that Eugene Mann had continued and indeed greatly expanded. In his first week as proprietor an editorial in this section deplored the practice of scandal-mongering and declared, "All honest people will find *Town Topics* at all times ready to elevate and purify our civilization." By early 1886, however, the moral tone of this department—now known as "Saunterings" and signed "The Saunterer"—had noticeably lost altitude. It described itself as "an *olla podrida* of gossip, comment, and anecdotal paragraphs of contemporaneous interest . . . not for babes, prudes, idiots or dudes." By the middle of 1887 "Saunterings" regularly occupied half of the magazine's twenty pages and had so far departed from its original prospectus that the *New York Star* was denouncing it as an instrument of blackmail.

Whatever its corollary financial returns under Eugene

Mann's direction, in an era when the society pages filled most of their space with such items as "Mrs. Ogden Goelet is giving a dinner of eighteen covers on Tuesday next," *Town Topics'* reports of strip parties along Bailey's Beach, public neck-biting of a female member of the Four Hundred by a male member of the club, and other intimations of Colonel Mann's "Saunterings" to come were not likely to go unread. "Up to the time *Town Topics* took its place among the prominent journals of the time," the Colonel declared in "Saunterings" in 1916, "society in New York received little or no attention from the newspaper press." Society affairs had, in fact, been on the agenda of the American press for generations before the Saunterer entered the picture, but most of the coverage had been stately and discreet to the point of flunkeyism. Even this degree of publicity was so generally deplored by society leaders that guest lists—the meatiest part of such court-calendar accounts—were often hard to come by. The frequently quoted edict of a dowager of today's Old Guard that in her youth the name of a true gentlewoman appeared in the paper but three times—when she was born, when she was married, and when she died—was liberal compared to the notions of what was *comme il faut* up through the 1870's when it was considered indelicate for a newspaper to mention that a child had been born to a lady of quality. After James Gordon Bennett arrived on the New York scene and launched the *Herald* in 1837, he had carried impudent and even scandalous accounts of society doings from time to time, but after a few years, as soon as his society editors began to be invited to attend the grander affairs, his reports bowed and scraped like all the rest. Not only tradition and a fear of retaliation in the advertising department but the personal social ambitions of many newspaper owners of the day, including the younger Bennett, encouraged this ceremonial approach to the private affairs of the rich. Against such a background *Town Topics* under the Manns flourished by following the lead of the *World* and *Truth* in London, refusing to treat *arcana imperii* as more sacrosanct than kitchen gossip.

"I made society the talk of the town," the Colonel boasted in Saunterings in the nineties. "Were it not for *Town Topics,* Mr. McAllister, Mrs. Astor, . . . the Bradley Martins and numerous other show figures of the social musée would not be known outside their own small and select circle of friends. I set this statement down rather with regret than pride. When I contemplate the strange and ridiculous order of things of which I am the cause, when I find the ornamental dolls of our most unimportant fashionable world being discussed and pictured over whole pages of sloppy journalism, gushed over, dressed, undressed, and often followed through the pangs of childbirth, I am compelled to pause and ask myself if I have not considerable to answer for. . . . Nearly every Sunday paper in New York now devotes a full page to the movements of society people. The matter is prepared as nearly like mine as possible, being set forth in paragraphs, and, as a rule, my manner of expression is clearly imitated. This system of emulations has grown to such dimensions that at this moment no society in the world is discussed so extensively as the little knot of individuals in New York known as the Four Hundred. Had I not gaily set the puppets to dancing," the Saunterer concluded, "the newspapers of the town would never have seen fit to do more than make formal mention of the occasional entertainments among the rich, and we should not be regaled with momentous arguments concerning . . . Mrs. Bradley Martin's capacity for terrapin."

The Colonel was, of course, never one to underestimate his contributions to contemporary civilization. Surely there were other factors besides the Saunterer's contagious literary style that brought about the revolution in society journalism and banished the court gazette brand of reporting from most society pages not only in New York but in other large American cities during the final two decades of the last century; there was, for example, the sudden influx into resorts like Palm Beach and Newport of unprecedented numbers of new millionaires not well enough brought up to deplore the uses of publicity. But once society's kings, queens and court favorites were out where the plain folks could get a good look at them, *Town Topics'* was the shrill voice pointing out that many of them had no clothes on.

This *lèse-majesté* began to draw a crowd almost as soon as Eugene Mann took the magazine over. According to a house audit, the circulation was then about five thousand; by 1891 it had risen to sixty-three thousand. In the same period the advertising rate went from ten to seventy-five cents an agate line. But over the same years there was a corresponding rise in the perils of ownership and, indeed, of being on the *Town Topics* payroll. Subjects of the Saunterer's attention often took exception to the editorial policy that was proclaimed, for a time, just under *Town Topics'* masthead: "What's Worth Reading Is Worth Printing." Horsewhips were also prescribed on this side of the Atlantic—and they were ready to hand in the eighties. Apoplectic husbands and fathers began to appear with them so regularly at the *Town Topics* office that the staff devised a routine for dealing with such uninvited guests. When one of them burst through the doorway, demanding to see the fellow responsible for a particularly ruinous item, the nearest editor was instructed to answer sorrowfully, "You can't—he died yesterday. Those were the last words he ever wrote," and to burst into tears. "Nobody ever licked a weeping man," was Eugene Mann's theorem and, more often than not, it seems to have proved out.

The more respectable members of the editorial board, however, began to regard these as rather sticky working conditions. Many of them deserted, and from this period on— and indeed throughout its career—the full-time staff of *Town Topics* was largely made up of journalistic castaways. These were men, often of considerable ability, who labored under some incubus (drink or dope, particularly awful woman trouble or even a police record) that made them unacceptable in other editorial offices with literary pretensions and thus willing to ally themselves with a widely denounced—though widely read—scandal sheet. "Literary flotsam, we had all slunk onto the magazine from some limbo, usually of our own creation," a junior editor of the nineties once wrote. Nursing a grudge against the general structure of society, they perhaps took a particular pleasure in spoiling the fun of those who lolled about in its upper reaches.

Among the early defectors was Paul Potter, who later had a successful career as an adaptor of such novels as *Under Two Flags* and *Trilby* for the Broadway stage. Potter, who had sold his one-third interest in the magazine to one or both of the Manns, told the *World* in 1887 that the immediate cause of his departure was a letter the publisher had written him outlining a blackmailing campaign against some leading New York political figures—a remarkable proposal for a member of the bar to have put in exhibit form. Indeed Eugene Mann, for all his legal training, showed a curious recklessness about what the law would allow. One evening in the fall of 1887 half the staff of the magazine was arrested, and a few days later Mann was convicted of sending obscene matter through the mails. The sentence was suspended, but in October, 1891, the publisher was arrested again on the same charge, probably as the result of an item in Saunterings—foolhardy for the time—concerning the prevalence of abortion among society women. Apparently the younger Mann recalled his legal studies sufficiently to mistrust his prospects as a second offender. As soon as he made bail, he arranged to have the case postponed, pleading that he was critically ill of consumption. A few days later he turned *Town Topics* over to Colonel Mann and moved to Citronelle, Alabama, where he was given a job on a newspaper founded by C. C. Langdon, the Colonel's old friend from his Mobile days. During the mid-nineties Eugene Mann's case was postponed again and again on the ground of his illness. In 1897 representations were made to the District Attorney's office that he had only a few weeks to live, and at the suggestion of James Osborne, then an Assistant District Attorney, the charge was compassionately withdrawn. Three days later the doomed defendant arrived back in New York and took over *Town Topics'* Wall Street coverage, remaining an active member of the staff for several years. By the fall of 1901, however, his legal ruse—if it *was* entirely a ruse—had become reality. On March 30, 1902, at the age of forty-six, he died of tuberculosis in Phoenix. The *Times* found room for a brief report of the event on its front page, but no notice of it was taken in *Town Topics*.

According to a document filed by one of Eugene Mann's sons in a court proceeding in 1925, no money changed hands at the shift in *Town Topics'* ownership in 1891. Instead Colonel Mann agreed to be responsible, if the need arose, for the support of his brother's wife and children. Perhaps he had not counted on there eventually being five of these nieces and nephews, one of them born only five weeks before Eugene Mann's death in 1902. In any case, according to the document, he had lived up to his agreement. The Colonel always publicly dated his association with the magazine from this 1891 transaction. In his formal review of *Town Topics'* history twenty-five years later he entirely omitted his brother's part in its early career. Having mentioned Townsend and Keller and their financial troubles with the society journal, he wrote: "Afterward it had a varied career under different editors. I purchased it in 1891." In fact he had owned a third interest in it since the fall of 1885 and possibly a share of Potter's third after December, 1886. Beginning with his brother's first issue in May, 1885, he had been sufficiently close to the administration to make sure that the gossip department ran regular editorial puffs for the Mann Boudoir Car ("Its air is fresh and clean as the sea"). From time to time paragraphs in "Saunterings" even in its earliest years under Eugene Mann bore the Colonel's earmarks of composition. There were comments on conditions at West Point, for example, during the period when he had a cottage there, and on other occasions complaints about the personnel of the West Point Board of Visitors, which the Saunterer felt deserved to have members with actual combat records. Surely, he suggested in 1887, there must be *some* qualified person who had served with distinction in battle and, living in the neighborhood, would be happy to do his bit. (It took twelve years of such elbow-digging, and perhaps other means of persuasion, before a Secretary of War finally took the hint and appointed the Colonel to the board in 1899.)

Whether or not Mann had realized from the outset that his younger brother had come upon a gold mine and had helped supervise its exploitation from 1885 on, it wasn't a project he was free to devote his full attention to until the spring of 1889 when his sleeping car empire fell in ruins. Presumably during the next two years he was more actively involved in the direction of the magazine. Certainly the tone of the Saunterer who took over in the fall of 1891 was not that of a newcomer to the cast but the practiced, proprietary manner of one who has been on the scene, perhaps occasionally playing that particular role, for some time. If he was a major power at *Town Topics* before 1891, however, the word was apparently not formally conveyed to all members of the staff, or not conveyed early enough to suit him, and this oversight, rankling over the decades, may have been what caused him to begrudge his brother any role at all in his later account of the magazine's history. At any rate, one *Town Topics* employee described him in late 1889 or early 1890 as "a military personage who had nothing whatever to do with the management of the paper, but had, instead, a habit of haunting his brother's office and harassing the editors with childish suggestions." This was probably the only recorded instance when the Colonel's improvisations at *Town Topics* reminded anyone of child's play.

The Recording Angel.

By Charles Raymond Macauley.

The Helping Hands.

By Campbell Cory.

"Saunterings"

BY THE TIME MANN ceased to be a supernumerary at the
magazine, the weekly, which had previously been published
at various addresses in the Park Row neighborhood, was
doing business in rather dim and dusty quarters on Madison
Square near the 26th Street Delmonico's, an outpost that was
closed down in 1899. Possibly there was a connection between
the latter event and *Town Topics'* removal three years later
to 452 Fifth Avenue, fourteen blocks closer to the new
Forty-Fourth Street Delmonico's, where the editorial staff so
often took refreshment and where the Colonel ate his bounte-
ous lunch. The new offices, grander than the old ones although not so luxurious as those of the *Smart Set* just upstairs,
occupied the fourth floor of the Knox Hat Building, a narrow
nine-story structure with a steep mansard roof that today
still stands just south of the Public Library. Whenever the
Colonel's spirits plummeted because of new evidence of diplomatic incompetence among the Republicans in Washington
("We insist upon an Open Door in China, but keep our own
door closed and barred"), or grammatical incompetence
among leading social figures of the day ("The first thing a
reader must do with one of Mr. [Ward] McAllister's statements is to find out what it means since he cannot write
intelligible English"), a deep draught of the pollen of nature
seemed to revive them. Handy for this purpose just outside
the windows of his old quarters had been the lofty English
elms of Madison Square. At Fortieth Street he could resort
to the same remedy by craning his neck and peering past the

foundations of the new library to sniff the Chinese ginkgoes of Bryant Park.

During the first two working days of each week, however, not only did any messages of affection from nature go unacknowledged but the office blinds were often drawn against their distracting influence. These days were dedicated to getting *Town Topics* into the hands of the printers. The ladies in the fruited hats then prudently kept their distance while the free loaders, along with the office cats, slunk into out-of-the-way corners of the editorial rooms. By ten o'clock on Monday mornings Mann and his staff—in the warmer months just back from Saunterer's Rest—would be passing from hand to hand whatever information had arrived in the morning mail about weekend misconduct among the nation's best people, particularly items that would support the view of society set forth by the Saunterer in his declaration of war against the Four Hundred a few weeks after the Colonel took full command of *Town Topics*. "I believe," the Saunterer wrote in the issue for December 13, 1891, "that the possession of great wealth, the presence of continual luxury and an existence of sybaritic ease are sufficient to lead voluptuous natures into a system of sensual gratification more intensely and ingeniously base than is found in humbler walks of life. . . . The Four Hundred of New York," he concluded therefore, "is an element so shallow and unhealthy that it deserves to be derided almost incessantly."

Town Topics had staff correspondents in most large cities and important resorts, but much of the choicest evidence in support of the Colonel's view came from informers who, in their own minds at least, retained their amateur standing. From one source or another, if there was a Saturday dinner dance at Mrs. Belmont's Marble House or Mrs. Vanderbilt's The Breakers, "something spicy"—as Mann's onetime Newport correspondent described it from happy memory—was sure to be delivered to the Colonel, often by hand, by Monday afternoon. Years later, Ludwig Lewisohn, a frequent contributor of fiction to *Town Topics,* recalled the office on such a day. It was "heavily carpeted in red," he wrote. "Footfalls were to be deadened. The stealthy atmosphere was dense with cigarette smoke, and in and out stole society reporters with shifty eyes, correct clothes and heavy perfumes." For the most prolific of these fifth columnists, a prominent clubman who stood in well with the Social Register but was off balance at the bank, the Colonel himself would form a one-man reception line. When the monocled young gentleman stepped through the office doorway, the Colonel would welcome him with a bonecrushing handshake while he made a grab for the copy. Disengaging his hand and keeping a firm grasp on the envelope, the clubman would rattle it significantly. The Colonel, getting the message, would then slump over to the cashier's desk and return with a check. The exchange safely made, he would usher the visitor out, hissing just before the door closed: "I wouldn't deposit it for a few days, my boy."

Once the raw material for the next issue was safely in hand, the Colonel and his staff went to work to shape it into the leering and impertinent (or unaccountably flattering) paragraphs to which the Saunterer's readers were accustomed. Discounting the Colonel's potpourri of political bombast and oldtime reminiscence at its close, "Saunterings" devoted about two-thirds of its space to items about prominent society figures in New York and its satellite resorts and the other third to their opposite numbers in such cities as Philadelphia, Boston, Baltimore, Charleston, Mobile, San Francisco, or, during particularly arid weeks, Chicago or Pittsburg, as it was then spelled. The Saunterer's social scene was populated by individuals who gave receptions, tea dances, and tennis parties, and got married and engaged much as they did on the town's other society pages. It was also populated by charlatans, transvestites, adulterers (often incestuous), nymphomaniacs, lesbians, and cuckolds. It was the Saunterer's custom to run news of the routine social engagements of his weekly cast of characters directly after reports of their indictable pursuits, which usually left out names but provided instead such do-it-yourself clues as the subject's precise address or such information as, "The young man's last name, incidentally, is the same as the title of the leading primate of the Church of Rome." With the help of this literary counterpoint *Town Topics'* subscribers had no difficulty identifying the bride of the season who had once borne twins out of wedlock, the cotillion leader down with syphilis, or the prominent Philadelphia matron against whom divorce proceedings were being brought because of her passionate friendship with a female librarian. Often the Saunterer's stance was more flat-footed: "All that is necessary to learn Mr. Cochran's character is to look him straight in the face and watch the little, closely-set, beady eyes roll in his head as he attempts to deceive." "The erotic southern novelist, Amélie Rives, has a kink in her hair that extends well into her brain." "Harry Lehr's proud parade of his many sissy qualities, . . . his pink complexion and golden hair, his thin voice, his peculiar gestures, the feminine prettiness of his general make-up . . . has gone beyond the limits of tolerance by decent society." "Mr. Henry Sloane has been looked upon as a complaisant husband who wore his horns too publicly." And when a child was born to a recently married couple before the conventional interval, the Saunterer rarely failed to call attention to their wedding date as well as to have a good laugh over the subterfuges the family had resorted to in trying to cover up the premature arrival. Even when no moral lapses were involved, his comments on those who had in some manner lost his favor could leave scar tissue: "Mrs. Belmont dyes her hair. Though covered with diamond rings, her hands are wrinkled like a washerwoman's." "Mrs. Frederick Nielsen has aged a good deal lately. Her complexion has become almost blue, and the crows' feet are visible at a distance." "Miss Van Alen suffers from some kind of throat trouble—she cannot go more than half an hour without a drink." "Seldom does a brunette make a pretty bride, and Miss Maria Arnot Haver was no exception." It was perhaps not surprising that those readers whose families or dear friends were eligible for mention in *Town Topics* opened the magazine each Thursday with unsteady hands or that a regular contributor of fiction, after insisting that he rarely read the social notes, added that whenever he did, he "searched the realms of conjecture in vain for a reason why the editor should be permitted to live."

The subjects of the Saunterer's nastier attentions, who could be counted on to join in this sentiment, would presumably not have regarded it as a mitigating circumstance that a large share of the two days before *Town Topics* went to press was given over to double checking the informers' gossipy reports. "Above all, the Colonel insists upon accuracy," his onetime managing editor testified in court. "The influence of the magazine sprang almost entirely from fear, but its prestige was due to its never-failing accuracy," another former editor wrote. The reckless tale-spreader, no matter how racy and amusing, is in danger of losing his audience after a few flighty performances. The Saunterer held on to his through his reputation for purveying truths, however unpalatable. From time to time, for reasons of his own, he might shift his point of view on an individual, transforming one week's unspeakable lecher into the next week's devoted family man and philanthropist. (There were occasions, in fact, when the Colonel seemed to endorse, in spirit, Samuel Butler's remark that although he couldn't stand inaccuracy, he didn't mind lying.) But the truth, after all, has many aspects. Before Eugene Mann had got around to "What's Worth Reading Is Worth Printing," he had indicated some nostalgia for his days at the bar by announcing as *Town Topics'* motto "The Truth, the Whole Truth, and Nothing But the Truth." His older brother was more discriminating.

The burden of such editorial discretion weighed especially heavily on the Colonel's massive shoulders during the hours on Tuesday nights before the last *Town Topics* galley proof went off to the printers. At this time he amended or expanded his own contributions to "Saunterings" and wielded such a vigorous blue pencil on those written by others that an unwary reader might assume that one pair of malevolent eyes had observed the sinners in half a dozen resorts and a dozen cities in the course of one weekend. He also took charge of putting the items in order, although when opposing counsel during the later libel trial called attention to the significant juxtaposition of a pair of paragraphs, he pronounced it the result of the inherent malice of inanimate objects. During these stressful hours the Colonel's usual paterfamilias attitude toward his staff utterly vanished. Creaking back and forth in the swivel chair beyond the spreading rubber tree he would shout them in and out of his office like Nubian houseboys when something displeased him.

"What damn fool wrote this? My Lord, it doesn't even parse!" he would roar at them. Or "This office is infested with dashes. Dashes (waugh!) and more dashes (waugh!)" After one especially trying evening he banned all dashes from the magazine for a period of three months. He also once

fired on the spot an editor who let Rhinelander go through
without the "h." His epithets for such blunderers were reportedly even more withering than the ones he dealt out to
editors who passed along scandalous items without consulting
the list posted on the wall of the editorial room of those who,
for reasons best known to the Colonel, were currently safe
from exposure or ridicule. The Colonel's reprimands for
these latter slip-ups were explicit, matter of fact, and without
any trappings of hypocrisy. "When he was aware that a
person knew him and his weaknesses," Harold Vynne wrote
of a fictional character based on the Colonel, "he never
attempted to deceive or cozen that person into a belief either
in his greatness or his sincerity." His expression during such
discussions would be "cold and unscrupulous," Vynne recalled, and if the listener in any way demurred, the publisher
would say only, "How painfully moral you are," and turn
back to his galleys.

The ominous quiet of the *Town Topics* office on these
crucial nights, broken only by the Colonel's shouts and the
scurrying of editorial feet, was occasionally shattered by a
thunderous pounding on the outer door. Whoever opened it
would be nearly trampled down by unscheduled visitors, who
had got word from one source or another that a certain
factually accurate but hideously inconvenient report was about
to be dispatched to the printers. These invaders (after dark
no one seems to have come alone) would take a sweeping
look around the outer editorial room and, clearly beyond the
reach of the sub-editor's tears that had turned the trick in
simpler days, would advance through the open door of
Mann's private office. By this time the old Colonel, suddenly
agile as a stripling, would have sprung to his feet, reached
out one hand for his Scotch fir walking stick—"a weapon
that might have floored a mule," as one employee described

it—and with the other hand have grabbed the pistol from his top desk drawer. So far as the record shows, however, no blood was ever shed on such occasions. The high drama was swiftly transformed into a business negotiation. At its conclusion a check changed hands, marked down as a loan or stock purchase or perhaps an advertising contract, the offending item was removed from the next week's edition (though not from the *Town Topics* files), and the visitors retired, sighing the long sigh of the reprieved.

After their departure, the Colonel would resume his reading of "Saunterings," now chuckling to himself from time to time and in a mood to correct after only a minor explosion such a gaffe as the spelling of Duryea with two e's. An occasional groan would signify that he had encountered one of the two-line jokes that were customarily scattered among the Saunterer's deadly earnest paragraphs. ("What caused his downfall? A slip of a girl." "What is political economy, Pop? Buying votes as cheaply as possible.") After this, with his blue pencil poised at the ready, he would settle down and read every word of the proofs for the second, non-Sauntering half of *Town Topics,* material that, more often than not, he had never laid eyes on before. It was frequently three o'clock in the morning before he initialed his last galley and bundled the lot of them off in the arms of the printer's messenger. As the little band of editors shuffled down the stairs and out of the gloomy office building, the Colonel's tired old face would be wreathed in smiles, and, as they said good night, each editor was again his "dear boy." But one of his sometime companions on these overwrought evenings had insisted in an article published in the *Morning Telegraph* in 1898 that, for himself, he had often brooded over the fact that "the peace or misery of many individuals occupying lofty places in society was directly dependent upon what these

sleepy-eyed men had been doing." They were, Harold Vynne
had written, "like a gang of small-calibre conspirators who,
having laid their dynamite, were departing stealthily to their
holes."

The hole to which the Colonel himself departed on those
early mornings was no shabby hideout but a five-story,
seventeen-room brownstone with an oblique view of the Hud-
son River. Its address was 309 West 72nd Street, in the early
1900's a highly fashionable one; in fact the house stood only
two blocks from Charles Schwab's seven-million-dollar granite
château. Mann had bought it in 1899 after an adult lifetime
of making his headquarters in hotels ("I have passed far too
much of my life in caravansaries," he noted in "Saunterings"
in 1905). He lived alone in the new house with his daughter
until August, 1902, when he was married at All Angels
Episcopal Church on West Seventy-seventh Street to one
Sophie Hartog. The marriage was at least the Colonel's third.
Perhaps there had been others during the nearly four decades
that separated this ceremony from his second excursion into
matrimony, but if so the evidence has apparently long since
been filed and forgotten. Except for the reference during the
U.S. Petroleum trial to his second marriage and the tangible
evidence of a daughter, who was certainly the product of his
first, even the Colonel's two earliest wives might never have
existed. In the press accounts of the numerous events that
brought him before the public eye during his lifetime and
in his own *Town Topics* reminiscences, which occasionally
verged on total recall in the case of matters he cared to leave
a record of, there is no trace of either lady. The only wife
taken note of in his obituaries was the former Miss Hartog,
who otherwise has left vestiges only a little less dim than
those of her predecessors. Rumored to be the daughter of
an old army friend of the Colonel's, she is revealed in court-

room sketches of his 1906 trial for perjury—her only important public appearance with him—as a small, dark haired, rather pretty woman, much younger than Mann and noticeably younger looking than his daughter. According to later accounts, his marriage had no effect on the Colonel's established midweek practice of allowing the decorum of the *Town Topics* office to be disrupted by swarms of lady callers or his habit of carrying some of the winsome invaders off for weekend houseparties at Saunterer's Rest. Moreover, when less informal social events at the Lake George farm were reported in the columns of *Town Topics,* his daughter Emma continued to be referred to as the hostess, with the new Mrs. Mann "among those present."

Of Emma Mann more substantial evidence survives. This is partly the result of the Colonel's attentive coverage of her summer tea parties and other Lake George affairs, often having to do with the annual Regatta, which would give him the opportunity to note in passing that the vice-president of the Lake George Regatta Association was Colonel William d'Alton Mann. This information may have been intended to confound such disparagers as those at *Collier's* who had written that "we can hardly imagine that many decent men would consent to meet the [*Town Topics*] editor. . . ." Items about his daughter's soirées always appeared toward the end of the Saunterer's social chronicles, even after the dispatches from Chicago and Pittsburg, and are the only instances of Mann's laying claim to any social significance for the comings and goings of his own household. The principal testimony about Emma Mann, however, is that of Harold Vynne, who was her first husband, and appears in his fictional account of life at *Town Topics* that was published in 1900. Called *The Woman That's Good,* the novel's subtitle was *The Undoing of a Dreamer.* Beginning in the late eighties,

Vynne was on the *Town Topics* staff off and on for nearly a decade, first as an editorial assistant in New York during the Eugene Mann era, then as Chicago correspondent, and, after he returned to New York in 1893, as a general editor, music critic, and fiction writer. The female paragon of his title is the first wife of the novel's writer-editor hero who divorced him—as Vynne's first wife had divorced *him*—in the early nineties. The book is such faintly disguised auto-biography that Mann, who appears in it as Major John Plum, is sometimes forgetfully referred to as "the Colonel." In this novel Plum is the hero's employer, the proprietor of *The Fang,* a magazine "fashioned somewhat after the lines of Mr. Labouchere's *Truth.* Written from beginning to end in English absolutely without flaw" and "covering every phase of life and sphere of human thought in a way at once master-ful and exhilarating," in the novel's words, "it would have found an honored place among the sparkling publications of the country if it had not been for the foundation of social gabble on which it was built."

Of the publisher's daughter, Agnes Plum, Vynne wrote that she had a face "not wholly unattractive in profile. . . . Only the sixteenth of an inch of space that separated her two front teeth lent her smile a suggestion of ravenousness." Miss Plum "had reduced the mixing of cocktails to a most rare and delicate art," and enjoyed the result which, in the early nineties, "occasioned some surprise in a lady of degree from the East." She dressed with elegance, set an excellent table, and ran her father's staff of Negro servants, as well as her father, with an iron hand, deftly subduing him in his more boisterous moments by murmuring, "Papa, your brain is softening." In his first years with the magazine, Vynne noted, it was the doting father's custom to pretend indignation when a man approached his daughter with even a hint of amorous purpose. In January, 1896, however, when she was in her late thirties, the hero suddenly found such rhetorical overtures interpreted—and accepted—as a proposal of marriage. It was in early 1896 that Vynne was married to Emma Mann. The latter half of Vynne's novel is devoted to an account of the disintegration of the marriage as the result of the Major's insistence upon spending most of his time with the newly-weds, of his daughter's evident preference for the company of her father,* of the increase in the hero's drinking at the behest of a father-in-law who regarded a man without a glass in his hand as a threat to his way of life, and of the hero's eventual realization that the basic charge preferable against the gossip department in the Major's magazine was not just malicious mischief but blackmail.

Vynne and Emma Mann, even as their fictional counterparts, were divorced late in 1898. Emma added a hyphen to her name and became Mrs. Emma Mann-Vynne. (Apparently she liked the look of this since she reverted to it in 1912 after her divorce from her second husband, Albert Wray.) Meanwhile Vynne took a job with the *Morning Telegraph* for whom he began to write a series of articles telling the inside story of where the Colonel's money came from. Mann instituted suit for libel. His price for withdrawing the legal action (duly paid) was a retraction and apology from the *Telegraph* and the firing of Vynne. Thus in the only effective libel suit filed during Mann's first decade and a half as publisher of *Town Topics,* the Colonel appeared as the plaintiff.

Defeated in his attempt to publish a factual account of his *Town Topics* years, Vynne went back to Chicago and wrote the fictional version of his experiences with the wicked warlock of the East. His novel was not a success, nor was it even widely reviewed. Toward the end of the book he con-

* "Watch the Major fumble Agnes," said an onlooker during a drunken interlude in the book.

cludes an episode in which the hero's first wife declines to return to him or even to let him see his child with: "After that he broke some furniture and went to dine with some irresponsible people." In June, 1905, just before the Colonel's own serious troubles began, Vynne, according to a story in the *World,* died of drink in a midwestern asylum.

There was no question of who had undone the dreamer in Vynne's fictional account of things. Yet, like many of the Colonel's victims, the novelist was not always able to maintain his stern prosecutor's countenance toward the old man. Despite his bitterness, he managed to make rather poignant a description of the noon scene at Delmonico's on Wednesdays after the scandal magazine went to press. The publisher, his spirits at high pitch, would sometimes forget himself and wave across the room at one of his fashionable informers, perhaps the monocled dandy who was such a prolific contributor to the gossip department. The clubman would slowly adjust his eyepiece, stare the old man full in the face, and, with exquisite insolence, cut him dead. Giving a short laugh, the publisher would turn back to his mutton chops and order himself an extra plateful of biscuits to salve his affronted feelings.

In real life, outside of anybody's novel, the Colonel on Wednesday afternoons might make the rounds of his clubs— the Manhattan, the Lotos, the Press, the Transportation, the Army and Navy, and perhaps search his calendar for a scheduled meeting of the Ohio Society, the Southern Society, the Loyal Legion, the Knights Templars, the Elks, or the Old Guard, to most of which he had belonged for many years before he had got into his current line of work. Except at the comparatively relaxed Lotos Club, whose members seem to have had a high regard for his entertainment value and whom he rewarded with reams of deferential notices of club affairs in *Town Topics,* his appearance at any of these oases was likely to be followed by a sudden silence and the ostentatious closing of ranks. Although "he was never known to display indignation when treated with palpable disrespect," Vynne noted, it was an awkward situation for a gregarious man. He was back in the Strangers' Rooms of Europe, but without a club member to vouch for him. By the end of the day he had usually settled for a game of pool with Justice Deuel or had rounded up the *Town Topics* staff for an evening of compulsory gluttony at his town house, often on the eve of carrying them off for more of the same at Saunterer's Rest. "We live quietly, but we feed well," the Colonel liked to say, and Vynne once estimated that "the herds of kine, the droves of deer, the flocks of canvas-backed ducks consumed at (Mann's) table in the course of one short week would have fed a city in a siege." The Colonel apparently never confronted head-on the probability that, along with his habit of tying up so much of his cash in real estate, this dispensing of prodigal and almost continuous hospitality might leave him—and his staff—once again temporarily embarrassed on pay day. ("I may be drunk on your whisky, but is that any reason why I shouldn't be paid?" an editor once sobbed toward the end of such a party.)

By the weekend, as he continued his strenuous revels, *Town Topics* readers had surreptitiously fetched their copies from kiosk or letter box, and its messages were being decoded, as necessary, "upstairs, downstairs and backstairs." The assignations, gaffes, and untoward incidents were taking place at Newport, Bar Harbor, and elsewhere on which the Saunterer would rest his case in the following week's issue, and Mann's agents—upstairs, downstairs, backstairs—were taking notes. Certain objects of his attention in the current issue were deciding to consult their lawyers and, on second thought, deciding not to. Several of their neighbors were crumpling—and then smoothing out—polite letters on *Town Topics* stationery requesting an interview "on a matter of considerable importance." ("Only the heedless or the ignorant refused," recalls Edwin Post, Jr., in *Truly Emily Post.* "This kind of thing had been going on for almost twenty years. . . . Everyone knew about it. Everyone loathed and feared it. But nearly everyone yielded.") On Monday morning, having put aside his clown's mask, the Colonel would be back at the Knox Hat Building and his serious business in life. It was this weekly routine that the Colliers, Norman Hapgood, and William Travers Jerome hoped to see undergo drastic revision as the result of the trial that opened in the New York Criminal Courts Building in January, 1906.

The Witness
for the State

THE REPORTER FOR the *New York American,* who had been
so overcome by the theatrical aspects of Mann's earlier appearance in court that he had called for an interpolated song
by the Colonel, was hardly the first to see dramatic possibilities in a criminal hearing, whether as musical comedy or
something more profound having to do with pity and terror.
Among the complications that would foul a conventional plot
line, however, in any full-scale stage version of the series of
legal proceedings in which the editorial and fiscal practices
of Colonel Mann were spread across the public record over
a period of thirteen months in 1905 and 1906 was the circumstance that during the trial in which the leading character's villainy was most dramatically exposed he was not the
defendant or even the plaintiff but a witness for the prosecution.

The trial in which the Colonel played this anomalous role
opened on January 15, 1906, in the criminal branch of the
New York Supreme Court. This arm of local justice met in
the Criminal Courts Building on Centre Street, a vast, hideous red-brick barrack that had been built in 1885 and two
decades later was in an advanced state of decrepitude, its
buckling walls constantly being denounced by civic reform
groups as a menace to human life. Arthur Train, the novelist
who was then on the District Attorney's legal staff, called it
"one of the gloomiest structures in the world. Tier on tier,"

he wrote, "it rises above a huge central rotunda, rimmed with mezzanines and corridors, upon which the courtrooms open, and crowned by a glass roof encrusted with soot, through which filters a soiled and viscous light." The air, he added, was "rancid with garlic and cigar smoke," and from the ceiling of the main courtroom on the first floor flakes from dim frescoes of seedy-looking cherubs sifted down from time to time onto those in the seats below.

Despite these hazards of attendance, what went on in this chamber, gloomier than ever in the abbreviated midwinter days, was treated as the best show in town during January, 1906, by throngs of spectators who began to assemble in the murky corridors early each morning before the court was called to order at eleven. As the legal drama approached its climax, the number of available general admissions seats dwindled. Social and literary celebrities bearing *laissez-passers* from Hapgood, Collier, or Jerome, virtually filled the gallery. In one corner of the room, within the rail marking off the judge's realm, was a special section the press called the Royal Box, unofficially reserved for groups of young society matrons shepherded by Mrs. Rob Collier, the granddaughter of Mrs. Astor. "Dressed as if for the theatre," noted the *Times,* they would drop their lorgnettes and gasp in unison at indelicate references in the testimony and after each recess would pose for newspaper photographs whose captions dwelt on their fashionable costumes. Often their escorts would be allowed to take ringside seats on the steps leading up to the judge's bench, and court attendants would be called to the telephone during the proceedings to ask if they could make room for an additional party of ten or twelve. Meanwhile hundreds of the less favored were each day turned away at the door. The otherwise dull time of the year, the spiciness of the promised revelations, and the great names involved would have brought out a crowd in any case, but the accompanying newspaper hoopla turned it into an attraction of carnival proportions. Day after day every paper in town devoted half to three-quarters of its first two pages to the performance, and on several afternoons Hearst's *American* found room for little other news before page five. When, on the trial's first day, the man chosen as foreman of the jury turned out to be F. T. Richards, a cartoonist for *Life,* the *American,* not content with its vantage point in the press section, signed him to an exclusive contract to sketch the principals from the jury box. Judge James Fitzgerald took no recorded exception to this unusual bit of moonlighting.

Indeed Fitzgerald, a large, chubby-faced man with a wispy black moustache, was apparently dazzled by the visiting company and intruded little into the proceedings throughout the trial except occasionally to quell the more unseemly hilarity on the part of the spectators, who sat along the left side and across the back of the dingy room with the jury box to the right. Within the railing in front of the judge's bench was a table for Jerome and his assistants. Immediately outside the railing on the jury side of the courtroom was one reserved for the defense, and to its right a much larger table for the press. Near the press table, beyond a low rail, two front seats in the stalls were set aside each day for Justice Deuel and the Colonel. Deuel dressed with some elegance, but his wardrobe got indifferent notices beside that of his neighbor. The Colonel's arrival in court each day, carrying a high silk hat and wearing his Prince Albert coat, pin-striped trousers, and either a bright red or yellow vest, was always good for a colorful paragraph to balance another going into the dreary technicalities of the legal goings-on. His favorite tie, it was noted, was also red and seemed to bore a hole through his beard which, worn in the split-chin fashion of two decades earlier, "gave him a fierce, buccaneering air," reported the *American*. Against the brilliant white of this beard and of his long, silky hair, the publisher's complexion appeared as "a tasteful shade of port wine." It was not only as a study in still life, however, that he drew the eyes of the assembled crowd. When a witness was on the stand, the Colonel's eyes never left his face, but in other respects he reacted so histrionically to each turn of the testimony—groaning, smiling, stamping his foot, clenching his fists, or tearing at his whiskers—that the reporters just beyond the barrier and even some of the figures at the tables reserved for Jerome, Hapgood, and their cohorts often turned their backs on the witness box to attend to the man who was officially only an innocent bystander in the case.

During this main event Peter Collier was again off foxhunting in Ireland, but he had provided Hapgood with two stellar defenders, who apparently shared equal responsibility for the conduct of the case. The defender who had by far the greater number of lines, however, was the jovial, noisy James W. Osborne. Three months earlier the Saunterer, in his role as political as well as social arbiter, had formally endorsed Osborne, then the Democratic candidate running for District Attorney against Jerome. When he had been roundly beaten, Mann had expressed regret but added that "in view of the wide field in New York for a great criminal lawyer, he ought, perhaps, to be congratulated on his defeat." A few weeks later the Colonel must have been affronted by the news that the very next move of the great criminal lawyer was to join the war against his own magazine. Co-counsel for Hapgood was Edward M. Shepard, a small, wiry man who wore his thin hair long and his collars high and, in contrast to Osborne, rarely raised his voice above a reedy conversational monotone. Shepard, like Osborne, had occasionally been accused of acting as a respectable front for Tammany, and it was under these auspices that he had unsuccessfully run for Mayor of New York against Seth Low in 1901. After some backing and filling ("Shepard has all the virtues of a Brooklynite, also all the defects, and one of these is a lack of popularity") the Saunterer had also endorsed his candidacy. It would undoubtedly have made the staunchly Democratic Colonel happier to have found the enemy camp at the Criminal Courts Building peopled by Republicans for whom his favorite group epithet was "megatherium"—a megatherium being a genus of giant ground sloth of the Pleistocene Age. As it was, he could only reiterate for the rest of his life that the ingratitude of men in public life would never cease to amaze him.

Also occupying a prominent place at the defense table, of course, was defendant Hapgood, "that lean, keen, ascetic student," as the *American* called him under a sketch of his long, equine face and aloof eyes behind pince-nez, an aloofness he did not seem tempted to relax in these legal surroundings in spite of his Harvard law degree. As an undergraduate, Hapgood had been editor of the *Harvard Monthly,* and although he had practiced law for a year after receiving his LL.B. in 1893, his interest in journalism had turned out to be the stronger. Before joining *Collier's* as editor in 1902, he had worked for the New York *Evening Post* along with Lincoln Steffens and, with Steffens, had shifted over to the local *Commercial Advertiser* as dramatic critic. At the time the *Town Topics* trial began, however, the thirty-seven-year-old Hapgood was still regarded as a somewhat cerebral and cautious, rather than a crusading, type of editor. He had just turned down a chance to serialize Upton Sinclair's *The Jungle* for example, as not being *Collier's* type of thing. One of his *Collier's* colleagues, Finley Peter Dunne, made fun of him about this time in one of his Mr. Dooley articles as "Norman

Slapgood" whose motto, he said, was "Yes—and no."

Additional, unofficial counsel was available to Hapgood throughout the trial from Rob Collier, who was continually diving in and out of the courtroom, racing around it, hallooing at acquaintances, and giving the impression of a young man having the time of his life. Regularly accompanying him on these revels was a college classmate whom young Collier had brought to New York as advertising manager of *Collier's*. The added starter was Condé Nast, the dapper *boulevardier* and future publisher of *Vogue* and *Vanity Fair* who, like Hapgood, was a non-practicing member of the bar. Hovering rather tentatively about the edges of this splendid group were the chief defense witnesses, Irving, Wooster, and Wayne who, two months before, had written a letter to a friend in which he declared that he "still had some honor" and "hoped not to have to accept Collier's blood money."

Despite the variegated cast of characters at the defense table, the center of attention within the enclosure was the tense, muscular figure of William Travers Jerome. Jerome, then forty-six years old, was six feet tall, with a square face, brooding, heavy-lidded eyes behind round glasses, and a small, neat moustache. He rarely smiled, his rather stern expression relaxing rather than changing when he was amused, like that of a man who was leading a complicated inner life. Yet his movements about the cramped courtroom were large and swashbuckling, those of a *beau sabreur* or conscious folk hero. Someone once described his personality as having the changeable luster of a cat's eye in the dark. Milton McKaye, interviewing him for *The New Yorker* a quarter of a century later, described Jerome in 1906 as having been, with Bryan and Roosevelt, "one of the three most famous men in America." He was the only man who had ever been elected to important public office in New York without the support of either major political party. In 1901 he had beaten the Tammany candidate for district attorney, running on a Fusion ticket, and four years later, "running wildcat," as he described it, he had stood off both Tammany and the Republicans, although the Democratic candidate for Mayor had been over-whelmingly elected. Jerome was a first cousin of Jennie Jerome, Winston Churchill's mother, and, in all but the most nobbish judgments, a birthright member of the society that many of the Colonel's clients were trying to crash. (Later in the trial he asked Robert Irving about the rules for eligibility in *Fads and Fancies.* "Well, I wouldn't be eligible, but you would," said Irving. "God forbid!" was Jerome's response.)

Jerome's public career had begun with a Tammany appointment as Assistant District Attorney in 1888. A few years later, kicking over the political traces, he had taken a job with the Lexow Committee of the State Legislature that exposed police corruption in the city and in 1895 had helped elect a reform mayor, who immediately appointed him to a judgeship on the newly created Court of Special Sessions. During the next six years he flung himself into his judicial duties with such rampant moral indignation that, as his obituary in the *Times* described it in 1934, "a sort of a thrill ran through the city," and he soon was known "throughout the country . . . as a spectacular crusader against vice, crime, and political corruption." Almost nightly he would descend from the bench, raid the town's leading gambling houses with his hatchet brigade, and would then, wrote *Collier's* in October, 1905, "hold court upon a table in the captured stronghold, surrounded by the spoils of victory. At the end of his term not one known gambling house was left open in New York." Even the notorious Richard Canfield had been driven upstate to the more receptive judicial atmosphere of Saratoga. Yet, in the days when a yellow finger was the symbol of depravity, Jerome's nickname was "Cigarette Willie." This evidence of human fallibility, along with his open indulgence in whisky, friendly card games, and elaborate profanity, took much of the curse off the term "reformer," which he professed to detest. ("If there is such a thing as a perfect sport, Jerome was that," Hutchins Hapgood, Norman Hapgood's brother, wrote many years later.) Having acted more prosecutor than judge while on the bench, Jerome, once he was elected District Attorney, had rejected the more melodramatic possibilities of his new role and, while maintaining his public image—"a combination of Savonarola, St. George and D'Artagnan" as Arthur Train once described it—had left the trying of cases to his assistants. The trial of Colonel Mann was the first he had personally conducted during his four years in office.

The prosecution's first witness, sworn in on the morning of January 16, was the complainant, Judge Deuel. Deuel spent much of the day reviewing his career of public service, beginning with a carpetbagger appointment as commonwealth attorney in Virginia in 1869, shortly before his admission to the New York bar. During one period in the eighties, he admitted, he had collected four separate federal paychecks each month as simultaneously a Master in Chancery, Examiner in Equity, United States Commissioner, and Clerk of the United States Circuit Court. During the nineties he had served as a New York police magistrate and in 1903 had been appointed to the Children's Court, a branch of the Court of Special Sessions. He confirmed the Colonel's story to the press that they had first met twenty-three or twenty-four years earlier when he had done some legal work for the Mann Boudoir Car Company. He and Mann were excellent friends, he testified, in spite of their political differences. He himself, Deuel said, was "the very image of a Republican."

It was merely as a token of their friendship, he said, that the Colonel had, in 1896, given him thirty shares of *Town Topics* stock and five years later had made him vice-president of the Town Topics Publishing Company. Jerome then turned his witness over to defense counsel for cross-examination.

Osborne began by reading aloud Section 1416 of the City Charter, which provided that "no justice shall receive . . . any fees or perquisites . . . nor carry on any business or practice as an attorney." Jerome gave "a rather ironic smile" as the statute was read: he had, in fact, composed it ten years before as chairman of a Bar Association committee delegated to do so by the state legislature. Deuel conceded the existence of the regulation but denied that when he appeared in the *Town Topics* office each week he read over its galleys for libel. He agreed that he "might put in a few exclamation points." It was true that he had a desk at the magazine, he said, but that was because he had been writing a series of articles for *Town Topics* about crime in New York, and the office was "a convenient place for research on the subject," a remark that, according to the *Tribune,* caused Osborne to "simply roar with laughter." Immediately afterward, however, the defense attorney plucked the *Town Topics* minute book from among the papers on the table in front of him and began to read aloud "with a drawling and raucous emphasis" a report of a 1901 corporate meeting when Deuel himself had moved that *Town Topics* pay him $1,200 a year for his services and a second session a few months later when he had proposed that the *Smart Set,* another Mann publication, pay him an $1,800 annual retainer. Both motions had passed, Osborne noted, and then introduced a number of ledger pages showing the payment to the judge of additional bonuses from time to time. "Deuel placed his hand over his eyes, and his mouth trembled nervously," reported the *Globe.*

"Do you admit the record?" Osborne asked him.

"I'll have to," said Judge Deuel just before court recessed for the day. Deuel then joined Colonel Mann and drove uptown with him in the Colonel's shiny black Pope-Toledo.

The following day two dozen letters were read into the record that had been sent by Deuel to Moses Wooster between 1901 and 1903 during the membership drive for *Fads and Fancies.* A few of these were on the stationery of the City Magistrate's Court, where Deuel had then been sitting, and the rest on the letterhead of the New York Republican Club; clearly the Judge believed in the virtues of a low overhead. "You are seeding the garden, and I trust with gentle cultivation, of which you are capable, we will yet fill our basket quite full of either flowers or fruit," he had written in August, 1901, to Wooster, who was off prospecting in Newport. "I want to see some big money," he had written later that fall. "Have you run down Marshall Field? If you get them all, we'll have a spree when you get back." ("Here Mr. Osborne chuckled, Colonel Mann looked daggers, Jerome looked disgusted," noted the *World.*) A few months later Deuel had expressed the hope that Wooster would have "not only pleasant weather but pleasant people to see and to meet, and that all of them will be like Davy Crockett's 'coon—all you need to do is point your gun and every high-toned desirable citizen at Palm Beach may tumble instantly into your basket." "As the day wore on," reported the *American,* "Judge Deuel appeared to shrink and age before the very eyes of the crowd."

After the noon recess Deuel was asked whether it was true that society leaders had ever come to the *Town Topics* office on the night it went to press and paid $10,000 to have an item removed. Deuel thought it was never more than four thousand—and that in payment for a perfectly legitimate advertising contract. He had "no distinct recollection" of how many times this might have happened. Was he aware that during the summer of 1905, while he was occupying the Colonel's office, a paragraph had appeared in *Town Topics* that had caused a well-known society figure to commit suicide? Deuel said he had read about it in the papers. Osborne then put to him an involved series of questions about the piece of property on West Thirty-eighth Street owned by the Town Topics Corporation and a mortgage on it given by the Equitable Life Assurance Society. Jerome interrupted to say that "we have no objection to admitting that *Town Topics* borrowed $165,000 from Equitable."

"On unimproved property?" asked Osborne, his voice rising in astonishment.

"On unimproved property," Jerome agreed "in his mellifluent contralto." Osborne then read aloud a number of flattering references to James Hazen Hyde, Equitable's leading stockholder, that had appeared in *Town Topics* after this transaction. Later in the trial it was brought out that Equitable's return on its investment had included more than the nourishment of a young man's vanity. In 1904 a minor employee of the insurance company had come to the Colonel with the details of scandalous corporate shenanigans at Equitable. Mann testified that after the mortgage was granted he had decided not to publish the story, which thus did not break until almost a year later, possibly after some Equitable officials had had time to cover their tracks and thus escape their share of the legal retribution exacted of other insurance executives following the spectacular investigation by the state legislature. While Judge Deuel was on the stand, however, Osborne's only further question on the Equitable matter was whether, about the time the Colonel got his $165,000 mortgage, the company hadn't also run a series of $6,000-a-page ads in the magazine, printed in several languages, including Russian. Was *Town Topics* widely read in Russia, he asked Deuel.

"*Town Topics* is widely read *everywhere*," said Deuel, retrieving a little of his accustomed spirit.

The following morning, in an effort to recoup further, Deuel went on the stand at his own request to read a prepared statement allotting himself credit for numerous humanitarian legal reforms over the years. During the long, droning narration Juror Number 12 fell asleep, Osborne left the courtroom, and Jerome sat in conversation with some friends. When the Judge finished at last, he was allowed to step down and return to his place beside the Colonel without further questioning. At the beginning of the afternoon session the jury was handed copies of twenty-four paragraphs that had appeared in *Town Topics* after the individuals concerned had refused to subscribe to *Fads and Fancies*, paragraphs that both sides in the case had stipulated were too scandalous to be read aloud in open court. The jurors' gasps and giggles as they read these over continued for some time. There were various procedural delays, and it wasn't until late in the afternoon of January 19 that Colonel Mann was called to the stand. After establishing that Mann had been editor and publisher of *Town Topics* since 1891, Jerome's direct examination consisted of two questions: "Does *Town Topics* print scandal?" ("No."), and "Has it ever been guilty of levying blackmail . . . or publishing anything in consideration of money being paid?" ("Absolutely not!"). Jerome then delivered his second witness over to the defense. Before court recessed for the day Osborne had time only to have the Colonel identify the *Town Topics* style book with its notation in block caps on the cover: "Remember that ridicule is more effective than abuse. Use a rapier rather than a bludgeon."

When his cross-examination got into full swing the next day Osborne was so ferocious that the Colonel's plight reminded Julian Hawthorne, the novelist's son who was covering the session for the *American,* of "Andromeda chained to the rock in the act of being devoured by the dragon." During the morning several paragraphs published in *Town Topics* in 1901 and 1902 were introduced into evidence. All of them dealt with Reginald Ward, a high-flying entrepreneur from Boston who had invaded the international financial field. Somewhere along the way, perhaps from some obliging Balkan principality, he had picked up the title of Count. One *Town Topics* item referred to Ward and "a scandal that savors strongly of the Oscar Wilde type." Another read: "I hear from London that Reginald Ward is soon to wed a widow of title who has seen at least sixty-five winters. Mr. Ward is more of a dandy than ever and affects the dress and manners of the fops of the last century. He wears his fingernails long, and each finger is loaded with rings. He is a great friend of Mrs. Ronalds who, I hear, arranged his coming marriage." A paragraph was then read from "Saunterings" for July, 1903, reporting that Ward had arrived in this country where he had "received notable social attention. His old friends in the Union and Metropolitan Clubs, where he has always been very popular, were glad to have him with them. . . . Few men have gone from the states to London and established themselves more successfully in both the social and financial worlds than Reginald Ward." Did Mann deny that shortly before the appearance of the last paragraph Ward had transferred to him ten thousand shares of stock in the Rico Syndicate, a copper mining enterprise? The Colonel could not recall. Letters reporting the transfer were then read as well as a tremulous note from Ward to say that he was "looking forward with much interest to the paragraphs to which you refer. I wish you would please put my name down on the regular list of *Town Topics* so that I will get it regularly, if not too much trouble." At the bottom of this were the letters "OK—W.D.M." Mann denied that he had written them or that he had ever laid eyes on the letter, assertions that would be of subsequent legal interest.

Several items from "Saunterings" during the late nineties that concerned Perry Belmont were then passed to the jury. Only one of these, published in 1899, was read aloud. "I really think he did the honorable thing when he married Mrs. Sloane as soon as the law would permit," it concluded. Had he borrowed money from Perry Belmont in June, 1900, Osborne asked the Colonel. "Yes, $4,000." Without security? "Yes." Had he also got from the same Perry Belmont $10,000 for a hundred shares of United States Steel whose value on the Exchange had never gone above fifty? The Colonel agreed that he had. Had *Town Topics* thereafter always referred favorably to the banker-diplomat? Mann could not remember. A long series of flattering paragraphs about Perry Belmont, published after the financial exchange, was then introduced, along with a letter the Colonel had written to editor Wayne from London only the previous July, stating that "I wish to show that the Perry Belmonts are invited to all the best affairs here." Had he ever tried to borrow money from Perry's younger brother, Oliver Hazard Perry Belmont, Osborne asked. The Colonel did not think he had.

After the noon recess Mann was temporarily excused, and O. H. P. Belmont, "wearing the highest standing collar that was ever seen in public" and carrying a glistening bell-crowned silk hat, was called to the stand. "Colonel Mann had become agitated and nervous as soon as he saw Mr. Belmont enter," reported the *American*. The younger Belmont testified that in 1899 Colonel Mann had come to him and asked him for $5,000 in return for some shares of *Town Topics* stock, that when he refused Mann had written a letter, which Belmont produced in court, soliciting a straight loan of $2,000, and that after Belmont had again refused (and also turned down an invitation to appear in *Fads and Fancies*) some fifty abusive items about him had appeared in the magazine. Recalled to the stand, the Colonel found his recollection refreshed and admitted that he might have dictated most of the paragraphs.

As the long examination continued, a heavy rain began to fall outside, the courtroom grew increasingly dark, and, in the ominous gloom, Mann's rasping voice gradually lost its strength. Osborne kept leaning toward him, cupping a hand behind his ear, and demanding that the Colonel repeat what he had just said, that he speak loud enough for everyone to hear.

"Did you ever borrow money from E. Clarence Jones, the broker?" was the question Osborne had just asked him when Mann turned to Judge Fitzgerald as if requesting the protection of the court, and said in a weak voice, "I don't want to answer." Ordered to respond, he said he had borrowed $10,000 from Jones. Had he repaid it?

"Probably not," said Mann. After Osborne's next question—an insignificant one—the Colonel whispered that he did not care to answer further.

"On the ground that it would degrade you?" snapped Osborne.

"Yes," said the fallen warrior, and a recess was called until after the weekend.

The next morning Osborne told a group of newspapermen that a series of *Town Topics* attacks on Senator Russell Alger in the late nineties when Alger had been Secretary of

War had ceased after Alger had turned over to the Colonel $100,000 worth of Alger-Sullivan Lumber Company stock and, in addition, had named him in 1899 to the West Point Board of Visitors. The *World* reported that, in view of the calamity of the previous day, the defense was now fearful that at this eleventh hour Judge Deuel would withdraw his complaint and ask to have the proceedings stopped. Apparently he concluded that it was too late now, and the trial resumed Monday morning as scheduled. Richard Harding Davis, the celebrated war correspondent, turned up in the front row of the civilian skirmish "wearing wash leather gloves and carrying a small cane upside down," noted the *World*. The Colonel appeared defiantly in his brightest yellow waistcoat.

During the course of the day Mann agreed that since the mid-nineties he had received and failed to repay individual loans of $25,000 from William K. Vanderbilt; $14,000 from Dr. Seward Webb, Vanderbilt's brother-in-law; $1,000 from William C. Whitney; $2,500 from J. Pierpont Morgan; $3,000 and $2,500 respectively from George and Howard Gould, sons of Jay Gould; $5,000 from Collis P. Huntington; $76,000 from James R. Keene (plus $14,000 he had paid back); $20,000 from John (Bet-a-Million) Gates, the barbed-wire king; $3,000 from Roswell Flower, the broker and former Governor of New York; $1,500 from Grant B. Schley, another broker whom *Fads and Fancies* had described as "large-framed, large-minded and large-hearted"; and $10,000 each from Charles M. Schwab and Thomas Fortune Ryan. Along with the $4,000 from Perry Belmont and the $10,000 from E. Clarence Jones, about which he had already testified, the outstanding loans came to $187,500. The total did not include his outsized profit on the stock sale to Belmont or other loans the defense didn't happen to ask him about, or loans that were understated or not mentioned at all because of someone's lapse of recollection. (When asked whether it could have been more than $25,000 he got from William K. Vanderbilt, Mann himself said that he did not know. "I have borrowed so much money from people . . . that I can't remember it all.") The total did not include the hundred thousand dollars or more that had been his estimated profit on *Fads and Fancies,* contributed by many of the same large-hearted millionaires, or the hundred thousand dollars worth of lumber company stock for which he testified he had made "some payments" to Alger. Left out of the reckoning was the steady advertising in *Town Topics* by corporations in which his benefactors had a controlling interest, ads for which he had on occasion exacted four-figure fees although the specified page rate in the *Town Topics* masthead was seventy-five dollars. Also omitted from the total were his profits over the years from various special *Town Topics* projects such as the December, 1902, Wall Street Issue. In a statement of contributions at the end of this edition, Charles Schwab, for example, had been put down for twenty-five hundred dollars. Presumably in return, the Wall Street Issue had published a reverent account of his financial acumen, an A rating whose value to Schwab in his trade cannot have been readily apparent. But even without these addenda, by the sixth day of the trial the courtroom response would probably not have been disrespectful had the Colonel repeated his claim of the summer before that *Town Topics* was "the best paying weekly newspaper in America, bar none."

"Judge, jury and learned counsel," reported the *American,* "listened aghast at the mysterious power of the bearded old man" who, with his eyes on the scabrous courtroom ceiling, now stated that at the time he had borrowed these sums and at the present moment he held no assets whatsoever in his own name. He received an annual salary of twelve thousand dollars from *Town Topics*, but his daughter, as chief stockholder, could withhold it any time there was danger of attachment. "You could not collect a judgement against me in the last ten years," he testified. Nevertheless, he insisted that the "loans" made to him had been ordinary business transactions.

"Is this the way these business deals went?" demanded Osborne, " 'I want $90,000.' . . . 'Certainly,' said Mr. Keene." At this point "the air was so full of merriment that Justice Fitzgerald got out of his chair, turned his back on Colonel Mann, and shook with silent mirth for some time," reported the *Times*. "No one even remembered to rap for order."

"Mann's face was purple above his bushy, angry-looking hedge of white beard, and for several minutes he was unable to speak," was the way the *American* went on to describe the scene. "Then he made a noise like a walrus for a few seconds" before he answered with a No! that "made the windows rattle." He explained that he had given Keene a second mortgage on the same unimproved lots on West Thirty-eighth Street on which Equitable held the first mortgage of $165,000. He conceded that none of the loans had required elaborate negotiations. He had simply called up Schwab, for example, and the ten thousand dollars had been delivered to his office that afternoon. Ryan had apologized for being very busy that day but had the ten thousand ready the next morning. Senator William A. Clark of Montana had come to the magazine office himself to complain about a series of articles about his family, and the two men had become friends. After this development the Colonel agreed that the Saunterer's paragraphs about the Clark family had taken on a new and highly favorable tone.

"How did you become friends without money changing hands?" asked Osborne, and the Colonel, apparently missing the heavy irony, explained that the Senator had agreed to turn over to him an unspecified number of bonds of one of his railroad enterprises, making him the fourth member of the United States Senate to enrich Mann's (or his daughter's) portfolio. With former Governor Flower he had "exchanged checks." In the case of Gates, Howard Gould, Webb, and Vanderbilt, he had sold them stock in *Town Topics* at a thousand or fifteen hundred dollars a share, although its par value was ten dollars, and it had never paid dividends. To Morgan and E. Clarence Jones he thought he might have given notes. After Jones had paid over his ten thousand dollars hadn't he stopped referring to the broker's wife as "a former Bowery girl," Osborne asked him.

"Why shouldn't I?" inquired the Colonel, raising his eyebrows.

The next morning's newspapers fell delightedly on the Colonel's testimony that some of New York's leading society figures were secretly part owners of a publication they publicly deplored. None of them ever appeared as stockholders of record, however, and it seems probable that if any shares in the magazine actually changed hands, they were soon, on reconsideration, returned to sender. At any rate, such was the case with William K. Vanderbilt. Mann himself took the stand later that day at his own request to testify that Vanderbilt was no longer one of the proprietors of *Town Topics,* having returned the stock, which the Colonel now described as "collateral" for the twenty-five-thousand-dollar loan. He had known Vanderbilt's grandfather, Mann said, as, in the days when he had been a power in the railroad business, he had known the parents and grandparents of many of his present creditors. On returning his stock, Mann told the court, Vanderbilt had said "he did not care to lend me any more money, but he said he hoped I would get on." At this point, reported the *World,* "Colonel Mann shed genuine tears. They were not very plentiful, it is true, but he did weep when he spoke of Mr. Vanderbilt's kindness to him." Unmoved, Jerome asked him why he thought Vanderbilt had returned the *Town Topics* stock.

"I suppose he thought it was not worth anything," said Mann, in a low voice.

Just before the prosecution rested its case, Jerome asked the Colonel why he thought the notoriously unapproachable Pierpont Morgan would lend $2,500 without security to a comparative stranger. The Colonel's mumbled response lacked the rigorous clarity and grammatical impeccability that were his editorial earmarks of composition.

"I went to Mr. Morgan," he said, "the same as I did to the other men of prominence, and asked them because I felt they were of such standing that if they accommodated me there would be no occasion for me to criticize them."

The next day James I. Montague celebrated the conclusion of the prosecution's case with a poem that appeared on the editorial page of the *American:*

"If I should ever pen by chance some actionable skit,
And, by a luckless circumstance, get hailed to court for it,
I hope that William T. Jerome will try the self-same plan
Upon the people's witnesses he works on Colonel Mann.
For as he's run the present trial of Hapgood up to date
I'd rather be defendant than the witness for the state."

NINE

"Town Topics Convicted"

IN HIS OPENING STATEMENT FOR THE DEFENSE Osborne, without mentioning the Dickensian aptness of the name of Deuel, described the Judge as a man "whose duty it is on the bench to preserve the innocence and purity of childhood," but who then under cover of darkness would steal down to help edit a paper "whose direct purpose it is to destroy the purity of the youth of the land." The first witness called for Hapgood's side was Robert Irving, who was still out on bail on the charge of attempting to blackmail James Burden. Shortly after he began to testify Jerome made the curious move for a prosecutor of breaking in to remind the defense witness that he had been promised immunity by the state. "All you have to do is tell the truth," he informed Irving. At the request of Shepard, who now moved to stage center for the defense, Irving named the stalwart souls who had refused the *Fads and Fancies* proposition. These included Andrew Carnegie and Henry Frick of United States Steel; Townsend Burden as well as James Burden, Jr.* ; the banker Ogden Mills; H. O. Havemeyer of the sugar trust; William Rockefeller of Standard Oil; Peter Cooper Hewitt, grandson of the founder of Cooper Union and son of Abram Hewitt, former mayor of New York; James Roosevelt, half-brother of Franklin; "and the Rhinelanders." Two of the figures Irving named as having turned down a chance to appear in

* James Burden Sr., however, subscribed.

Fads and Fancies, Mrs. Potter Palmer and James W. Gérard, who would later serve as United States Ambassador to Germany during World War I, had apparently been given reason to think better of their defiance and had turned up among the subscribers to *America's Smart Set*—which, of course, had been represented to them at the time as a *Town Topics* enterprise. Cornelius Vanderbilt, cousin of William K., had not been pursued further by the *Fads and Fancies* promoters, Irving testified, after it developed that he had had a stenographer hidden behind a screen throughout his audience with Irving. He had sent the Colonel a transcript of the interview, adding that he would "take measures" with his own copy if he were troubled again. On cross-examination Jerome asked Irving whether those who *had* subscribed had done so after he had threatened to "roast them" in *Town Topics.*

"Never," said Irving. "It was never necessary. It was all done by flattery."

Wooster, the next witness, began by announcing that he was helping the Colliers with the case to "get myself right before the public." ("I make no contention that Wooster and Wayne were not common blackmailers," Jerome broke in gratuitously a few minutes later.) Wooster declared that he had seen Colonel Mann sign the initials "O.K.—W.D.M." to the significant Ward letter. Asked for further details about *Fads and Fancies,* he reported that ninety-three prominent citizens had paid their subscription fees to this volume but ten had preferred to conceal their co-operation by stipulating that their names not appear in the exclusive book. Asked for examples, he mentioned William White of the White Sewing Machine Company, whose anonymous contribution had amounted to $2,500. Most of the contributions had gone directly to the Colonel in cash, he said, and it was his opinion that many of them had amounted to more than the standard subscription charges. He repeated his estimate of the publication's profit as $200,000. The original title of *Fads and Fancies of Representative Americans at the Beginning of the Twentieth Century,* Wooster went on to testify, had been *Fads and Fancies of the Four Hundred.* It had been amended, he said, after Thomas Lawson, the Wall Street plunger who in 1904 had set downtown New York on its ear with a series of articles in *Everybody's* magazine called "Frenzied Finance," revealing the crookedness of the New York stock market, had declared that he would be glad to contribute to the scheme but that he would feel like a damn fool appearing in a volume that identified him as one of the Four Hundred. Anyhow, by this time, Wooster said, the canvassers had already discovered that there were many more obliging prospects off Mrs. Astor's select list than on it. The Colonel had kept "an ornate and modern" card file on all likely subscribers. The information on the cards, Wooster testified, was not about their financial condition. Samples of *Town Topics* paragraphs that might be compiled from these files were sent to all prospects before a solicitor visited them.

A clue to Mann's definition of "representative" emerged from Wooster's report of the Colonel's sales talk on John R. Hegeman, president of the Metropolitan Life Insurance Company (who apparently did not subscribe). "He said that Mr. Hegeman was a very wealthy man, an old bandit who had been robbing widows and orphans and a very representative man who should be captured." Excerpts from Mann's written instructions to Wooster were then read aloud: "General Fitzgerald is a very pompous and vain man and very rich, and I think, if approached in the right way, can be captured. . . . You did not go to Boston, but Thayer, Henry H. Higginson and Bigelow ought to be good victims. . . . If you can discover any way on earth to get two minutes with Frederick O.

Bourne, you could catch him. . . . Spencer Trask of this city is rich and vain. . . . Did you get Amzi L. Barber? He has been trying to creep out. . . ."

As soon as Wooster stepped down there was a great stir in the chamber as a tall man with a vast, walrus moustache, wearing a fur cap above his ruddy, jovial face, stomped down the aisle to the front of the courtroom. This was the famous Commodore Elbridge T. Gerry, grandson of the originator of the gerrymander, corporation lawyer, and founder of the Society for the Prevention of Cruelty to Children. Removing his fur cap, Gerry testified that early in 1901 he had been visited by Wooster, bearing an introduction from Deuel, and sounded out as a *Fads and Fancies* prospect. ("The best way is to tell him he has been a benefactor to the human race," the Judge had written to Wooster.) The Commodore had sent Wooster packing in language that, he now testified, had been "somewhat emphatic." Later he had received a series of letters from Deuel begging him to reconsider, and defending the Colonel as one "who has been maligned and misunderstood beyond measure. A man with a purer, more magnanimous, generous, humane heart I have never met." To his knowledge, wrote the Judge, Mann had on occasion been offered at least $20,000 to suppress items in *Town Topics,* but he "never takes a position for mercenary motives."

After the merriment in the courtroom had subsided this time (the only sober faces in the courtroom, the *World* noted, were those of Colonel Mann and Judge Deuel), the Commodore's place was taken by *Town Topics'* former managing editor, Charles Stokes Wayne. As Mann and Deuel leaned forward in their chairs, he listed for Shepard those individuals whose names were posted on the wall of the editorial office as immune to criticism in the magazine. "Immunes came and went," he said, but among those solidly entrenched as of the previous summer had been the entire paying company of *Fads and Fancies* as well as Senator Alger; Stuyvesant Fish, of the Illinois Central Railroad; August Belmont, brother of Perry and O.H.P.; and Creighton Webb, an in-law of the Vanderbilts. Immunes paid for their immunity to inconvenient gossip either in cash or in kind, he said. Those who were in a position to have inside information about scandalous goings-on in society could qualify for the list by passing such items on to the Colonel. Among the most useful tipsters, he said, were those who hadn't quite made the social grade themselves and who could thus kill two birds with one stone, simultaneously bringing down those who had snubbed them and winning for themselves immunity from the Saunterer's rapier. Another sort of immune, Wayne testified, was Abe Hummel, the celebrated trial lawyer, who sometimes told on his clients. (Had Hummel, a good friend of Mann's, been available, he would surely have given the Colonel better legal advice than he had had so far in the trial. But as the result of a lengthy and vigorous prosecution by Jerome's office, Hummel had recently been sentenced to two years on Welfare Island for subornation of witnesses.) Another immune, Wayne reported, was Harry Lehr, the champagne salesman who had caracoled his way into society as Newport's court jester ("I took up where Ward McAllister left off," he liked to boast) and who would be upgraded three decades later in a biography by his wife entitled *King Lehr and the Gilded Age*. Lehr had received rough treatment in *Town Topics,* said Wayne, until he had begun paying frequent visits to the Colonel's inner office. Soon afterward his name had gone on the immune list. "The Colonel said he was a clever young man who had given him valuable information."

By January 24, the eighth day of the trial, Hearst deemed the courtroom theatricals to have reached such a pitch that he dispatched the *American*'s regular dramatic critic, Alan Dale, to cover the proceedings. Hundreds of would-be spectators were turned away at the door, and beyond it "the scramble for seats was almost appalling," Dale reported. "The lackey-heart, which palpitates so quickly in the presence of the gilded few, palpitated yesterday in the Criminal Court." Among the unlikely pulsators was Death Valley Scotty, the near-legendary California miner, sporting a blue lumberman's shirt and an enormous red tie to match the Colonel's. Mann took his accustomed seat, wearing a haughty expression, but in a few minutes "his Polonius-like visage was quivering" over the testimony of Bernard Baker, a stout, worried-looking Baltimorian who was president of the Atlantic Transport Lines. In the late nineties, he testified, *Town Topics* had run a number of articles damaging to his family's reputation. He had visited the Colonel and asked that they be stopped. Mann had told him that only the very best people were attacked and that he should consider himself complimented. Other steamship lines had advertisements in *Town Topics,* the Colonel had then reminded Baker. "He said that all steamship men were after something, and that I might want something which *Town Topics* could help me to get. He said there ought to be reciprocity." Baker had signed an advertising contract, and the objectionable items had ceased, but the week the contract ran out they had started up again. His lawyers had advised him that there was no recourse but to visit the Colonel, this time carrying a cane. When he had done so, the Colonel had once more mentioned reciprocity. Baker had not taken any further ads, and the attacks had continued, but he had not been able to bring himself to use the cane. "It was a very small cane," added Baker, apologetically.

After the steamship owner's departure, Edwin Post had appeared to describe how he had been blackmailed by Charles

Ahle. ("He said I couldn't afford to pass this opportunity by.") "Virile and snappy, Post entered into the spirit of the plot with fervor and good elocution," reported Dale, adding that "the stock exchange broker in New York is what the Fairy Prince is in childhood's realm." (The Fairy Prince's testimony was later disallowed as irrelevant.) Wayne, however, who was now called back for cross-examination by Jerome, "played a character bit," according to Dale. "He was insulted by all the cast—like the poor fat woman in comic opera." After a lengthy airing of his drinking problem, Wayne, on request, listed some additional *Town Topics* informers, including dressmakers, governesses, officers of leading local clubs, a defrocked Episcopal curate, "Mrs. Goelet's servants," and Robert R. Rowe, the Newport telegraph operator, as well as the society editors of the *Globe, Herald, World,* and *Sun,* who apparently passed along items their own papers declined to print. No matter where it came from, however, Wayne testified, a *Town Topics* item was always checked with a second source—often an obliging servant in the household concerned. It was then that he added: "Above all, the Colonel insists on accuracy." Wayne's successor on the stand was Peter Cooper Hewitt, who had not only eminent relatives but a distinction of his own as the inventor of the mercury vapor lamp. "The solicitor told me that Colonel Mann had always treated me well in *Town Topics,*" said Hewitt, "and I replied that I saw no reason why he should not."

The headlined witness in most newspaper reports of the day's events, however, was Harry Lehr, a rosy-cheeked young man, faultlessly dressed, who, after the recess, appeared at his own request to declare that he had never been a spy for *Town Topics.* He had merely "had several earnest talks" with the Colonel and had explained that after the Saunterer's attacks on him ("Harry Lehr's proud parade of his 'sissy' qualities has gone beyond the limits of tolerance by decent society") he had "been ashamed to go among my friends."

"Why didn't you thrash him?" Jerome demanded, clenching his fists.

"It never occurred to me to thrash Colonel Mann," said Lehr, his voice trembling. Osborne then leaped to his feet to point out that thrashing was a crime.

The next witness was Creighton Webb, another whose name was on *Town Topics'* immune list and who also pleaded not guilty to having been an informer. He acknowledged, however, that during the summer of 1904 after the magazine had published an article about him and a young lady "which caused me to leave Bar Harbor," he had visited the Colonel and, by presenting him with a copy of his war record, had persuaded the old cavalry veteran to let up. Webb insisted he had paid no money for this respite. ("I'm just a $30,000-a-year man.") He agreed with Jerome that *Town Topics'* immunes were "a fluctuating army." "But I hope I am still immune," he added fervently.

The final witness of the day was Robert R. Rowe, "a smooth-faced, innocuous young person" as Dale described him, who admitted having found his job as Newport's telegraph operator ideal for *Town Topics* purposes, though whether his line of work had led to his employment by the magazine or the other way around was not established. He testified that when he had attended the Newport ball in honor of the Duchess of Marlborough he had been disguised as a tambourine player and that on another assignment he had spent several days posing as a visiting professor of mathematics at Exeter, not only to spy on the young gentlemen there but to poll them on the behavior of the young ladies at Miss Ely's school nearby. "A delightful little intimate domestic society comedy," Dale pronounced the day's entertainment, "quite on a par with *Man and Superman*. It achieved the rarest of all combinations, for it was vulgar and funny at the same time."

The following morning Norman Hapgood, the almost-forgotten defendant in the case, was at last called to the stand. The courtroom was "crowded to suffocation," but one face was missing—that of Judge Deuel. "The chair beside the mighty form of the Colonel was empty except for his high silk hat. Eventually the seat was taken by a short, stout man whose professional business it is to furnish flowers for funerals. Some said this was a bad omen," reported the *World*. As he called Hapgood to the stand, Shepard said joshingly, "I believe you are the defendant, although I am not entirely satisfied of it." After the alleged libel was read, Hapgood was asked where he had got his information for the editorial. From the District Attorney's office, Hapgood answered, and from a discussion with Jerome himself. "The consensus between the District Attorney and myself," he explained, after noting that he was expurgating somewhat, "was that the important thing would be to strike at the root of the trouble and get the man who was the fountainhead. We were entirely in accord."

"Then your judgement was based on the District Attorney's?" asked Jerome, rising for cross-examination. "Then it turns out *I* am the writer of this article?"

"Yes, in a measure," agreed Hapgood. At this point "everyone laughed to such a degree," reported the *Tribune*, "that Justice Fitzgerald rapped violently for order."

After a recess Shepard delivered a two-hour closing address for the defense. Speaking in a low, biting voice, he declared that Hapgood had "rendered the best, the truest, the divinest service to this city and to this nation." *Town*

Topics had been shown to be not a literary publication but "a conspiracy to produce money in large sums," making use of "sneaks in the clubs, sneaks in the kitchen, sneaks in the churches." Deuel was "a corrupt judge" and Mann "the master craftsman of blackmailers." ("The Colonel threw back his head with a jerk as though struck in the face, and his face turned crimson," reported the *American*.) Shepard dwelt at length on the tragedy of families attacked by "this vile pair." "Don't say a man who kills himself under such circumstances is a coward—you haven't been there yourself," Shepard said. "You have had two cross examinations in this trial," he went on, "one by the prosecution and the other by the defense, which will make this trial memorable. It is a splendid thing that there is an act which can be used to make a man, against his will, tell the truth about himself."

Jerome delivered the closing address for the prosecution the following morning. "He was aggressively honest," Arthur Train once wrote of him. "If there was an inopportune occasion for speaking the truth, it seems as if Jerome always selected it." During most of his public career his vaudeville turns in the cause of righteousness had made him the darling of the press. "Everything Jerome did was news, and the reporters never left his heels," Train recalled. Now, in his opening remarks to the jury, he declared that the loudly-deplored crimes of *Town Topics*—"that *Police Gazette* of the Four Hundred"—were standard procedure for all newspapers. Every paper in town printed atrocious scandal, he said. And was there one that would claim it did not, as a matter of course, treat its financial supporters with flagrant favoritism? Indeed, he recalled many cynical comments to this effect made by reporters present in this very courtroom, he said, swerving about to look several of them straight in the eye. Advertising revenues were widely regarded as corruption funds. "Every paper in New York, almost without exception, is run from the counting room."

Turning on the more official referees of his future public life, Jerome then conceded that Judge Deuel had violated the city charter, but added that, as everyone in the room well knew, nearly all other judges in town were similarly guilty, that indeed "one jurist rules a banking house from the Supreme Court bench." ("I have no reverence—I have not even everyday common respect—for the Supreme Court Justices of the First Department," he had announced in his speech accepting the nomination for District Attorney the fall before.) He regarded his own witnesses, Mann and Deuel, with "utter loathing and contempt," Jerome said, "but don't say a man is a vampire and sucks human blood because he has violated the city charter. With the shadows lengthening in his life, broken in health, his back to the wall," Judge Deuel might have broken the law "in the endeavor to provide for himself in his old age," but the point to remember, he said, was that "Colonel Mann never borrowed money from anybody who hadn't got any."

Moving on to a dissection of these alleged victims, Jerome declared that in his seventeen years of legal experience he had "never listened to such a story of weakness and degradation." He sighed for a Thackeray to put the trial's revelations in permanent form. The most powerful men in the nation had meekly submitted to the depredations of a New York editor who "west of the Appalachian mountains or south of the Mason-Dixon line would not live forty-eight hours." Yet where was the proof of blackmail? There was "not a scintilla of evidence" of it. Indeed, who could imagine old Colonel Mann blackmailing J. Pierpont Morgan?

"If there is a man on God's footstool who carries a fiercer eye, I don't know him," he said of Morgan. "Facing a cannon's mouth would be nothing to that fierce gray eye of Mr. Morgan. And if Mr. Morgan was blackmailed, why was he not called at this trial? I know he is in town. And why was Mr. Vanderbilt not called?" Not one *Fads and Fancies* subscriber had appeared to testify that he had been the prey of an extortionist, he pointed out. Yet, "you could go right in the next room and get Thomas Fortune Ryan on the phone." And, for that matter, Jerome went on, how could Ryan— whose operations in the street railway and insurance fields were currently being investigated to the accompaniment of screaming newspaper headlines—be blackmailed over something that might appear in public print? "Every terrible thing has already been printed about him." Was such a man "who has been dealing with financial guerrillas . . . liable to be shaken down by some society editor?" Was it possible to believe that "this old warrior of the boudoir car robbed James Keene, that rough-and-tumble fighter of the financial world, of $90,000 in a single night?" On the contrary, he said, Colonel Mann had simply cashed in on the knowledge that the titans of American industry were spineless men "with more money than brains and more vanity than either." "Why blackmail anybody?" Jerome demanded. "You just shake the hat, and it drops in." ("Blackmail," the *Evening Post* commented the next day, "has, in fact, become so ridiculously easy an occupation that we seriously doubt if any gentleman of good intellectual parts should condescend to pursue it so long as the higher forms of burglary and forgery shall offer a career open to talent.") In his hour-and-a-half philippic, the prosecutor reserved his only kind words for the defendant— "one of the best of my friends in the world"—and never at any point called for Hapgood's conviction.

At the conclusion of what the *World* described as "one of the most extraordinary summing-ups ever made," Judge

Fitzgerald, blinking rapidly, reminded the jury that newspaper editorials were frequently the only weapons against "odious tyranny" and explained that if they believed the alleged libel had a reasonable basis in fact, they must find the defendant not guilty. At 1:07 the jury complied after being out only seven minutes, most of which, as the foreman later reported, they had spent waiting for the bailiff to fetch them back. Just before their return Fitzgerald—turning a stern eye on the ladies to his right—had forbidden any demonstration over the verdict. Nevertheless, as Foreman Richards, grinning broadly, pronounced the words "Not guilty, your honor," there was a burst of applause that the Judge silenced with a bang of his gavel.

Those whom the *Times* described as "the fetching coterie in the Royal Box" rushed forward exuberantly, many of them throwing their arms around Hapgood, who "bore his honors easily," reported the *American,* declaring that it would be in poor taste for him to make a statement. "A magnificent triumph for public decency," said the less-inhibited Shepard. "I am overjoyed," said Osborne. "Get out of here, you criminal—you've had your day in court," said Jerome, reaching over and clapping Hapgood on the back. Arm and arm, he and Hapgood left the courtroom, followed by Collier, the lawyers, and many of the coterie, an assembled company that immediately retired to Delmonico's for a victory feast.

In the corridor the triumphal caravan passed Colonel Mann, standing alone with an unlighted cigar between his teeth. At the words "not guilty," the Colonel had sat down heavily in his chair. After a moment he had made his way into one of the private chambers of the Special Sessions judges and called Deuel. "It's not guilty," he said, and hung up. "Why should I say anything? I wasn't the prisoner," he now told reporters, crowding around him for a statement.

Then, pulling his silk hat down around his ears, he stomped out of the courthouse and into his waiting car whose departure, noted the allegorist on the *World,* was for some time blocked by an undertaker's wagon. This macabre delay may

DAY, JANUARY 24, 1906.

THE KEEPER OF THE SKELETON.

have given the Colonel—a tireless commemorator of anniversaries in his role as the Saunterer—time to realize that the crucial verdict had been handed down forty years to the day after the judge's decision in another of his legal ordeals, that of the oily gammon, when he *had* been the prisoner.

During the long ride uptown in the solitary confinement of the Pope-Toledo's back seat, the Colonel must have pondered grimly on the origins of his present predicament. "Why did Colonel Mann and Justice Deuel ever allow the case to get into the courts? They must have known the situation and the evidence that could be presented against them . . . ," read an article that at that very moment was being prepared for the *American* to appear next day over the signature of its talented hireling, the foreman of the jury. The Colonel was, of course, not the first man, or the last, to come to grief in a court of law as the consequence of legal processes he himself had rashly initiated: the case of Oscar Wilde must still have been fresh in his mind. "The libel suit against Mr. Collier was the supreme mistake of the Colonel's life," wrote Newport correspondent Rowe in the *American Mercury* twenty years later. "It was the brilliant mind of Magistrate Deuel that persuaded Mann of the wisdom of the suits," Rowe asserted, and, when they came to trial, "the Colonel, who was forever accepting poor advice from third-rate lawyers, foolishly took the witness stand, thinking he could bluff his way through anything." Rowe also had the impression, from talking to others on the *Town Topics* staff, that Mann had been "partly tricked by the District Attorney," and that he had seriously believed that the case might bring him a fat out-of-court settlement from the Colliers. Possibly, as a major participant in what Alva Johnston described as "the vast, honorable, high-minded, complex frame-up" to get the Colonel on the stand, Jerome did encourage the editor in this fantasy. Certainly he withheld the information that he and defendant Hapgood were longtime friends, and this circumstance seems to have eluded Mann's network of spies. "As

Jerome's promises are worthless, his professions are meaningless," wrote the Colonel in *Town Topics* the following
year. "Everyone who has ever trusted the District Attorney
has found this true." As he got out of his car in front of his
town house on the afternoon of Hapgood's acquittal, he told
the waiting reporters that in view of the evidence of collusion
between the *Collier's* editor and Jerome, he didn't see how
an intelligent jury could have reached any other verdict.
The verdict, as reported in the *New York Evening World*
banner headline the following afternoon was TOWN TOPICS
GUILTY.

"Judge Deuel's continuance in office is unthinkable,"
declared a *World* editorial the next day, a sentiment echoed
by the press all over town. The resignation of the man the
Evening Post described as "this wretch" was predicted mo-
mentarily. Jerome, who only the day before had come near
to bringing tears to his own eyes with his description of
Deuel "broken in health, his back to the wall," ordered his
staff to get busy preparing an accusatory brief for presentation to the Appellate Division of the Supreme Court, which
had the power to remove judges of the Court of Special
Sessions. Meanwhile, Deuel's family announced that he was
"an extremely sick man. It will be days, weeks perhaps,
before Justice Deuel is well enough to recognize anyone."
The following afternoon, however, the gregarious old jurist
turned up, hearty and hale, in the bar of the New York
Republican Club, where he announced he had no intention
of resigning and pronounced Jerome's behavior in the trial
"the most flagrant example of malfeasance in office ever seen
in this city."

"Judge Deuel was murdered in the house of his ostensible
friends," wrote Julian Hawthorne in the *American* the same
day. "Nobody was ever before so hocus-pocused, fooled and

betrayed" as Deuel had been by "Brutus Jerome, flourishing his snickersnee. If the District Attorney were ever out of accord with his audience, it might begin to criticize him," added Hawthorne ominously, "as the public has before now criticized persons apparently entrenched as popular favorites." Many questions might be put to him, Hawthorne went on, concerning Jerome's own immunes, "the many alleged criminals in high places" and particularly "the validity of his sweeping charge against the press of the country." The *Daily Mail* denounced his attack on the newspapers as "a *Town Topics* type of mud-slinging" and the *Globe* called it "the work of a common scold," an observation that suggested the *Globe* editors were closer students of the Saunterer's work than they might have admitted: Mann had used this phrase to describe Jerome as early as October, 1902. Many elements brought about Jerome's eventual political decline, but among them was the fact that during the few years that remained of his public career a sulking press was inclined to take a disenchanted view of its former folk hero of the Criminal Courts Building.

The evening after the Hapgood verdict, however, reporters were still following Jerome around in droves to remind him that he had just lost the first case he had personally tried as District Attorney. "I am much depressed," he told them, smiling broadly, and departed for Grand Central, where he took the train for his weekend home in Connecticut. Apparently a frontal attack on the Colonel had already been set in motion at the victory luncheon. At noon the following day, though it was a Saturday, young Collier, Osborne, Wooster, a handwriting expert, and Assistant District Attorney John W. Hart appeared in the chambers of Justice Charles McAvoy of the Court of Special Sessions. Here Collier and Wooster swore out a perjury complaint against Mann, charging him with having "wilfully, knowingly, corruptly and feloniously testified falsely" that the letters "O.K.—W.D.M." had not been written by him on the Ward letter introduced in the Hapgood trial.

Rumors of this enterprise had reached Colonel Mann, and he sent word that he would be at his *Town Topics* office, awaiting arrest. His daughter and son-in-law and several reporters attended him, killing a bottle of Scotch in the process. Jerome's office had just released a copy of a letter sent to the Colonel from the White House six weeks earlier after the publication of *Fads and Fancies,* returning the President's presentation copy and stating that Mr. Roosevelt wanted nothing to do with the volume. The contents of the letter could only have reached Jerome by way of Washington, the Colonel now pointed out. The knowledge that the nation's chief executive was part of the enemy conspiracy seemed to improve his spirits mightily. "All the tergiversations, twistings and blame-it-on-me's . . . cannot confuse the truth that the White House itself is enlisted with the Colliers Rough Riders in an attempt to destroy this newspaper," he announced to the members of the press who were on hand. But, as the afternoon wore on, he began to lumber restlessly about his office.

"By George, unless they hurry up, they will seriously interfere with my dinner," he grumbled at a quarter to five. By this hour forty more reporters and photographers were blocking the sidewalk outside the *Town Topics* offices. Finally, at five o'clock, the indefatigable Detective Flood appeared with a warrant for his arrest. The Colonel introduced him all around, offered him a drink, and, when Flood regretfully refused, invited the detective to ride downtown with him in comfort. At the Criminal Courts Building bail was set at ten thousand dollars. As bond security, Mann offered, over his daughter's signature, the same lots on West Thirty-Eighth Street whose value the Equitable Life Assurance Society as well as James R. Keene had previously endorsed. Pleading not guilty, he commented, "My day will come. There is nothing to it," and asked that his trial not be put down for the following Tuesday since that was the day *Town Topics* went to press. He did not add that that was the day when he *wrote* his libels. Lighting a large black cigar, the Colonel then walked slowly down four flights of stairs, alone, to his waiting automobile.

"I must say that I admire his courage," said Rob Collier, gazing after him. "I only wish the fight could have come ten years ago when he was younger and more vigorous."

The following month the Colonel began running at the beginning of each issue of "Saunterings" the reminder that under the common law an accused person is innocent until proven otherwise. "This fundamental principle of right is forgotten," his weekly sermon concluded, "only when an epidemic of injustice, born of fanaticism and made contagious through an overheated consciousness of one's own tendency to moral obliquity, sweeps over the land, twisting and distorting for the moment the people's usual sanity and calmer judgement."

A Gratifying
Verdict

AFTER THE COLONEL HAD INSISTED during one cross-examination that *Town Topics'* mission was not blackmail but "the elevation of society," the Louisville *Herald* commented that at any rate he had certainly "held society up." But other publications viewed the trial's revelations as too serious to make jokes about and seemed genuinely distressed by their implications. The *Nation* deplored what it called *"richesse oblige,"* which it defined as "the huge delusion that makes its victims subject to all kinds of strange attacks and seizures . . . that obliges the rich man to surrender to every impudent confidence man that comes along." A cartoon that appeared in the *American* in January, 1906, bore the title "A 'Colonel of Industry' " and the caption "He Makes the 'Captains of Industry' Surrender." It showed a gleeful Colonel surrounded by the leading robber barons of the day, all kneeling and offering him tribute. "Why did they so humbly unbutton their pocketbooks?" asked the *Globe*. "How can such things be?" echoed the *Evening Post* with a troubled air. "There were our hardest-headed men of business, our keenest speculators, our grimmest promoters, our coolest brokers . . . all classed as ready dupes of a transparent bunco game. Why could Colonel Mann count so safely upon finding so large a proportion of gulls among the men of great wealth?"

Possibly he could not have counted upon it so safely at any other time or place in history. The Colonel's gulls knew, to begin with, that the avid attention that Labouchere, Yates, and their successors on both sides of the Atlantic had accustomed the reading public to pay to their affairs left them no hope of invoking the right of privacy that had shielded their privileged predecessors until a generation before. During *Town Topics'* heyday, long before the apotheosis of the Hollywood starlet and other symbols of national progress, the gilded world of New York society was, as the Saunterer had noted, an extraordinary cynosure. The degree of public preoccupation with what he had called "the show figures of the social musée" is difficult to imagine today, but it helps explain the power and wide audience then commanded by an elderly tale-bearer. In Tennessee mountain towns in the nineties crowds swarmed to the depot to catch a glimpse of the Four Hundred's self-appointed referee, Ward McAllister, as his train hurtled by. ("There are only about four hundred people in fashionable New York society," the fatuous McAllister had told the *Tribune* in an interview in 1888. "If you go outside that number you strike people who are either not at ease in a ballroom or else make other people not at ease.") Little girls on isolated farms in upstate New York in those days pasted in scrapbooks pictures, cut out of the illustrated weeklies, of James Hazen Hyde and his latest lady friend. Manhattan sightseeing guides spent much of their time herding their blinking charges up and down Fifth Avenue, identifying for them the homes of the socially mighty. After the marriage of Consuelo Vanderbilt to the Duke of Marlborough in 1895, the throngs lining the streets outside the church were in such a state of excitement that, according to the *Times,* "they seemed almost ready to fling themselves under the feet of the horses" drawing the nuptial carriage. The morning after the announcement of May Goelet's engagement to the Duke of Roxburghe in 1903 the sidewalk in front of her Fifth

Avenue home was impassable. When a young woman was seen moving past the drawing room curtain—carrying a copy of *Town Topics,* according to the Saunterer's account—the crowd began to shout hysterically. As the couple emerged from St. Thomas's after their wedding a few months later, people in the street, who had been waiting in place for hours, tried to tear their clothes, seeking souvenirs of these godlike creatures.

"The pursuit of money has indeed become so much the dominating influence of the mass of Americans that its prize-winners stand to them for all excellence," was the sorrowful judgment of Constance Cary Harrison, a financially under-privileged descendant of the celebrated Fairfax family of Virginia and author of *The Well-bred Girl in Society.* Mrs. Harrison's judgment appeared in the remarkable—and probably little read—introduction with which Colonel Mann, presumably with coin of the realm, persuaded the blue-blooded lady to honor his literary monument to the pursuit of money, *Fads and Fancies.* In this altered world, she noted bitterly, "the men and women who, knowing themselves well-born and believing themselves well-bred, yet have not money to compete with the others, submit to be pushed into outer darkness. Nothing of moral worth, of intellectual supremacy, of great philanthropy, of achievement in art or letters, of military glory, or of scientific discovery counts as 'success' with our general public," she went on. "These conspicuous people . . . concerning whom every detail is of interest to the public . . . are followed and revered by the weak-minded among their less fortunate fellow countrymen for their wealth alone." Then, almost audibly gritting her teeth as she lived up to the letter of her bargain with the Colonel, she concluded that nevertheless, "it is well worthwhile to record in permanent form instances of some of the men who by their personality, influence and surroundings, as well as wealth, give character and form to American society of this period."

But the major element in the Colonel's curious success was probably the fact that the rich at the turn of the century were not only different from us, but different from most of the rich men who came after them: indeed, they had more money. Not yet halved by taxes or hampered by presumptuous laws or burdened by the need for justification, despite the hoarse cries of reformers in the distance, their wealth appeared to be unlimited and the heedless dispersal of it a natural right. One of the baubles many of them set their hearts on buying with it was social prominence. The frontier societies where many of their fortunes had been made were too easy to crash, and around the social enclaves in Procrustean cities like Charleston and Philadelphia, the walls were too forbidding. From the 1880's on, therefore, wave after wave of what one of the old guard called "the suddenly rich" made like lemmings for New York ("the great social centre of the Republic" as Frederick Lewis Allen described it) where a successful siege was known to be vastly expensive but not beyond price. New York's elite in-group was no aristocracy in the Old World sense of the term. As in most American cities, it was made up of descendants of the more prosperous of the lower-middle-class adventurers who had been the town's early colonists (as has frequently been pointed out, Earls Don't Emigrate), augmented every few decades by beneficiaries of the later real estate, trade, and shipping fortunes. In nearly every case, however, the family money had been given two or three generations to cool off before the social gates had edged open. But whereas at the time of the Civil War the country was said to have only three millionaires—Vanderbilt, Astor, and A. T. Stewart, the department store king—by 1900 there were nearly four thousand of them, products of the new age of railroads, mining, steel, and oil; and the clamorous pile-up around the entrance to Fifth Avenue society had reached epic proportions. In their campaigns, often victorious, to dazzle their way past the gatekeepers, these latter-day Visigoths, usually under the shrill guidance of their wives, fitted themselves out with the palaces, jewels, equipages, stables, horses, yachts, private cars, country places, shooting lodges, game preserves, and opera boxes, the "very carmagnole of display," as Mrs. Harrison described it, "that in earlier days was supposed to be the appanage of royalty alone."

Nearly all who took part in this glittering stampede complied with what the *Times,* reviewing Ward McAllister's autobiography in 1895, declared to be the first requisite of the society personage: intense mental earnestness. "No suspicion that he is making a continental laughing stock of himself must disturb his mind," the *Times* concluded. The leading characters in one story that suggests the deadly seriousness with which the social musée was regarded are Mrs. Stuyvesant Fish, the queen of Newport and wife of the president of the Illinois Central, and E. H. Harriman, the railroad czar. On one occasion Mrs. Fish failed to invite Mrs. Harriman to a ladies' tea at Crossways, the Fish cottage on Bellevue Avenue, and, so the story goes, a few days later Stuyvesant Fish was found to be no longer president of the Illinois Central, a railroad in which Harriman held a substantial interest. This roster of rich men who could afford almost anything on earth but to be made fun of or to have their womenfolk socially slighted served as a ready-made sucker list for a society editor whose sense of humor and contempt for the *arriviste* were repressible for a price. What the total price was will never be known, but it seems certain that the Colonel's charge for protecting the little woman's feelings or for general peace of mind—"innocent luxuries," as he had once indirectly described them—was not, in his clients' terms, any great sum. The twenty-five-thousand-dollar contribution mentioned in the libel trial did not, after all, significantly reduce the circumstances of William K. Vanderbilt, who had laid out between ten and fifteen million dollars to be able to count a ducal son-in-law, the Duke of Marlborough, in the family inventory. James Keene may have noticed the absence of the ninety thousand dollars he pressed upon the Colonel at one point; on the other hand, he had only shrugged his shoulders when, not long before, he had lost four hundred thousand at Canfield's in a single evening. Another of Mann's benefactors, Senator William Clark, was said for a time to have an income of a million dollars a month from his Montana copper mines. His house at Fifth Avenue and Seventy-seventh Street reportedly cost six million dollars, as did those of Charles Schwab on Riverside Drive and Clarence Mackay in Roslyn, Long Island (designed in Mackay's case by another contributor to the Mann exchequer, Stanford White). It was an era when favors for the women guests at parties might be diamond bracelets, and cigarettes beside the place cards came wrapped in hundred-dollar bills. August Belmont, a *Town Topics* immune for one reason or another, was said to have paid ten thousand dollars for a gilded suit of armor to wear for a few hours at the Bradley Martin ball. These recurrent fancy dress bashes, recreating the court of Louis XVI or Charles II, might cost the host upwards of a hundred thousand. "It was a strange complex," the widow of Harry Lehr wrote many years later, "that made us, who belonged to a society so new, seek always inspiration from our ancients in the past . . . like children playing some fascinating game of make-believe." She added that Mrs. Pembroke Jones, wife

of the North Carolina rice king, had once remarked to her
that at the beginning of each social season she set aside
$300,000 for entertainment—and the Joneses, the former Mrs.
Lehr added, were nothing like the most extravagant enter-
tainers of the time. If Mrs. Jones's husband, in pursuit of
some make-believe of his own, got a better night's sleep after
handing over $1,500 to Colonel Mann for a subscription to
Fads and Fancies, it was not, as Jerome had pointed out in
court, as if the Colonel ever took money from anybody who
hadn't got any.

As for those unrepresentative Americans who could well
have afforded it, but declined to humbly open their pocketbooks—men such as Frick, Carnegie, Cooper Hewitt, and
the Rockefellers, for example—their notions of the satisfac-
tions money could buy had simply never included the suffer-
ance of the gilt-chair and cotillion set and in most cases *had*
included some form of philanthropy, art, scientific research,
or other longer-range type of fulfillment. Rejections came
also from Rhinelanders, Hyde Park Roosevelts, and the like,
whose family affluence reached far enough back for them to
be able to view an upstart gossip sheet in perspective. And
yet it wasn't invariably the suddenly rich who lent the Colonel money they never expected to see again or bought
their way into *Fads and Fancies.* For reasons perhaps buried
in *Town Topics* paragraphs whose distressing overtones are
no longer audible, the *Fads and Fancies* table of contents
included a Van Rensselaer and a Pell and a grandson of John
T. Calhoun. It included William C. Whitney, whose social
security long antedated his bankroll, and a Belmont, whose
mother had presided over New York society in the 1860's,
as well as Colonel John Jacob Astor, son of its reigning queen.
And perhaps most remarkably of all it included J. Pierpont
Morgan, the elder, a man whose social rank was as high as

he cared to fix it but who appeared totally indifferent to the
opinion of either Mrs. Astor or Mrs. Grundy. "Imagine Colonel Mann blackmailing J. P. Morgan!" Jerome had challenged the jury. It was apparently all but impossible for even
the most cynical figures in the courtroom to picture the
terrible-tempered banker being either frightened into buying
silence or seduced by the flattery that had brought other
prospects into line. Jerome went so far as to suggest in the
same address that Morgan's loan, along with many of the
others, possibly represented not blackmail but compassion
on the part of those who had made a vast fortune in railroads
for one who had pioneered in the field and lost. ("Isn't it a
better solution of it that this old man had been in the railroad
business and had been crushed to the wall . . . and that
there was, after all, a heart in the railroad magnates?") It
may even be that a few of Mann's victims—men, including
Morgan, who had ruthlessly used all powers at their disposal
to get what they wanted in the course of their own careers—
had paid over their comparatively piddling tribute to the
Colonel out of a kind of wry amusement at the spectacle of a
minor brigand who had found a way of beating their sort at
their own game. Like most of the Colonel's creditors Morgan
never cared to shed any direct light on the subject. In the
1913 Pujo Committee hearings investigating his influence
over the railroad business, however, he was asked whether
he extended credit primarily on the basis of property or of
money. "The first thing," retorted Morgan, "is character. A
man I do not trust could not get money from me on all the
bonds in Christendom."

Even the trusting Morgan would probably have had difficulty seeing much resemblance between the character of
the *Town Topics* publisher and that described in the italicized
quotation that, off and on during the long months after the

Hapgood trial, replaced at the beginning of "Saunterings" the reminder that a man is innocent under the common law until proven guilty. "The man who allows his life to justify itself and lets his work speak and who, when reviled, reviles not again, must be a very great and lofty soul," was the alternate quotation, attributed to Fra Elbertus. In fact, the lofty soul who wrote "Saunterings" was so preoccupied during this period with justifying and reviling that he had little "Sauntering" space left for purveying gossip. Having denounced the "brutality" of *Collier's* references to himself, he reprinted all of his previous attacks on Pat (Fagin) Collier, concluding with "He is a vain, egotistical, ignorant, self-glorifying man, sillily ambitious to shine for a set for which neither family, breeding, mental attainments nor manners fit him." No one could describe these paragraphs about Collier as "brutal, malicious or libelous," he added, since they were the simple truth. As a contrast and at what he declared to be popular demand, he provided a lengthy list of his own military and commercial achievements, including a replica of his 1878 patent for the vestibule car. (The account omitted, however, any mention of his foray into the oil business.) He reprinted the laudatory editorial from the *Birmingham Ledger* and another from the *Fort Worth Record,* which took his side against Jerome although it finished off rather unsatisfactorily with "We . . . admire a clever faker. We despise a whining hypocrite." He offered to pay $1,000 to the favorite charity of anyone who could prove he was blackmailed by a bona fide representative of *Town Topics.* He jubilantly reported the success of a libel suit he had filed against the Paris edition of the *Herald,* which had printed a letter describing *Town Topics* as being run by "a gang of blackmailers guilty of most shameless slander and of revenging themselves upon those who refuse to pay for their favor."

The French court had directed the *Herald* to print a retraction, assessed costs against the newspaper, and awarded *Town Topics* two-hundred francs in damages, which the Colonel had grandly contributed to the *Herald* Free Ice Fund. After this victory the Colonel was in a sufficiently cheerful frame of mind to announce in "Saunterings" that he was now resigned to the erection of the main Post Office at the Thirty-third Street site. Indeed, he reported that he had called upon the Postmaster General in Washington and had personally given his blessing. He added that after the new building was completed real estate values in the entire neighborhood all the way up to Thirty-eighth Street would undoubtedly rise appreciably and suggested that certain lots he happened to know about on West Thirty-eighth Street would make an ideal spot for the new County Courthouse. However, the President of the United States, whom he had blamed for the choice of the Post Office site, remained in the doghouse. The Saunterer's latest thumbnail sketch of Roosevelt was: "T.R.—up like a rocket! Fizz! Down like a stick."

There is some evidence that the President of the United States was following the *Town Topics* affair with close attention, as one might fairly expect of a man whose name had been mentioned, in one connection or another, in news stories about it every week or so since the previous summer. On March 5, 1906, Roosevelt made a speech before the Gridiron Club in Washington in which he declared that the reporters of the day who were writing distressing revelations of Congressional corruption, the power of the trusts, and the shame of the cities, reminded him of the Man with the Muckrake in *Pilgrim's Progress,* who "could look no way but downward." The term "muckraker," attributed to Roosevelt, thus came into the language. The fact is that a sensational journalist had already been put forward as the contemporary version of the Man with the Muckrake, and the nominee was not Lincoln Steffens, David Graham Phillips, or any of their partners-in-exposé. "Nobody can have observed the aged but unvenerable figure of the editor of *Town Topics* without being reminded of Bunyan's 'Man with the Muckrake,' " read an editorial in the January 23, 1906, edition of the *New York Evening Post*. "He 'could look no way but downward,' and his continual occupation . . . was raking 'to himself the straws, the small sticks and dust of the floor.' . . . The symbol is evidently appropriate to the minor activities of a successful society journalist, who deals in trash for lucre, but we should do a grave injustice to our new-style Mann with the Muckrake if we did not acknowledge how greatly he has improved upon his primitive prototype. Bunyan's man collected nothing more offensive than litter; our Mann deals in filth . . . our Mann brandishes his rake on the highroad, bespattering the bystanders as chance or self-interest dictates, and takes handsome toll of those who value their petticoats or gaiters. That is the superiority of muckrakism militant." The *Post* editorial was reprinted in the February 10 issue of *Collier's,* a magazine of which the President was an avid reader. It is hard to avoid the conclusion that Roosevelt, casting about for a term that would be effective ammunition against a group of writers who were beginning to embarrass him politically, was delighted with the analogy and shamelessly filched it for his own purposes.

Mann, who must have noted this sequence of events, would presumably not have held the substitution of villains against his old antagonist. He continued, however, to regard Roosevelt as an active member of the Collier-Hapgood-Jerome conspiracy against him. "It is not necessary to recall," he wrote a few years later in a résumé of the case in *Town Topics,* "that which must be in everybody's memory, how for weeks and months discussion of Colonel Mann . . . afforded column after column of copy to the newspapers of America and Europe. Admittedly no *cause célèbre* has ever received more extended and widespread attention from the press in headlines, in interest, in features, in cartoons, and in caricature." The *cause,* he explained, "grew to its immensity . . . simply because of the connection of the President of the United States."

On other occasions Mann was willing to concede that some of the unwelcome attention paid to his case might be explained by the fact that national and international news had continued in the doldrums during the early months of 1906, leaving an undue share of the front pages available for the Colonel's troubles. Whatever the reason, members of the press were out in full force on February 1 of that year when a preliminary hearing began in the Criminal Courts Building on the charge that Mann had committed perjury in the libel trial in which Hapgood had been acquitted. On the premise that by acquitting *Collier's* editor of libel the jury in the Hapgood trial had, in effect, upheld his contention that *Town Topics* dealt in blackmail, Bourke Cochran, a Democratic member of the New York congressional delegation, had introduced in the House a resolution to bar *Town Topics* from the mails. It had failed to pass, but if the Colonel could be convicted on the current perjury charge (resulting from his denial on the stand of having had anything to do with the letter from Reginald Ward and, by extension, with Ward's miraculous character transformation in the pages of *Town Topics* after his transfer of ten thousand shares of copper stock to the Colonel's account) the implication of blackmail would at any rate have been brought home to the big spider. Apparently Mann endorsed the theory that his weakness for free legal advice had been largely responsible for his personal

SOCIETY.

disaster in the previous trial. Now that he faced indictment, the old soldier had sent an S.O.S. for Martin Littleton, the famous legal dreadnaught, whose salvage fee was rumored to be $75,000.

In his book *The Art of Advocacy,* the celebrated trial attorney Lloyd Paul Stryker, named half a dozen "great advocates" he had known in his years in the criminal courts. Of this number three—Jerome, Osborne, and Littleton—were directly involved in the *Town Topics* trials. Osborne and Jerome were over-sized, flamboyant figures in the courtroom. ("Always shouting, snapping and slamming, together with his hissing, yawning, bullying, grimacing, screaming and weeping . . . he is like a bad actor who chews the scenery," ran a later *Town Topics* notice of one of Jerome's performances.) Littleton's manner was stately and his voice low-pitched; somebody once said it had the timbre of a cello. In 1906 he was thirty-four years old. Not tall, he had powerful shoulders, a huge head, a profusion of black hair, dark eyes set wide apart, shaggy eyebrows, and a towering forehead. Watching him in action, Stryker was reminded of Sydney Smith's exclamation when he met Daniel Webster: "Good heavens, he is a small cathedral in himself!" Born in the Tennessee hills, the ninth of nineteen children, Littleton had had less than a year's schooling, but he obviously never found his lack of formal education inhibiting. Years later the non-scholar described his own oratory as "an unparalleled aggregation of sibilant synonyms, antonomastic antonyms, contumelious caconyms, tuneful tropees and vorticular verbs." Each tuneful tropee, declared Stryker, "pierced like a sword." He named Littleton "the greatest American jury lawyer of his generation." Littleton had been chosen to nominate Alton B. Parker for President of the United States at the Democratic Convention in 1904, and at the time he was called to the rescue of Colonel Mann reckoners of his own political future didn't boggle at the highest office in the land.

Jerome who at this time, according to Arthur Train, also "had one eye on the governorship and at least one on the White House," chose at the start to present the case for Mann's indictment in a hearing before a magistrate, rather than to bring the matter before a grand jury. Witnesses against the Colonel were heard at a dozen sessions during the month of February. Littleton, reported the *Tribune,* "made objection to every particle of evidence introduced." He was particularly inhospitable to the testimony about compound curves, double twists, loops, mergers, and up-and-down strokes of the fifty-dollar-a-day handwriting experts. (Indicating the newspaper-reading public's over-familiarity by this time with details of intercorporate skulduggery, the entire courtroom burst into laughter when the experts mentioned "mergers.") These specialists had been hired, it was reported, by a young Rob Collier who, continuing his campaign against the Colonel, was footing all but the routine bills of the prosecution. There were only ten handwriting experts of national reputation, noted the *Tribune,* and nine of these were said to be on the Collier payroll. Littleton singled out for two days of the court's attention Colonel Edwin B. Haye, who described his knowledge of handwriting as having "come by nature" and his military rank as "inherited," and who interrupted the cross-examination to nominate himself for Police Commissioner of the City of New York.

Deeming it safe to refer at regular intervals thereafter to "the inherent infirmities of expert evidence," Littleton then turned his sardonic eye on Moses Wooster, still holding down his hundred-dollar-a-week job as "advisor" to the Colliers, who was the single formal witness to the Colonel's having initialed the Ward letter. Wooster's previous checkered career had involved not only dubious financial schemes and brushes with the law but extra-marital excursions. Littleton's interest in the details of each of these chapters in his life was insatiable. On the sixth day of the hearing, advertised as involving an editor's alleged perjury with under-and-overtones of blackmail, the assembled company found itself listening to an account of a *ménage à trois* that Wooster had maintained on Staten Island fourteen years earlier with a couple named Wendel. (Q. Did you not run away with Wendel's wife to New Jersey? A. I did not. That is absolutely untrue. Q. Then if you didn't go to New Jersey, where did you take her? A. I don't recollect. . . . Wendel was only a choir singer.) At this juncture Jerome offered to stipulate that *Fads and Fancies* was not a blackmailing enterprise but a master literary work, if Littleton would only desist. Littleton replied that he intended to keep on asking questions as long as there was any information outstanding. Jerome and Littleton spent much of the rest of the month wrangling with each other in the middle of the courtroom, "seemingly with nothing between them," noted the *American*, "but the smiling face and stalwart figure of Mr. Collier." After a few days of Littleton's exhaustive and exhausting cross-examination, the audience, along with the press, had begun to defect in droves. The petulant expression on the magistrate's face apparently told Jerome that his chances for an indictment were also dwindling. On February 27 in a three-hour speech Littleton made a motion to dismiss the charge. When the magistrate granted a two-week recess to allow Jerome to reply, the District Attorney, in one of those maneuvers that confounds the layman and that apparently confounded Littleton as well, secretly hustled his witnesses before a grand jury which, without the benefit of Littleton's searches after the whole truth, handed down an indictment on March 2. The case was not called until the following December, by which time local front pages were heavily committed to details of the impending trial of Harry K. Thaw for the murder, the previous June, of Stanford White.

The selection of the jury began on December 17 in the Court of General Sessions, presided over by Recorder John A. Goff. Recorder, as the senior judge of this court was then known, was an ancient judicial title going back to the Dutch days in New York. Goff, who had come over from Ireland in the 1860's, was a tiny man whose voice rarely rose above a whisper. "His head . . . framed in an aureole of satin hair, his silken beard a sheen of spun silver, his ruddy cheeks and his piercing blue eyes made him resemble a medieval portrait of a saint," Newman Levy wrote many years later, in his review of the Nan Patterson murder trial, over which Goff had presided. Goff was also, said Levy, "the cruelest, most sadistic judge we have had in New York in this century," a judgment affirmed by Stryker. Entering his courtroom, Stryker wrote, "I felt like some four-footed denizen of the jungle that suddenly stares into the cold visage of a python." Jerome, who had been a colleague of Goff's on the Lexow Committee twelve years before, had probably deliberately steered Mann's case into Goff's court, relying on the hostility the Recorder might be counted on to feel for an editor who over the years had declared in the columns of *Town Topics* that the Recorder's continuance in office was "a menace to the community," that his "place is in a freak museum or a loop-the-loop circuit, not on the judicial bench," and that his inhuman treatment of prisoners before him had caused him to be reversed so often that he should be permanently seasick.

Among the reasons for Goff's being reversed in the later trial of Lieutenant Charles Becker for the murder of gambler Herman Rosenthal ("Have the shades drawn low. There is not enough gloom in the courtroom," he ordered during one session of the case) was his insistence that on the trial's final day the defense lawyer sum up for his side from two-thirty in the afternoon till nearly nine at night with no departures from the courtroom for dinner or any other purpose. A sufferer from ulcers, Goff ate almost nothing, contenting himself with a bowl of crackers and a swig of Irish whisky at mealtimes. He saw no reason to make allowance for defendants or counsel with stronger stomachs or weaker kidneys than his own. However, the speed-up order, including compulsory evening sessions, that he now imposed in Mann's case had a logical basis. A month earlier Goff had been elected to the New York Supreme Court and would take office the first of the year. If *The People* vs. *Mann* lasted beyond that date it would be declared a mistrial. In mid-afternoon of the first day when the weeding out of the jurors was proceeding too torturously to suit him ("Have you ever been a juror in a trial where public witnesses were paid by a private prosecutor?" Littleton asked each of them), Goff suddenly hissed that no further excuses would be accepted, and an hour later the jury was complete. Among the two hundred names on the panel had been, by an odd chance, that of private prosecutor Collier. Probably assuming his disqualification would be automatic, he had stayed away from court. He was fined $100 as a delinquent, an expense to be added to the $100,000 that, according to his father's statement to the press, the case had already cost the Collier family.

The following morning and on each of the twelve days of the trial the defendant Mann was preceded into court by his daughter, looking indignant, and his wife, looking rather pale and wan. Both ladies were dressed in the height of fashion. Son-in-law Albert Wray was also on hand, though not at the defense table. As for the Colonel himself, he again flaunted each day a different sample from his wardrobe of waistcoats. He tipped the elevator men a dollar a trip, and as he moved in and out of the courtroom, he would bow to the right and left at the crowd and lavish special smiles, followed by dollar bills, on the court attendants. The *World* reporter declared his beard to be "the largest growth of whiskers ever seen in a courtroom," and after some further study called the trial "a notably hirsute proceeding" with not only the Colonel and Goff but the third, eighth, and twelfth jurors contributing to the display. (*World* employees had a special interest in beards and such, since Pulitzer wouldn't allow a man on the premises who wasn't clean-shaven. For that matter, neither would James Gordon Bennett over at the *Herald,* although Bennett himself sported a vast and elegant moustache of his own.) The *World* reporter also noted that not one of the lawyers involved on either side wore even a moustache, unless one counted Jerome, with his modified toothbrush, who dropped in only occasionally, having largely left matters this time in the hands of Assistant District Attorney Francis Garvan while he worked on the case against Harry Thaw, scheduled to open in the same courtroom on January 21.

Soon after the Colonel's trial got under way Garvan, a tall, boyish-looking man who, years later, became an enormously prosperous figure in the chemical industry, lost a major decision to Littleton, who was able to prevent the admission of Mann's unfortunate peripheral testimony in the Hapgood trial. Littleton dwelt at length on the treachery of those proceedings, declaring that the Colonel had been "stripped of his skin a half-inch at a time" while Jerome had not only failed to protect his witness but had "sat back and watched in the very echo of the crushing bones." Wooster then took the stand to declare once again that he had seen the Colonel sign the Ward letter. During Littleton's scathing cross-examination that followed, Mann smiled broadly. Charles Stokes Wayne was then called although he agreed that he had *not* seen the Colonel sign the letter. (After Wayne's appearance Rob Collier was asked outside the courtroom what Wooster and Wayne had done to earn their $100-a-week wages for the past year. "I never saw them do anything," he said glumly.) Detective Sergeant Flood made positively his last appearance in the case, testifying that he had traced W. L. Daniels, who *might* have seen the Colonel sign the letter, to a hideout in New Jersey, but that when found Daniels "declined to cross on the ferry." After the Christmas recess six of the handwriting experts—not including the birthright Colonel—testified that the initials were in the publisher's hand. At noon on December 28 the prosecution rested.

After a quick bowl of crackers Goff delayed the afternoon session in order to hear new testimony and, at its conclusion, to uphold a conviction and $10 fine in the case of Enrico Caruso, accused of having annoyed a Mrs. Graham in the monkey house at the Central Park Zoo. During the afternoon Littleton put on half a dozen witnesses, all currently under wages to *Town Topics,* who denied that the initials were written by the Colonel. (It is noteworthy that none of Mann's employees, who could well have used the Colliers' informers' fees, came forward to testify against him, and that even the discharged Wayne had expressed distress at the prospect of doing so.) Shrewdly taking note of the change of venue, Littleton then rejected the delaying tactics that had nearly turned the trick for his client at the preliminary hearing ten months before and won a faint smile from Goff by announcing that the defense rested.

At five o'clock that afternoon Littleton began his summing up. If it was blackmail the Colonel was guilty of, why wasn't he being tried for that crime, he asked gently. As for perjury, the only proof hung on the word of that "smooth, oily, subtle, sinister, slick fakir," Wooster. The Colonel, on the other hand, was widely known as an exemplary citizen, a brave soldier, and the best friend Wooster ever had. Although for years afterward the Colonel pressed on his dearest friends and barest acquaintances copies of Littleton's address, bound in gold-tooled crushed levant morocco, little more of its substance survives. Its effect was evidently powerful, however. "When Littleton told how good a man he was, the Colonel wept," said the *World,* "holding his hands to his face and sobbing violently;" many years later Alva Johnston described the tears of "the wicked old rogue" as having "rattled and clanged as they hit the floor." "Spectators wept," reported the *Telegram,* "some jurors wept, and . . . the Colonel's wife and daughter became so hysterical it was feared they would break down completely."

The case went to the jurors at seven in the evening. In spite of the damp eyes among them and Goff's final counseling that a perjury conviction was impossible on the testimony of one witness, they remained out for four hours. Their ultimate verdict, however, was "Not guilty." At the words the Colonel, who had dressed entirely in black just in case, opened his eyes wide in triumph and threw his arms around Littleton, "letting his wife's and daughter's tears of joy trickle down his coat." Goff banged impatiently for order and pronounced this his final case as Recorder and, indeed, the final case for any Recorder in New York City, the office having been abolished as of the end of the year. He then delivered a curious valedictory in which he declared that the prevailing criminal law made it almost impossible for an innocent man to be convicted but could not prevent an occasional guilty man from being acquitted. Undismayed, the Colonel, in the opening paragraph of the issue of *Town Topics* that reached its subscribers two days later, gave full credit for the gratifying verdict to Recorder Goff "and the kindness of his great, fatherly heart," and nominated his former candidate for a freak museum for the position of Chief Justice of the Supreme Court.

ELEVEN

The Back of
the Book

IN HIS AUTOBIOGRAPHY, *The Changing Years,* Norman Hapgood recalled that Finley Peter Dunne, in 1905 also an employee of *Collier's,* had advised him not to let himself get arrested as part of the plot against *Town Topics.* The memory of the public in such matters was so untidy, Dunne warned him, that in a few years' time people would remember him as the fellow who had written an editorial insulting Alice Roosevelt. Sure enough, reported Hapgood, a man he later encountered on a Pullman car expressed his pleasure at the opportunity of shaking hands with the colorful editor of *Town Topics.* Colonel Mann was similarly afflicted by the public's disorderly memory as well as by its feeble grasp of the subtleties of legal proceedings. During the years after his formal vindication he frequently felt it necessary to remind his readers ("I am compelled to speak plain words that border on brusqueness . . ." he would begin) that he had not been convicted or even tried for blackmail but had been acquitted of perjury. Apparently he saw nothing relevant to his plight in his 1907 comment opposing a Georgia plan to erect a monument to Warden Wirtz of the infamous Confederate prison at Andersonville. "History is full of injustices," he wrote, "and possibly Wirtz may have been an angel. But mankind has made up its mind." The notoriety of the front-page morality play in which the Colonel had been cast as predatory Evil caused another of history's minor inequities. In addition to almost totally obscuring the occasional excellence of *Town Topics'* departments that were not concerned with society gossip, it misled those historians who like a place for everything and everything in its place. Identifying the Colonel only as a grotesque symbol of a decadent social era, they failed to credit him with certain forward-looking contributions to the literary scene.

If *Town Topics'* role in the development of American letters were to be officially forgotten, Ludwig Lewisohn wrote in 1932 in *Expression in America,* later reissued as the *Story of American Literature,* it would be "a great absurdity and a grave injustice." Until the end of the First World War, in his view, the magazine served as a continuing school of critics and short story writers. Its columns, he added, "should one day be sedulously analyzed for the brilliant light that would thus be thrown upon our cultural history during certain years." Perhaps because reading *Town Topics* is still regarded as no occupation for respectable persons, no historian seems to have adopted Lewisohn's suggestion. Should its columns ever receive the attention he recommends, the ensuing report would probably dwell longest on *Town Topics'* critical departments. There is no reason to suppose that this outcome would have surprised Colonel Mann. *"Town Topics* is essentially a journal of criticism,"* the Saunterer wrote in the fall of 1905. "While it gives much attention to the news, especially concerning the great social world, that feature is but a minor incident of its distinction and important character." Many of the critical departments of the magazine were, in fact, of a remarkably high calibre during the period when the Colonel was its presiding genius. At first glance it is hard to imagine what attracted able writers such as James Huneker to the staff. The association carried with it the opposite of prestige, and the Colonel's rate of payment was hardly persuasive: in the early nineties he paid a half-penny a word or five dollars a column, and the later increases he put into effect never went higher than a penny a word. (By 1905 *Collier's,* for example, was paying five times this rate.) Probably the compelling factor that brought Huneker and others into the fold was Mann's *laissez-faire* policy. Busy devilling the Four Hundred, he left those department editors who dealt with extraneous aspects of civilization such as art, music, and literature to write—and to live—as they pleased.

Huneker, in the *Town Topics* tradition, was enjoying some highly unconventional domestic arrangements when he joined the magazine in 1897. A noisy, exuberant, intrepid man, he served as its music critic, signing himself "The Melomaniac," for the next five years and for several years after his formal departure from the Colonel's weekly payroll in 1902 continued to contribute articles on the theater as well as music. Indeed, a Huneker review on any subject customarily took on several other artistic fields before it subsided. Years later he called his autobiography *Steeplejack* and explained in a preface that he regarded himself as a critical steeplejack of all seven arts. Later students of the time have generally had harsh words for the popular artists, the critics, the publishers, the powers-that-were of the American creative world who controlled its genteel, Anti-Saloon League climate just before the turn of the century when Huneker began writing his pieces for *Town Topics.* In this "tragic aesthetic wilderness" (H. L. Mencken), this "refined and bloodless atmosphere" (Malcolm Cowley), "perhaps the most provincial and uninspired moment in the history of American society" (Edmund Wilson), Huneker, in essays that reminded Wilson of "the floral bombs and the close-packed rockets of fireworks," was enlightening the Colonel's readers about such disturbers of the peace from abroad as Moussorgsky, Wagner,

Richard Strauss, Debussy, Berlioz, Schönberg, Ibsen, Nietzsche, Huysmans, Verlaine, and Cézanne. "If a merciful Providence had not sent James Gibbons Huneker into the world," Mencken noted in the *Smart Set* as early as 1909, "we Americans would still be . . . sweating at Chautauquas and applauding the plays of Bronson Howard." George Jean Nathan called him "the greatest of American critics," adding, extravagantly, that "he did more to free America from its slavery than any Lincoln." More recently Alfred Kazin wrote of Huneker that "almost single-handed he brought the new currents of European art and thought to America and made them fashionable."

The critic most often cited for abetting Huneker in his campaign of liberation in the literary field is Percival Pollard who, writing under the pseudonym of "The Ringmaster," was *Town Topics'* book reviewer for all but two years of the period between 1897 and his death in 1911. He was one of the significant figures who "contributed to the intellectual ferment," who "troubled the waters," notes Cowley. Lewisohn describes Pollard as having "in the columns of *Town Topics* . . . showed the first American awareness of the great movements that were transforming continental literature." In these columns, which were his only forum (Huneker's directives were available in other publications), Pollard also went out of his way to berate most contemporary American authors for "browsing forever on the complacent plains of mediocrity," and maintained that the most important American writer of the day was not F. Marion Crawford but Henry James (then in a critical eclipse), with Ambrose Bierce as runner-up. Whatever Colonel Mann thought of this view, he must have been happy to harbor a critic who shared his convictions about the importance of syntax. Pollard (who, though fervid and persuasive, was not a particularly good writer himself) dismissed one book as having been "written almost without verbs" and being "rank with dashes. The construction was not English." Far from chafing at the knowledge that the average reader of *Town Topics* had bought it only for its scandal department, Pollard insisted that he had no desire to be one of the esoteric group of critics who "just mumble and maunder polite shop talk one to the other" with "no public in mind but themselves." His ambition, he said, was "to write of art or of letters so tellingly that persons not intrinsically interested in art or letters will stop, look, and listen." *Town Topics* subscribers who strayed past "Saunterings" and into the Ringmaster's circle were generally treated to a good show. No disciple of the *nil nisi bonum* school that made much criticism of the day so banal, Pollard called Frank Norris's *McTeague* "a mixture of dentistry, dust and alkali." ("Things are continually 'transpiring' with Mr. Norris," he added contemptuously.) He offered as his interpretation of the moral of a Jack London novel: "If you want to succeed with women, you must wear the muscles of your neck outside of your collar." He also boasted shortly before his death of having "waved the banner of Shaw in the faces of the public" at a time in the nineties when Shaw was "a phrase to frighten fools with," and essayed one of the earliest translations of André Gide, running excerpts from it in *Town Topics* in 1905. In a mealy-mouthed age, the editorial leeway at the magazine allowed him to discuss in detail Schnitzler's eroticism and to devote a whole column to a review of books on what was then known as "sex hygiene." And in January, 1901, immediately after Oscar Wilde's death, in an era when it was considered indiscreet to mention that writer's name except with loathing, he published in *Town Topics* a long essay entitled "Our Descent into Indecency," in which he held that a worse crime than any Wilde had committed was that of regarding the cloud over the Britisher's name as having any relevance to his artistic achievements.

Pollard had been involved in a squalid divorce scandal just before he went to work for *Town Topics* and socially was a loner, "taciturn, rather morose, suspicious . . . inordinantly stingy" and "without respectability," or so Mencken pronounced him in *A Book of Prefaces*. Mencken also described him as being "apparently without the slightest affection for any human being." He does not suggest that Pollard made an exception of Colonel Mann. However, in his book, *Their Day in Court*, which was largely made up of his *Town Topics* pieces and was published in 1909, Pollard gave the *Town Topics* owner a testimonial that might well have astonished followers of the headlines about the venal Colonel in the Hapgood libel case, had they been in the habit of reading collections of essays written by irascible critics not in favor with the literary Establishment.

An ad for *Town Topics* that ran in the *Smart Set* in 1900 boasted that its critical departments were "absolutely independent. The critics who write for *Town Topics* have but one rule: Be honest, fear none, favor none." Pollard vigorously upheld this claim. "I have as critic of letters been singularly fortunate," he wrote in his book. "For more than a decade I have reviewed current literature through the columns of . . . one weekly newspaper which never gave me anything but a free hand. It supposed me to be honest; after that it asked me no questions. Never, in all those years, have I been asked to trim my opinions to suit the advertising columns." He sometimes filled in for the theater critic, and when, on one occasion, he had panned a play, he recalled that the producer (and frequent *Town Topics* advertiser) had made a charge of personal prejudice. "My employer believed my honesty before the other's chicane," wrote Pollard, "and I was left unmolested as a critic." As book reviewer for the same publication, he went on, "I had the satisfaction of seeing a cheap sort of pirate publisher practically kicked out of the office for insinuating that certain published censure had for object only the forcing of him into advertising. The fellow, after that, could not have bought space in those columns for love or money." In fact, Pollard reported, the proprietor of the magazine was so anxious to avoid the possibility of undue influence that "to all intents, publishers' advertisements were excluded from the paper's columns." There is no evidence that most publishers were clamoring to advertise in *Town Topics* which, besides its other disabilities, was a competitor in the publishing trade, occasionally persuading one of its regular contributors to expand a piece of fiction into a full-length novel and bringing it out in that form. Nevertheless, "the list of American newspapers who maintain a critic independent of the business office is so small that I do not trust myself to hint it," Pollard went on and, indeed, suggested that the "absolutely free hand" that critics were given at *Town Topics* was unique in contemporary journalism. The staff writers of that magazine would presumably have been the last to argue with the premise that the character of William d'Alton Mann was not a simple one.

Among those who shared the heady editorial independence as well as the unimpressive pay scale of the critical departments at *Town Topics* was Edward Ziegler who succeeded Huneker as music critic, moved on after some years to the *Sun* and the *Herald,* and eventually became assistant general manager of the Metropolitan Opera Association. Also on the roster was Charles Frederic Nirdlinger, a lively and forceful writer who was *Town Topics'* theater critic for much of the first decade of the century. "Nirdlinger," Pollard once wrote in an intrafraternity plug, "first raised dramatic criticism in America to the level of permanent literature." He professed admiration for Nirdlinger's "Attic elegance of style," although complaining that the play reviewer was overly partial to such words as "ambiency," "trope," and "pudicity." Another *Town Topics* critic of some stature was Willard Huntington Wright, who succeeded Pollard as book reviewer. And Ludwig Lewisohn, an intense, oracular writer, an early Freudian who became a stormy petrel in the American critical world of the 1920's before he veered into Zionism, first sold some verse to *Town Topics* in 1904 and over much of the next two decades continued to contribute not only poetry and fiction but critical essays to the scandal sheet, serving as its theater reviewer during the Colonel's final years. Lewisohn's convictions about the significance of *Town Topics* in the American literary scheme may have had some relation to his habit of interpreting the development of American literature in terms of the literary progress of Ludwig Lewisohn. On the other hand, among the reasons why this significance, slight as it may have been, is now entirely forgotten, is the tendency of all other reputable *Town Topics* contributors to omit entirely from their official résumés any trace of their alliance with the *Police Gazette* of the Four Hundred.

Once in a while, when he thought the critical writing had got too fancy, the Colonel would send a piece to its author with a note saying, "This newspaper does not deal in Pactolian refulgence." For the most part however, his only stipulation was that anything due to appear in the magazine must parse and be spelled right. It was to make sure these conditions prevailed that, once "Saunterings" was out of the way, he conscientiously read over and initialled all other *Town Topics* page proofs on the night the magazine went to press. The poor view his house critics took of the status quo in the American arts apparently came as no great shock to him. In

December, 1891, soon after he formally took over the magazine, the Saunterer himself dealt rudely with Richard Watson Gilder, the poet as well as editor of the *Century* and at the time a ruling Pooh-Bah of the New York literary world. "Mr. Gilder," wrote the Saunterer, "is a poet of decidedly restricted talents who has never written four lines that are known or heeded outside of his own circle of friends. I understand all too well the sickly and shallow Philistinism that glorifies the Gilders and overlooks the true poets." In a case where he did take exception to a critical judgment, he seems to have handled the matter indirectly, inserting his dissenting opinion in a later issue among the final paragraphs of "Saunterings." For example, an unenthusiastic review of a performance by his old friend and boudoir car customer, Adelina Patti, would cause him to scratch around for an excuse to run a social item about the lady which would mention in passing that she was the greatest vocal artist in the history of the world. And a week after Pollard had engaged in some rather convolute discussion of Bernard Shaw's philosophy of life, the Saunterer offered his opinion that Shaw was "simple as a squash."

Except for such rare minority reports, Colonel Mann generally left all problems of artistic judgment, including the selection of poetry and fiction and the layout and style of the latter half of the magazine, to his associate editors. The foreman of this crew with the longest term of service, lasting from 1905 to 1919, was Charles Bohm, former *Town Topics* art critic, who succeeded the hapless Charles Stokes Wayne as managing editor. Lewisohn described Bohm as a small, bald, long-nosed man with pale, clever eyes who died young as a result of having "worked without moving such long hours and smoked so many cigarettes . . . in the service of the cruel pasha." Bohm had not only a shrewd editorial sense but highly developed protective instincts toward *Town Topics'* back-of-the-book contributors. According to Huneker's biographer, Arnold Schwab, Bohm saw to it "that blackmail never interfered with culture, and Huneker, Nirdlinger and Pollard had no inkling of Mann's extracurricular shenanigans." This version of events would have required the three men to have been in a catatonic state during 1905 and 1906. Moreover, when Harold Vynne spilled some of the beans in the *Morning Telegraph* in 1898 and a good many more in his novel two years later, it is hard to imagine that the revelations (if they were news to anyone on the payroll by that time) weren't considered required reading by all the Colonel's galley slaves. Probably Mann's distinguished staff of critics concluded that, in all fairness, the Colonel's live-and-let-live policy should cut both ways.

Distinguished, one should add in all fairness, was by no means the word for all of the *belles-lettres* half of *Town Topics*. The poetry the subeditors chose to help fill the concluding pages was strictly doggerel and, usually staff-written, had the hastily-contrived look of something turned out while the printer's boy stood by. In fact, it often had been. On Tuesday nights when he found he was short of material, perhaps because of a just-concluded treaty removing certain paragraphs from "Saunterings," the Colonel often suggested that the house poets call in a stenographer—they were called "typewriters" in those days—and start dictating. The persistently cheerful tone of the light verse ("We ask no gentle reader to be kindly and indulgent/ Since every member of this staff is sparkling and effulgent") was also notable in view of the Colonel's twenty-five-cent-a-line rate, which caused one editor to describe him as believing that "poets were born, not paid." As for the fiction in *Town Topics,* much of it was sentimental and stilted. Its heroes and heroines were typically not only well-born and well-bred but well-heeled, conditions that were endemic in most magazine fiction of the day even outside of the journal of society. Their heroines' conflicts—whether to marry the city fellow or the country boy or the dark stranger, who would turn out on the last page to be the multimillionaire yachtsman incognito—were in pointed contrast to the back street slap-and-tickle among the upper classes that the Saunterer had just described so graphically in the front pages of the same magazine. Along with reflections of the refined and bloodless literary age, however, *Town Topics* in the Colonel's day occasionally printed more full-bodied short stories by such writers as Gertrude Atherton, O. Henry, Ambrose Bierce, Jack London, and Stephen Crane, and importations from abroad by Israel Zangwill and Somerset Maugham. Crane's contribution in October, 1896, of which the Colonel specifically approved although he identified himself as not a particular admirer of the author of *The Red Badge of Courage,* was a story called "In the Tenderloin." Certainly well outside the genteel tradition, it dealt with a young punk who saved his mistress from a suicide attempt by pouring a quart of whisky down her throat. The next morning, it concluded ironically, "they were asleep, and this, after all, is a human action, which may safely be done by characters in the fiction of our time." All in all, wrote Lewisohn in his 1932 survey of American literature in which he paid tribute to his old literary outlet "one can imagine the scorn with which Mr. Brander Matthews [professor of literature at Columbia and a stately pundit of the *Saturday Review*] would have received the information that in 1905 the future of our letters was implicated with nothing that took place in his noble drawing room on West End Avenue and with everything that had its faint but definite beginnings in certain editorial offices, not in the best repute, in the Knox Hat Building at Fifth

Avenue and 40th Street."

"*Town Topics* is my baby," Colonel Mann remarked fondly during his troubled summer of 1905, and on his favorite publication he lavished the sturdiest bindings and the heaviest, glossiest paper that money could buy. The bound volumes of the magazine that survive in a number of the nation's public libraries today are thus in a far better state of preservation than are most of the more respectable periodicals dating from the same era. On the other hand the cheapest wood pulp of the sort that began to crumble the moment it hit the newsstands he considered quite good enough for the less-favored magazines in his publishing family.

One of his most unlikely literary offspring, short-lived as it turned out, was *Tom Watson's Magazine*. Watson was a fiery-tempered red-haired Georgian Populist who had been elected to Congress in 1890 on a ticket dedicated to more understanding of the problems of the Negro as well as those of the poor tenant farmer. A sworn enemy of rampant capitalism who favored government ownership of some utilities and all railroads, he was the Populist candidate for Vice-President in 1896 and for President in 1904. In spite of the Colonel's stated mistrust of Populism's "glittering mendacities" and despite the clear importance of rampant capitalism to his way of life, he approached Watson early in 1905 and offered to publish a magazine to be edited and largely written by the colorful Georgian, who would receive $500 a month and expenses. Watson's biographer, C. Vann Woodward, assumes that Mann's only interest in Watson had to do with the hundred and seventeen thousand captive subscribers who had voted for him for President the fall before. However, Mann had gone so far as to announce in the spring of 1905 that *Town Topics* endorsed Watson's socialistic policies "if necessary to prevent the robbing of the people by soulless monopolies." (Watson, he pointed out in passing, was "from an old Georgia family.") Probably the recent rousing success of *McClure's*, which had exposed the trusts and other injustices to the common man, had something to do with Mann's new venture. His gamble looked promising after the first run of 100,000 copies of the initial issue of *Tom Watson's Magazine* in March, 1905, was sold out in twenty-four hours. During the next eighteen months the Colonel's experiment in radicalism flourished. Each month it inveighed more strenuously against the sins of the same Wall Street moguls whose virtues his *Fads and Fancies* was simultaneously praising to the heavens. Watson called them all "shameless, unprincipled, lawbreaking robbers." If you don't drop the stolen goods," he would warn them editorially, "I will rouse your victims till they rise in the elemental wrath of human nature and string you up to the nearest lamp post." By the fall of 1906, however, Mann's trial for perjury was pending, and he may have felt it was no time to stir up the animals. Besides, he and Watson were no longer getting on. One of the Georgian's minor complaints was that the Colonel by this time owed him $9,000 and showed no signs of ever paying over a penny of it. In October, 1906, they parted company. Watson went on to become a powerful Southern demagogue, pathologically anti-Catholic, anti-Semitic and anti-Negro. Mann, after trying for two months to edit *Tom Watson's Magazine* without Tom Watson, permanently retired from the rabble-rousing end of the publishing business.

Tales from Town Topics, another magazine that went out under the Mann imprint, had a longer run. A twenty-five-cent quarterly launched immediately after the Colonel took over in 1891, it was originally an anthology of short stories from back numbers of his favorite journal. By the mid-nineties, however, staff members were picking up extra change by writing great, spongy, sentimental novelettes that were then bound in with the reprints. In 1905, just before the blackmail scandal broke, the intramural digest underwent a change of personality as well as name. It became *Tales,* amended a year later to *Transatlantic Tales,* and was now a twenty-five-cent monthly whose announced purpose was "to show that authors in other languages are quite as brilliant as those writing in English." A house ad described it as "the only magazine in the country devoted exclusively to translation and reviews of European literature. Before the publication of *Transatlantic Tales,*" the ad went on, "there was no way for cultivated American readers, unless they could read all languages and should pay a large sum of money, to keep in touch with European literature." Whether or not Mann's overriding motive was to cash in on the vast store of foreign fiction available for little more than translators' wages, the result was to import into the aesthetic wilderness some of the wildly fertile seedlings that Huneker and Pollard had set up a clamor about. A typical issue of 1907, "available at all newsstands," boasted of "fourteen stories from seven languages." Stories by such writers as D'Annunzio, Schnitzler, Südermann, Strindberg, Valdés, Anatole France, and Selma Lagerlöf were regularly featured. The largest share of the literary spoils, however, came from contemporary Russian fiction, including the works of Gorky and Chekov, whose names were an especially novel sight on America's corner newsstands. The Colonel's experiment in international letters, which had on its staff during 1907 a young truant from Yale named Sinclair Lewis, was closed down in 1908. Three years later Mann sold another of his brain children, though one rarely traced to him, the *Smart Set.*

Even when some acknowledgment is made of Mann's relationship to the magazine that many regard as a forerunner of the American literary flowering in the 1920's, the Colonel is often written out of the scene with unseemly—and inaccurate—haste. For example, the *Reader's Encyclopedia of American Literature* (6500 entries, 1280 double-columned pages), published in 1962 by Thomas Y. Crowell, describes the *Smart Set* as having been "founded in 1890 by William D'Alton, who called himself Colonel Mann and who had previously made large sums by publishing scandal sheets in New York." (*Town Topics* is not listed in the book at all.) The self-styled Colonel, according to this account, sold the *Smart Set* in 1900 to John Adams Thayer, under whose regime Mencken and Nathan were hired and who, the reference book goes on to say, eventually put these two men in charge of the magazine. Actually, it wasn't until March of 1900—the year Mann allegedly sold it—that publication of the *Smart Set* began. Mann's original conception of the twenty-five-cent monthly, to which he gave the subtitle *A Magazine of Cleverness,* was as a kind of house organ for fashionable ladies and gentlemen of literary bent (who presumably could not appear as contributors in *Town Topics* since they would then be suspected of collaborating with the Saunterer). Each issue was to consist of a hundred and sixty pages of poetry and fiction; illustrations were dispensed with, and there were to be no serials, a literary device that the Colonel had also stood out against in *Town Topics.* In the first issue (whose cover design, used throughout the Colonel's period of ownership, showed the sybillant initials of the title as long, swirling and brilliant red above a sketch of a couple dressed for the ball) the contributors duly included such *Social Register* names as Sara Van Rensselaer Cruger, Reginald de Koven, Caroline Duer, Hobart Chatfield-Taylor, and Sarah Cooper Hewitt.

The original prospectus had to be modified rapidly, however. The literary output of members of the local smart set was not all that publishable, and anyhow, as one observer suggested, "Fifth Avenue was too busy reading *Town Topics* to do any writing." During the next decade dilettante society writers continued to be welcome as contributors but were heavily outnumbered in the tables of contents by such professionals as Gelett Burgess, William Rose Benét, Edwin Markham, Lizette Woodworth Reese, Sara Teasdale, Vance Thompson, Zona Gale, John Hall Wheelock, James Branch Cabell, Rachel Crothers, Jack London, Damon Runyon, Theodore Dreiser, and Sinclair Lewis, making his second appearance in the Colonel's disbursement records. In the same period the former literary outlet for the Four Hundred was offering a haven to such leaders of Greenwich Village Bohemia as Inez Hayes Gillmore, Susan Glaspell, Harry Kemp, Louis Untermeyer, and Mary Heaton Vorse, who a few years later would be prominent contributors to *The Masses.* Most of the *Smart Set* writers were then young, obscure, and willing to exchange their best work—often their first published work—at the starvation rate of a penny a word. (On one occasion the editors relented and paid almost twice this rate to the unknown O. Henry, who had written that he would lose his mind if he didn't lay hold of enough money to get him out of Pittsburgh.) The magazine, printed on pulp and suffering from its reputation for frivolity and particularly from its association with *Town Topics,* was ignored by the leading literary nabobs of the day. Nevertheless, it was soon creating "something of the theatrical sensation of the *Yellow Book* of London," Charles Hanson Towne, who was on the staff during most of the Colonel's tenure and was editor-in-chief from 1904 to 1908 recalled in his autobiography, *Adventures in Editing.* By 1905 its circulation was a hundred and sixty-five thousand, well ahead of *Town Topics.*

It made money from its second year on, and Mann once declared that during its first eleven years it had brought him a profit of half a million dollars. "He was more surprised than anyone else when his new venture became an established success," Towne reported.

At this rate of return the Colonel apparently felt he could afford to accommodate himself gracefully to the alteration in his original plans for the magazine. In the issue of the *Smart Set* for August, 1908, a statement of policy appeared that gave a greatly-amended version of the *Smart Set*'s literary intentions. It also took a stand against the kind of editorial judgment, then prevalent in the publishing world, that had led William Dean Howells to refer approvingly to "the smiling aspects of life that are the more American." "An impression has gained ground that *The Smart Set* has published and is publishing only stories dealing with a certain aspect of society," read the statement. "Nothing could be more untrue. The aim of this magazine has always been to print the best fiction of the widest possible variety that could be procured; yet we have never hesitated, when the opportunity offered, to print a story that dealt with the deeper side of life or with life in its unpleasant aspects." The earthy and unfashionable subject matter of many *Smart Set* stories would have kept them out of any other magazine, the statement went on. "We do not believe it is unjust to say that if writers like de Maupassant, Poe and Balzac were living today, *The Smart Set* would be the only magazine that would have the courage to print their work." Whether or not this view was fair to such lively competitors as *McClure's* and *Ainslee's*, most critics today give the *Smart Set* high marks for boldness. "The *Smart Set* was a raffish magazine," Edmund Wilson notes in *The Shock of Recognition*, "but the old magazines with their editors of the type of Richard Watson Gilder were so paralyzed by their publics and their publishers that they could never have let down the bars and given the new American writers a hearing."

In deference to the style to which its early contributors were accustomed, the *Smart Set* office was more elaborately decorated than that of *Town Topics* on the floor below at 452 Fifth Avenue. Its desks were inlaid, its carpeting Oriental, and its curtains so ubiquitously beaded that the place reminded one editor of a Viennese bordello. From time to time literary teas were held there for contributors to both magazines. Carolyn Wells, whose light verse appeared frequently in the *Smart Set* and occasionally in *Town Topics,* referred to these affairs as Smart Settees. Except for these splurges, however, and for its décor, the editorial atmosphere at the newer magazine was not opulent. The staff was small, and many of its editors doubled in brass, writing articles under three or four names for each issue. After lecturing the staff on the absolute necessity of keeping the payroll pared to the bone, Colonel Mann would often arrive in the office the next morning convoying an impoverished family friend from the South who, in common decency, must be immediately accommodated with a desk and salary. He also made sure that his crony Justice Deuel drew a substantial retainer from the *Smart Set* as well as from *Town Topics.* But for the most part the Colonel, busy elsewhere, seems to have concluded that his handful of twenty-five-dollar-a-week editors in charge of the magazine of cleverness knew what they were doing. So long as they kept within the limit of the penny-a-word rate, he left them to their own devices. (He may have had some qualms about this policy after the line "My soul is a lighthouse keeper" in an Ella Wheeler Wilcox poem turned up in its pages in 1908 as "My soul is a light housekeeper.")

Emma Mann-Vynne occasionally read manuscripts for

the *Smart Set* although, as Towne wrote later, "she never forced her editorial decisions to become ours. I don't believe she cared much about her duties," he added, "and I always had a suspicion that manuscripts bored her, but, having some money invested in the property, she kept her fingers on the pulse of the paper. There was an element of humor in the situation. . . . Mrs. Vynne was not at all 'literary,' nor did she pretend to be. We gave her only what we wished her to read. . . ." Like the editors downstairs at *Town Topics,* those at the *Smart Set* were often conscripted to provide the Colonel with social companionship. Editorial conferences were regularly scheduled over enormous meals on West Seventy-Second Street and long weekends at Lake George. Staff members made special command appearances at the latter resort for the annual regatta during which the Colonel awarded not only a *Town Topics* but a *Smart Set* trophy. Towne also remembered elaborate Thanksgiving and Christmas dinners to which all employees of the two magazines as well as many contributors were invited. Towne was perfectly aware of what *Town Topics* was up to ("the most feared publication that ever appeared in our town," he called it), but he apparently had no trouble disassociating this terrorism from the publisher he knew. Colonel Mann, he wrote, was "as sentimental as a woman despite his outward manner of brusqueness. . . . He had a warm heart." The *Smart Set*'s proprietor, he added, "called us his 'family,' and we were literally that, as I have never known an organization that worked in such complete harmony."

Any reference to the *Smart Set* is usually closely followed by the names of George Jean Nathan and H. L. Mencken, a practice encouraged by Mencken who regularly informed his numerous biographers that before he and Nathan took over its control in 1914 the magazine had dealt only in "perfumed pornography." In fact, not only many of its contributors who made its literary venturesomeness a legend but Mencken and Nathan themselves dated back to the Colonel's regime. In the fall of 1908, when Mann added a department of literary criticism, Mencken, at Dreiser's suggestion, was hired as the reviewer. Much of the material for his early books was part of the perfumed pornography that appeared in the *Smart Set* during the next several years, the years during which Mencken was building his reputation as a great literary critic. Nathan's association with the Mann enterprise grew out of the fact that his uncle, with whom he was then living, was Charles Nirdlinger, *Town Topics'* dramatic critic. Nathan began writing for the *Smart Set* in the fall of 1908 and succeeded Channing Pollock as its theater reviewer a year later. Another important editorial figure at the *Smart Set,* Willard Huntington Wright, served on the magazine while continuing on the staff of *Town Topics.* Half a generation later Wright became famous as the detective story writer, S. S. Van Dine, in which role his financial returns were far more substantial than those he received as the editor-in-chief of the *Smart Set* during 1913, its "best year," in the view of at least one critic, Malcolm Cowley. During that year Wright was responsible for the appearance in its pages of such writers as D. H. Lawrence, Robinson Jeffers and Ezra Pound.

By this time Colonel Mann had departed the scene. In February, 1911, perhaps in a spirit of retrenchment after a spate of libel suits began to be filed against *Town Topics,* the Colonel sold the *Smart Set* for a hundred thousand dollars to John Adams Thayer, the former publisher of *Everybody's* magazine. He had originally offered a half interest to Thayer, but the latter wanted full control, and the Colonel had finally agreed. "I did not wish to sell *The Smart Set;* it has bulked large in my life for over a decade," he wrote sorrowfully in his farewell issue of April, 1911. Thayer liked to boast that he had made three million dollars as publisher of *Everybody's*. Apparently his financial acumen was no match for Mann's, however; he later claimed in court that just before the sale the resourceful Colonel had transferred a hundred and fifty thousand dollars in *Smart Set* assets to a dummy corporation headed by Mrs. Mann-Vynne. Thayer's interest in the magazine had been stimulated by the social aspirations of his wife and daughters, who somehow had got the impression that association with a periodical called the *Smart Set* would provide them with an entrée to the smart set. When this notion turned out to have been misguided—they might as well have been back with *Everybody's*—Thayer lost interest in his property and in the summer of 1914, after he got into financial difficulties, it was taken over, in default of a five-thousand-dollar debt, by the company that had been supplying its paper. The paper company named one of its own shareholders as publishers, and he, in turn, designated Mencken and Nathan as editors, giving them some stock and the right to a third— later increased to a half—of the magazine's annual profits. With his usual tact, Dreiser wrote Mencken a year later that he much preferred the Colonel's old *Smart Set* to their version. "Under Mann in its profitable social days," he wrote, "it had a glittering insincerity and blasé pretense which I rather liked . . ." Under Mencken and Nathan, he complained, it was "too debonair, too full of 'josh' and 'kid.'" Actually, although many new contributors' names turned up in the magazine's table of contents in the later years, many of the old ones—Huneker, Towne, Wheelock, Richard Le Gallienne, Teasdale, Cabell, Benét and the like—appeared and reappeared through the two decades no matter who was signing the pay checks. A reader, in fact, wrote in to complain long after Mann's departure that the *Smart Set* was full of "the same old names, the same old games." And in research for a 1956 doctoral thesis on the rise and fall of the *Smart Set,* C. R. Dolmetsch found that even during Mencken and Nathan's regime two-thirds of its romantic fiction dealt with life in high society. In the *Smart Set's* years under Mann, as later, he wrote, "more often than not one can discern in its yellowed pages a laudable effort to publish the best available writing."

Curiously, the *Smart Set* steadily lost readers in what are usually regarded as its years of greatest influence. In 1908, when Mencken joined the staff under the Colonel, its circulation was about a hundred and forty thousand, a total which dwindled each year until, in December, 1923, when Mencken and Nathan sold out, it was less than twenty-three thousand. The editors did not blame their withdrawal on vanishing readers. They were giving up the *Smart Set,* they announced, because "the purpose which they began in 1908 has been accomplished," that is, the American writer had been set free from the Philistine influences that had sought to intimidate him. The years between 1900, when the *Smart Set* began publication, and 1923, Mencken later noted, marked "the advance from *Sister Carrie,* suppressed and proscribed, to *Babbitt,* swallowed and hailed." After the *Smart Set* was conveyed to Hearst for sixty thousand dollars, its title, which Mencken had called "our biggest handicap," was attached for a few years to a true-confessions type of magazine of twice the circulation it had ever reached in the Colonel's day, and eventually, in the thirties, came to rest over a syndicated society column originating in the *New York Journal-American.*

"The Otherwise Pleasant Eventide"

AS MANN'S TRIAL FOR PERJURY had come to a close back in December, 1906, the chief movers and shakers of the vast, honorable and complex frame-up of Colonel Mann apparently had had some intimation that no victory celebration would be in order this time. Jerome was not in the courtroom for the near-midnight finale nor was either of the Colliers, *père* or *fils*. Some months before this, P. F. Collier had declared that, no matter what the legal outcome of the perjury matter, he was convinced that *Collier's* crusade had been worthwhile since, by bringing *Town Topics'* methods out in the open, it had already dealt "a death blow" to the Colonel's game of literary blackmail. "We take no delight in trying to send Colonel Mann to prison," the elder Collier had gone on to explain to the press, "for he will be dead in five years." In fact, it was Peter Collier who was dead in three years, keeling over of apoplexy on the threshold of the Riding Club on East Fifty-Eighth Street. The Colonel even survived Rob Collier, whose later publishing achievements included persuading the formidable Charles W. Eliot, President of Harvard, to edit "Dr. Eliot's Five-Foot Bookshelf"—more formally known as the *Harvard Classics*—for P. F. Collier and Son. However, the younger Collier's "dramatic nature" became more and more histrionic as time went on, and he eventually was deprived of editorial control over the family magazine. He died of a heart attack in November, 1918, the night after returning from a tour as a correspondent on the western front where his credentials had been suddenly canceled without explanation by the War Department. Besides his satisfaction, a dozen years before, over having publicly exposed the Colonel's extraordinary tactics, Robert Collier had had another reason not to regard the costly campaign against Mann as a poor bargain. "The *Town Topics* suit," wrote Mark Sullivan, who had been a member of *Collier's* staff at the time of the trials, "did for *Collier's* what Collier most desired and needed. The first page stories and heavy headlines with which the daily papers reported the trial"—he went on in his autobiography, *The Making of an American*—"the parade of names of the best-known figures in New York yielding to intimidation . . . all combined to give *Collier's* esteem, *éclat, kudos."* Other, less parochial crusades followed, circulation doubled, and, according to Frank L. Mott in his *History of American Magazines,* "few periodicals in America have exerted over any decade as strong and direct an influence on national affairs as that of *Collier's* during the Hapgood regime."

Norman Hapgood and Rob Collier eventually parted company over the election of 1912. With a nice sense of form the rambunctious publisher insisted that *Collier's* endorse Teddy Roosevelt while the more scholarly-mannered editor in the pince-nez favored Wilson. In addition, Hapgood complained that the editorial policies of *Collier's* were by this time largely dictated by its advertisers. He held editorial posts thereafter on *Harper's Weekly* and *Leslie's Weekly* and became active in Democratic politics. Wilson named him Minister to Denmark in 1919; he also helped run Al Smith's 1924 campaign for the Presidential nomination. During his *Collier's* days Hapgood had churned out biweekly editorials denouncing the philosophy, character, and journalistic methods of William Randolph Hearst. By the 1920's, however, he found he could accommodate himself to the publisher's ways and worked as an editor of Hearst's *New York American* and his *International* magazine. At the time of Hapgood's death in 1937 he was editor of the *Christian Register,* a publication of the Unitarian Church.

In the course of the Colonel's appearance as a witness in the Hapgood libel trial Osborne and Shepard several times indicated that Mann's way of life was particularly unbecoming to one who was about to meet his Maker. The Colonel survived them both. Littleton and Jerome, however, outlived him by fourteen years, dying in the same year, 1934. The two gladiators squared off against each other again in the second Thaw trial. Once more Littleton won out, wringing from the jury a verdict of not guilty by reason of insanity. His most spectacular feat in later years was his defense of Harry Sinclair in the Teapot Dome scandal: Littleton got Sinclair acquitted of the charge of tendering a bribe to Albert Fall who was later convicted of taking it. He served an uneventful term as a Democratic Congressman from 1911 to 1913 and lived long enough to denounce the New Deal but, like Jerome, never came close to the important national role that, in the early years of the century, his admirers had in mind for him.

"Jerome slips out of office," read the headline on a brief story on an inside page of the *Times* on January 1, 1910. He was succeeded as District Attorney by Charles Whitman, later governor of the state. Whitman had been the obscure magistrate who, beginning in November, 1905, had conducted the first hearing on the Colonel's libel charge against the Colliers, his rising political star thus crossing Jerome's as it began to fall. Jerome, wrote Arthur Train many years later, had "shot across the sky at a psychological moment, hung blazing for a brief period of almost unparalleled adulation, and then, unable to fulfill the exaggerated hopes which his personality and his own declarations aroused, faded from the public firmament." Helping to bring him down had been the combined thrust of the enemies the outspoken ("When I say a senator is unfit, I mean Depew") District Attorney had made over the years: the newspapers; the regular party heads whose indispensability he had flouted by winning office without their help; the captains of industry he had called "the criminal rich" and then had failed to prosecute, thus angering his liberal supporters; and the local judiciary for whom he had "no reverence . . . not even common everyday respect." By 1908 the vendetta against the recent object of hero worship had reached such proportions that he was formally accused on eight counts of misconduct in office. One of the charges, suggesting the desperation of his ill-wishers, was that, by joining in the ritual of flipping the dice box at the entrance to Pontin's Restaurant near the Criminal Courts Building to see who would pay for the noonday drinks, he had engaged in gambling in a public place. A referee appointed by the Governor cleared him on all counts, but the swashbuckling reformer had apparently gone out of style, and at the age of fifty Jerome's public career was over.

During the nearly a quarter of a century of his life that remained, Jerome quietly practiced law, pottered about his Lakeville chemical laboratory, and in his last years made a fortune as one of the moving forces behind Technicolor. After its publication in 1907 his favorite book was *Folkways* by William Sumner, who had rescued the word *mores* from the Latin dictionaries. Jerome carried a copy of it with him everywhere and often read passages from it aloud. Perhaps he noted particularly the one about the necessary decline of men in public life who fail "to gauge forces in the *mores* and to perceive their tendencies." He refused to reminisce about the past, however, seeming, reported Milton MacKaye, who interviewed him in the early ninteen thirties, "a little bored with the Jerome of twenty-five years before." The moral issues of the two eras were about the same, he told MacKaye. "The only difference is the stealing is more refined. In my day they took what they wanted and made no bones about it." Like the academic prodigy who in his later years shuns the written word, Jerome largely ignored the political arena, although in 1933 he made a few speeches praising the virtues of another political maverick, Fiorello LaGuardia. LaGuardia returned the compliment after Jerome's death, declaring that New York City had "not had a district attorney since William Travers Jerome." In recent years Jerome's friends and family have acknowledged another point of information on which the Colonel's spies failed him, one that he could well have used during the era when the Saunterer rarely let a week go by without denouncing "Flapdoodle Jerome." Early in the century Jerome, who was unhappily married, had formed a liaison with a handsome and cultivated lady named Mrs. Elliot, with whom he lived contentedly, though without bene-fit of legal sanction, for the rest of his life.

After Mann's acquittal in the perjury trial Amos Pinchot, who had been in the District Attorney's office with Jerome, suggested that the Colonel's victims should take the law into their own hands. He recommended that they get up a posse, shave off one side of Mann's monumental beard, and parade him down Fifth Avenue in an open car. This did not happen. "We know of no Society for Improving the Condition of the Helplessly Rich," the *Nation* remarked editorially during the Colonel's tribulations, but assumed that "a sudden conscious-ness that every man of sense is laughing at them will do them more good than all the preachers and satirists." For many of the wealthy and powerful figures who had followed the code of *richesse oblige* and had meekly paid the Colonel off, predicted the *Nation,* the exposure of *Town Topics* would serve as "a nail festering in a sure place." Yet after Mann's death in 1920 claims against his estate for loans made in the years following the great inquisition came to $5,000 from Judge Elbert Gary of United States Steel; $13,000 apiece from Henry Huntington of the Central Pacific Railroad and Harry Payne Whitney, the banker; $10,000 from E. Clarence Jones, the broker; $27,000 from F. De Courcy Sullivan of the Consolidated Cigar Corporation; $20,000 from Frederic Watriss, attorney and oil man; and $26,000 from Morton Plant of the Atlantic Coastline Railroad. The loans from Huntington, Sullivan, and Whitney, as well as the longer standing $2,500 debt to J. P. Morgan, had not been renewed in the conventional manner and were eventually outlawed by the statute of limitations. Since Mann never again testified under oath about his fiscal practices, the extent to which *richesse* otherwise obliged him in his later years isn't a matter of record.

In the spring of 1906 after the Hapgood trial, *Collier's* reported, as evidence of having dealt the Colonel that "death blow," that the number of advertisers in *Town Topics* between January and April, 1905, who were not represented in its advertising columns for the same period in 1906 was 78. The Colonel responded by making a survey of his own and announcing that the number of advertisers in *Collier's* for the first three months of 1905 who were not represented in *its* advertising columns for the same period in 1906 was 324. A few months later, after an agonizing reappraisal, *Collier's* complained that if *Town Topics'* advertising lineage was any indication, the Colonel was still doing business as usual, with his old patrons "abetting his crimes" by taking full-page spreads for their companies, followed by dazzling reports of their personal social progress in the editorial columns of the magazine. The Colonel might well have retorted this time by quoting the comment of Mrs. Pearl Craigie, an American expatriate living in England who wrote several novels under the name of John Oliver Hobbes. ("She cannot be forgotten in any study of her time," declared William Dean Howells after her death late in 1906.) In a dispatch in the *American* on the Hapgood trial that this Hearst publication had imported her to cover for them, she complained that the defense seemed to think that "no newspaper proprietor except Colonel Mann had ever suggested to his editors that he would like his friends well-used." Apparently Mrs. Craigie's observation had not struck the owner of the *American* as pertinent, and her byline had abruptly disappeared from the paper. Hearst, according to W. W. Swanberg in *Citizen Hearst,* was famous for his "Goodie List," on which the names appeared of people who "on Hearst's orders were to be mentioned only in flattering terms." He also had an "S-List" of persons to be mentioned only with scorn; at one time it ran to two thousand names. One reporter, reports Swanberg, had the fulltime job of reading over each issue to make sure the two lists were rigidly observed. For that matter Colonel Mann was presumably not the first and certainly not the last editor to run news in the form of cryptograms: "blind" paragraphs of scandal whose principals were named in another, innocent connection elswhere in the same article. And as early as 1837 a British commentator had insisted that "the only way of securing exemption from the scandalous attacks" of the *New York Herald* was "to advertise largely in the paper, at most extravagant prices, or to send the editor presents in money or other direct bribes." Nor was the Colonel's flexible editorial policy by any means the only such example to reach the headlines in 1906. The New York legislature's investigation of the insurance companies in that year revealed, for instance, that some of them were paying reputable newspapers handsome space rates for printing company handouts—including slanted accounts of the investigation itself—as if they were ordinary news. The unforgiving fury with which the local press responded to Jerome's charge that the newspapers of New York were run from the counting room may in many cases have been the result of another nail festering in a sure place.

By 1908 Colonel Mann was admitting in "Saunterings" that *Town Topics'* advertising revenues had, in fact, fallen off disastrously as the result of what he called "the Roosevelt-Collier conspiracy to destroy a newspaper conducted as honestly, as honorably and with as high a purpose and—with here and there a rare exception, unavoidable in the conduct of any paper—as cleanly as any paper printed in America." But this decline (which was possibly recorded with some idea of filing a damage suit, a notion that he apparently soon thought better of *) may have been due less to the trials than to changing times. As the twentieth century took firmer hold, fewer American corporations were any longer mere extensions of one man's all-powerful personality, as many of them had been a generation before. Advertising budgets began to be the province of committees, for whom the morale of the chief stockholder's wife was not so burning a concern. Whatever its effect on *Town Topics* advertising, however, the most damaging result of the libel trial in the Colonel's later history undoubtedly grew out of the audacious appearance against him in open court of a few of the men he had tried to shake down.

In the summer of 1905 a prominent figure in society who was known to have paid Mann off came to call on Jerome

---

* Sometime before he had quietly dropped his previous civil damage suits against the Colliers and withdrawn his criminal libel complaint.

at the Criminal Courts Building to give the District Attorney any private help he could. On his way out, however, when reporters asked him whether he would testify against the Colonel, he declared that he would perjure himself, denying the extortion had taken place, rather than risk any public reference to the scandal the Colonel had suppressed. With the exception of Bernard Baker, the shipping man, all of the individuals who had actually accommodated the Colonel in return for *Town Topics'* good conduct reports or for its silence on certain matters exercised similar prudence by remaining silent themselves during the libel trial. But in that trial a few men whom Mann or his agents had gone after— James Burden, O. H. P. Belmont, Peter Cooper Hewitt, Baker, and, of course, Edwin Post, who had started it all— had dared to risk the public implication that their behavior somewhere along the line might have been considered negotiable by a blackmailer. By mounting the stand and testifying about the Colonel's methods, they apparently broke the spell that, until then, had paralyzed the Colonel's victims and protected him from libel suits. In 1909 a Pittsburgh wholesale druggist named Samuel Dempster instituted a civil suit as the result of a *Town Topics* article charging him with philandering with "an ostensible seamstress" and was awarded $40,000 damages, a sum described by his lawyer as probably the largest ever given in a libel case in this country. "I have never tried a case in which the evidence more thoroughly warranted the verdict," declared the judge. "The defendants tried to play with fire and got not only scorched but burned." The award was later cut in half, but during the next decade "probably no publication in the world had more libel suits filed against it," reported the *Tribune* in 1920. Few of the suits reached the point of trial and those plaintiffs who were successful often ran into a collection problem, but litigation is expensive for the defendant as well as the plaintiff. A certain cautiousness, disappointing to its more fun-loving readers, invaded the columns of *Town Topics,* and circulation fell off. Meanwhile, a certain self-consciousness about the throwing around of money was beginning to invade the world the Colonel had found so ideal for his purposes. The era when Horatio Alger could solemnly write of riches as the reward of virtue was being overtaken by one in which it seemed that a rich man could do no right. When Frederick Martin, brother of the Bradley Martin who in 1897 had thrown a $369,000 fancy dress ball "to give an impetus to trade," brought out a book called *The Passing of the Idle Rich* in 1911, he was, perhaps, premature. But philanthropy and at least the appearance of industry were coming into vogue, and there was progressively less time and money left for breakfasting on horseback at Sherry's and other purely social games. After 1913 when that measure the Colonel had long advocated, the federal income tax amendment, was read into the law like a curfew tolling the knell of a departing age, *Town Topics* became more and more of an anachronism.

In 1911, the same year that he jettisoned the *Smart Set,* Mann had won a $200,000 civil damages suit filed against him by his son-in-law, Albert Wray, for the alienation of the affections of Emma Mann-Vynne Wray. He was less successful five years later, however, as the defendant in a case involving Saunterer's Rest. "The dear old Colonel would take your socks with his bluff, soldierly air. You know!" James Huneker wrote to a friend in 1905. It developed in this trial that what Mann had taken from the state of New York was a whole island. According to attorneys for the state, he had come upon it during a deer-hunting expedition in the early nineties, had leased it from the State Forest Commission for hunting purposes, paying an annual rental of $50 for a few years, and then, with his bluff, soldierly air, had simply expropriated it. The state evicted him in 1916 after an eighteen-month fight in the courts. Fortunately, by this time he had other recourse to the secrets of nature. Several years earlier he had given up his other longtime residence on West Seventy-second Street and moved with his wife to a farm near Morristown, New Jersey, where his daughter had settled after her divorce from Wray. Thereafter, on his weekly trips into the city to steer the final *Town Topics* copy to the printer, he would stay the night either at a hotel or with his old friend, Judge Deuel. Although the day following the Hapgood libel trial the *World* had called Deuel's continuance in office "unthinkable" and the *Tribune* assumed he had already resigned since "only the rhinoceros-hided could remain on the bench," Deuel had sat tight, the Appellate Court that had the power of removal had failed to act, and in time public indignation had found other targets. He had served out the remaining seven years of his term and, indeed, continued on the bench until 1917, although he was demoted to a magistrate during his last four years and soon after his re-appointment Mayor Gaynor, with whom he had quarreled, called him "a disgrace to the Magistrate's Bench." After his retirement from public life he went on reading *Town Topics* galleys for libel—or his own "delectation"—and represented Mann in the various real estate transactions that took up more and more of the Colonel's time during his later years. Mann's own rhinoceros hide served him well in this field. "He could ask for a third mortgage without blinking," Robert Rowe, the versatile Newport telegraph operator, reported in his 1926 article in the *American Mercury*. Rowe added that in his last five years the Colonel had appeared to be in a financial decline and that his flamboyant waistcoats "grew increasingly shabbier." Some of Mann's real estate deals were substantial ones, however, and Rowe noted that his holdings on West Fortieth Street, for example, were eventually sold to the *Tribune* and provide the frontage on that street of the present *Herald-Tribune* building. In 1917 he also leased to the Post Office for a badly needed annex a number of lots on West Thirty-Eighth Street. These were the same lots whose rejection as the site for the new main Post Office in 1904 had led the Colonel to take up arms against the daughter of the President of the United States which, in turn, had led him into a sea of troubles.

In the early years after his informal conviction as an extortionist and his formal acquittal as a perjuror Mann devoted considerable space in *Town Topics* to rejoicing over the eclipse of Jerome. He continued to attack Bourke Cochran, the New York Representative who in 1906 had tried to push through Congress the resolution to ban *Town Topics* from the mails. ("I have never known an honest streak in him.") He pointed out from time to time that the name "Norman" had no precedent in the Hapgood family, but was the given name of a very close male friend of Hapgood's mother. As for Commodore Elbridge Gerry, who had testified against him, he was "a constant grouch" and "the meanest man in New York." Gerry's rank, Mann enjoyed pointing out, was not the result of services to his country in time of war—as was, of course, the Colonel's own—but of seven valiant years at the helm of the New York Yacht Club. Mrs. O. H. P. Belmont was "unstable" and "irresponsible." (The Colonel undoubtedly regarded as primary evidence of her lack of balance the fact that she had divorced a man who had most generously accommodated him, William K. Vanderbilt, to marry one who had not only turned him down but had boasted about it in court.) Mrs. Belmont, according to the Saunterer, was putting on weight. She wore the same dress to every social affair for a week. She used "expletives of a character to turn all the milk in the refrigerators." Every few issues she was visited by the disaster that Mann once said caused more gnashing of teeth than anything he could say about a woman in society: her latest party was a total frost. As time went on, however, new vendettas overshadowed these tired old grudges, and by 1916 when a short-lived Broadway play called *The Fear Market,* written by Amélie Rives, the society novelist to whom the Saunterer had given the back of his editorial hand on many an occasion over the years, turned out to be based on the *Town Topics* trials, complete with courageous editor, feckless judge, corrupt publisher, and hapless women society leaders whose lives he ruined, the Colonel declined to use the occasion for another defense brief against the decade-old charges. His dramatic critic dealt with the play in routine fashion, pronouncing it "cheap, tawdry melodrama," a verdict not far from that of other critics in town. (Over at the *Smart Set* Nathan reported that despite its "wholesale perissology," it was "not without a certain piquant laboratory interest.") As for his old antagonist in the White House, the plight of the Rough Rider in his last years, relegated to the sidelines of a shooting war, clearly struck a sympathetic nerve in the Colonel. He wrote that "a great light—perhaps the most intense of the age— went out when Roosevelt died" in January, 1919.

In these last years the Saunterer was too busy setting the contemporary world to rights to spend time looking back in anger. He inveighed against "the unspeakable Comstock," wire-tapping, anti-Semitism in Russia, and the light-fingered attitude of society editors on other newspapers toward items first published in *Town Topics* ("If I chose suddenly to devote all my energies for a week to a description of the peaks of Popocatepetl, the amount of social news in the daily papers would be about one consecutive line.") For a time he conducted a campaign to have *Town Topics* used as a "model of diction" in the public schools. During the war he issued weekly bulletins advising the Allied Powers on the deployment of the expeditionary forces. He supported unconditional surrender, Al Smith for Governor of the state, and pensions for former Presidents. He came out strongly in favor of the Nineteenth Amendment (women's suffrage) and violently against the Eighteenth, "the law to make this country safe for hypocrisy." "I am resigned to everything," he wrote, "except this accursed Prohibition which has come to darken the otherwise pleasant eventide of a very eventful life."

Perhaps to show that he was not only keeping up with the times but to an extent anticipating them, he took note of a trend in public attention and in 1912 introduced into *Town Topics* one of the early columns of Broadway gossip under the heading "Broadway Banter" and over the signature "The Night Owl." In the same year, again rejecting his consignment to the backwaters of publishing, he launched a pulp magazine called, with his persistent fondness for alliteration, *Snappy Stories,* which he filled with lurid fiction, usually about bad women or good women tempted by bad men. From 1917 through 1919 it claimed an annual two hundred thousand readers, many of them, perhaps, soldiers far removed from accustomed restrictions, literary and otherwise, and its success persuaded Mencken and Nathan to rush to the presses with a reasonable facsimile. (With the return to normalcy and the home fires, however, circulation of Mann's last publishing venture gradually tapered off; by 1929 it was down to 45,160, and sometime in 1930 *Snappy Stories* disappeared from the newsstands.)

Mann's refusal to regard himself as a back number was shared to some extent by the world of society. John Jacob Astor, for example, provided him with a clear exclusive on the Astor divorce in 1908, and to the end of the Colonel's life many fashionable hostesses, although they gave little neighs of horror when his name was spoken aloud at the dinner table, continued to send cards to *Town Topics* reporters for their important social affairs. None of them could be sure that, if she neglected to do so, the newly discreet Colonel might not decide to make an exception in her case. Rearing back as of old, he would report that her latest gown made her look like the chandelier in a Broadway lobster palace or give a detailed description of the underwear worn at the latest cotillion by her marriageable daughter—kindly provided, he would add, by the stag line. As late as 1915 his poison pen was still virulent enough to cause consternation in the august precincts of the White House. The Saunterer's comments on Woodrow Wilson's ardent courtship of Mrs. Galt so infuriated Admiral Grayson, Wilson's aide, that he declared that he felt like coming up to New York and doing some shooting.

When Mann did indulge in editorial flashbacks, it was usually on a valid cue—the death, in 1916, of Mosby, for example, or that seven years earlier of Leopold II, King of the Belgians, who, he noted crossly, had never rewarded him with a proper medal for having designed the royal boudoir car. He reported fully on his attendance at the fiftieth reunion at Gettysburg, although complaining that he had not, as he had urged the Secretary of War, been named one of its principal speakers. During the encampment he returned to a Confederate delegation the flag of the First Virginia Cavalry regiment which the Seventh Michigan, under his command, had wrested from it during the fighting at Rummel's farm. Afterward he printed with pardonable pride a letter from a Virginian pronouncing the Seventh Michigan "the best regiment I ever met in battle." New York's preparations in 1919 for the arrival of the future Edward VIII reminded

him of the excitement he had witnessed in the same city
sixty years before over the visit of the future Edward VII.
The special issue in October, 1916, that celebrated the twenty-
fifth anniversary of his association with *Town Topics* coin-
cided with his fiftieth in the newspaper business. Except for
Colonel Henry Watterson of the *Louisville Courier-Journal*
he was, he noted, the only American still active in the field
who had been a newspaper owner in 1866, the year he had
taken over the *Mobile Times*. At his request Colonel Watterson sent a graceful letter for publication in *Town Topics,*
commemorating the anniversary. "I remember the old Mobile days very distinctly," he wrote the onetime carpetbagger,
"and remember all you did for our people. Be assured that
I have never ceased to be grateful to you and the brave and
loyal men who thought and acted as you did during those
bitter times."

The Colonel had cherished his special relationship to
Mobile throughout his life. About the time he returned from
Europe in the early eighties T. C. De Leon, a writer whom he
had brought to Mobile as managing editor of the *Register,* became entrepreneur of the Mardi Gras extravaganzas put on
by local mystic societies, and it was probably he who made sure
that Mann was on the annual invitation list for various balls
during the festive days before Lent—invitations not lightly regarded in southern Alabama. Curiously, two of the Saunterer's
favorite targets, Mrs. Belmont and Amélie Rives, had both
spent their early years in Mobile, but if his implacable dislike
of them had grown out of some family snub during his carpetbagger years, he was not likely to mention it. His *Town Topics*
items about members of the Mobile social order who remained
in the Gulf City had always been uncommonly gentle, and during his last decade, as he continued to make his yearly pilgrim-
age to his more respectable past, it seemed that they could do

no wrong. The *Register's* coverage of his courtroom ordeals had, in turn, given him the benefit of all doubts. In any case, many Mobilians who followed the trials presumably read with some satisfaction the details of how one of their temporary citizens had outwitted the flower of northern capitalism. Moreover, at the time of the scandal Mobile residents with long memories had had a recent reminder of the Colonel's role as a prime booster of their city. For in the summer of 1905 the same newspapers all over the country that were printing sensational charges against the proprietor of *Town Topics* also contained accounts of another event that Colonel Mann must have read about with some sense of irony. His "bold dream" of a railroad from Mobile to the western wheat fields had been revived by others in the late nineties, and in 1905 the two derelict ends of the Mobile and Northwestern track were to be joined at last. The three hundred and forty additional miles of railroad included sixty miles of a line beginning at Ripley, Mississippi, that had been built by William Faulkner's great-grandfather, Colonel William C. Falkner (as he spelled it), the model for the Colonel Sartoris of the Yoknapatawpha novels, in which his railroad serves as a recurrent symbol of past enterprise and affluence for the Sartoris clan. Falkner's charter for a road that he hoped would reach the Gulf had been granted in 1871, the year after that secured by Colonel Mann, and the two men had made rival appearances seeking appropriations from the Mississippi legislature. Over a generation later, in August, 1905, the last spike in what was by this time known as the Mobile, Jackson, and Kansas City railroad—now part of the Gulf, Mobile, and Ohio—was driven in a bridge over the Pearl River at an elaborate ceremony attended by officials of the line, municipal dignitaries, and governors of the states concerned. In surviving to read about the event from afar Colonel Mann may have concluded that he was at any rate better off than Colonel

Falkner, who had been shot to death in a duel in 1889.

Mann's last published communication outside of *Town Topics* was a letter to the *Times* in January 1919, defending the Allied leaders who were under attack for the heavy losses on the European front. Of the four hundred and seventy-six men in his regiment at Gettysburg he pointed out, "the losses . . . in killed and wounded were exactly one hundred, which fact is inscribed on the Custer monument on the battlefield. You can't do much fighting and 'go over the top' without loss of life." His final *Town Topics* editorial written three days before his death at eighty-one on May 17, 1920, of complications following pneumonia predicted a Republican victory in the coming election, an American reversion to isolationism, and a second war with the Germans "because of the war spirit, the naturally brutal, stubborn and overbearing nature of the race." At his funeral at the Episcopal Church of the Heavenly Rest the coffin was draped with an American flag on which had been laid his Gettysburg saber. It was attended by three Colonels and a Major-General, with a sergeant from the Seventh Regiment sounding taps.

The remarkable Colonel, like his magazine, had lived beyond his day. The *Mobile Register* was apparently the only newspaper that took editorial note of his passing. "Colonel William d'Alton Mann died Monday at something over eighty-one years of age," reported the *Register,* "and of him it can be said that he was fully alive the whole of that long period of time. He was gifted with extraordinarily vital force and was never seriously ill in all his long life; he was intelligent and quick to act and had a fine presence and affable manner." The editor noted that in the years after the War between the States "the Colonel made himself one of the people of this city and state," and endorsed Mann's chosen version of the outcome of his 1869 campaign for Congress, declaring that "he was elected from this district but was not permitted to take his seat." The *Register* made no mention of the Colonel's history beyond the borders of Mobile.

Early reports of his estate referred to the "Mann millions," but a final accounting in September, 1924, pronounced it, in fact, insolvent, with assets of $212,031—including an Old Guard uniform valued at twenty-five dollars—and debts of $287,094. Nearly two-thirds of the latter sum, however, turned out to be claims filed by his joint heirs, his wife and daughter, and obviously represented money he had transferred to them over the years in order to sequester it from damage suits and had then drawn on as he needed it. The two ladies bickered publicly over the will, and before the estate was settled Mrs. Mann-Vynne bought out the claim of her stepmother, who immediately departed the scene, settling down in a $50,000 house in Lewisboro, New York, where she died a few years later. Included in the Colonel's estate were a hundred and fifteen of the five hundred total shares of *Town Topics* stock, which Mrs. Mann-Vynne accepted as part of her claim, the remaining shares having been given to her sometime back, she stated. (Although during the libel trial Mann had insisted that all of *Town Topics'* stock except for the few shares given to Judge Deuel—by 1920 no longer a stockholder—were the property of Mrs. Mann-Vynne under "a perpetual trust deed," it appears that for the Colonel the word "perpetual" like the word "truth" was subject to revision.) In 1922 Mrs. Mann-Vynne agreed to sell the magazine to August Ralph Keller, a member of *Town Topics'* staff, for $100,000. The deal fell through when he was unable to raise the money, and in December, 1924, Mrs. Mann-Vynne died at the age of sixty-six. In her will, after bequests to various charities, most of the residue of her estate went to George Holbert, a Summit, New Jersey, attorney who had become her legal advisor sometime before and who, it appeared, had already come into possession of *Town Topics*.

Seven weeks later, in the last of the scores of legal actions that had thrust the name of William d'Alton Mann onto local front pages, beginning with his trial in the U.S. Petroleum case in the Jefferson Market Courthouse sixty years earlier, a suit was filed to overturn his daughter's will. It was brought by William d'Alton Mann II, who had been so christened in 1914 when, at the age of twelve, he had been formally adopted by Mrs. Mann-Vynne in Orphan's Court. Now twenty-two years old, he was the youngest son of the Colonel's brother Eugene and, according to the statement he filed with the Surrogate's Court, was the third of Eugene Mann's sons their cousin had taken on approval, the others having been found unworthy of inheriting the distinguished name. At the time of the adoption, the petition said, Mrs. Mann-Vynne had agreed to make him her heir, which made him, essentially, the Colonel's heir since to his knowledge, he declared in his affidavit, the publisher had turned over to her the bulk of his property to foil legal antagonists. The petition stated that his adopted mother had been "of unsound mind and physically incapacitated" when, late in November, 1924, she had signed over to Holbert the trust deed to *Town Topics* and made her will and that three days later she had been carried on a stretcher aboard a ship bound for South America in the custody of another, minor beneficiary of the will and had died en route. Young Mann's claim was quickly settled for $165,000 plus seventy per cent of any amount realized over the million dollar price at which Mrs. Mann-Vynne's real estate holdings were then being offered for sale by a syndicate to which Holbert had transferred his interest. It appeared that those who had seen the Colonel as growing threadbare in his final years might have saved their crocodile tears.

Late in 1925 Holbert allowed August Keller to relieve him of *Town Topics* for an undisclosed sum. Keller, no relation to Louis Keller who had given the magazine its name, settled in at 2 West 45th Street, to which Mann had moved his offices ten years before, and took over coverage of the new world of café society, whose members Lucius Beebe once described as being gratified and flattered if they were mentioned in print "no matter what the . . . editorial implications of the mention itself." Almost immediately after the Colonel's death the magazine had begun to change. The price had gone up to twenty-five cents, and fiction had almost entirely vanished from its pages. The department of literary criticism disappeared and was replaced by "In the Cinema World." The two stately young women reading *Town Topics* on the cover turned into flappers with marcelled hair. The cover ads now often touted theatrical companies, although Elizabeth Arden, Bonwit Teller, and Hattie Carnegie continued to regard *Town Topics* as worth an investment, and the advertisement promising "Club, Banquet and Holiday Headaches Quickly CURED with BROMO-SELTZER" appeared just left of the center of the cover as it had since the nineties. Every few weeks the old cover would be dumped temporarily in favor of something new and different. One of these change-offs in early 1925 showed a naked girl wrapped in an American flag with a dirigible cruising in the background. The editorial tone had declined markedly. There were references to "This here Psychoanalysis." "The people who buy the richest goods are readers of *Town Topics*," the magazine proclaimed in a house ad. Under August Keller's management its circulation apparently continued its steady downward trend. After 1895, when it was listed as having 63,500 subscribers, N. W. Ayer's *Directory of Newspapers and Periodicals* no longer reported its circulation, an action taken "when our information on local conditions creates a doubt as to the accuracy of the figures sent us"; during the Hapgood trial, however, without any formal audit, both sides of the law were willing to go along with the Colonel's estimate of its weekly run as about 140,000. No figures appeared after *Town Topics'* name in the directory until 1931 when the editors accepted 23,000 as a reasonable estimate. But in that year it developed that, as in the Colonel's time, circulation figures were an inadequate measurement of *Town Topics'* value to its owners.

On the afternoon of December 9, agents of the New York State Bureau of Securities knocked on *Town Topics'* door, following complaints that salesmen of the publication were using unlawful methods in their attempts to sell stock in the corporation. A face peered at them through a peephole, then vanished. A short time later the raiding party broke down the door and found Keller and his staff cowering behind their desks. The publisher and five associates were taken for questioning to the State Attorney General's office, which pointed out to the press that the *Town Topics* publisher had already been indicted on charges of extortion brought by a vice-president of RKO. The same afternoon subpoenas were served on the editors of the *Tatler* whose editor-in-chief, John Schemm, had founded it five years before after a tour of duty on *Town Topics*. Schemm testified at a hearing the following day that it was he who had for some years sorted the season's debutantes for *Town Topics* into grades A,B,C,D, and E–Z, which he described as "a collective term." Asked for his definition of society, Schemm replied without a moment's hesitation, "People who for several generations have lived a clean, decent life." The investigation revealed that although both the *Tatler* and *Town Topics* had lost money for several years, they had sold about $250,000 worth of stock apiece during the same period. "Money prominent persons are listed among the magazine's stockholders," reported the *Times* in an interesting typographical error. Among the *Town Topics* records subpoenaed was the famous card file, listing the transgressions of prospective financial supporters, that had been started by the Colonel some forty years before—the file that James Osborne had described in the Hapgood case as "an index of lechery, lust, dishonesty, beastliness and gruesome scandal . . . for use at a moment's notice." It had, of course, been brought up to date and expanded over the years. The Attorney General's office made available to the press what it called "expurgated" versions of several of the entries. "Most interesting society woman; fearful tantrums; Plaza incident; Mr. —and sweetheart at one door; Mrs.— and sweetheart at another; clever chauffeur," read one of these. Explained a *Town Topics* salesman: "We use the same methods as a salesman who, for example, sells pig iron. We want to know everything about a prospective customer before . . . trying to interest him in our stock."

On December 29 a "prominent businessman" testified in the Attorney General's office that he had bought a considerable amount of stock in *Town Topics* at $110 a share, but that when he refused to buy more an article had immediately appeared in the magazine scandalously linking his name with that of a young, married society woman. Three other "prominent men" contributed similar testimony, but before any further legal action was taken *Town Topics* announced on January 7, 1932, that it was suspending publication with the current issue. A few evenings later the old card index of lust and lechery was loaded into a wire basket, carted down to the State Office Building and tossed into the furnace in the presence of officials and the press. No one present inquired whether the wire basket was the same one that had stood so long by the Colonel's desk with the fir walking stick propped up in it for use at a moment's notice; indeed no report of the month-long investigation mentioned the Colonel's name or made any reference to relevant events of a quarter of a century before.

One of the men arrested, John Schemm, had been permanently enjoined from selling stock in the *Tatler,* but in November, 1936, he turned up as editor of a new monthly *Town Topics,* complete with a department signed "The Saunterer." *Fads and Fancies* was now the title of a department of pictures featuring young girls swinging tennis racquets. The style of the Saunterer was also new. "Maury Paul's name is not on Mrs. V. Beaumont Auguste's private list," he wrote in an early issue. "It's all right, Maury, ours ain't either. So we won't be invited to her griddle cake breakfasts, which leaves us still doing our stuff at the Automat." After a few issues the monthly became a bi-monthly. In the issue for November, 1937, it asked its readers, "How do you like the new *Town Topics?* The editors would appreciate any suggestions for further improvement." Apparently the response was discouraging. *Town Topics* hasn't been heard from again.